LIFE AND DEATH IN THE NEW TESTAMENT

LIFE AND DEATH IN THE NEW TESTAMENT

THE TEACHINGS OF JESUS AND PAUL

XAVIER LÉON-DUFOUR

Translated from the French by
Terrence Prendergast

1817

Harper & Row, Publishers, San Francisco

Cambridge, Hagerstown, New York, Philadelphia, Washington
London, Mexico City, São Paulo, Singapore, Sydney

Library of Congress Cataloging-in-Publication Data

Léon-Dufour, Xavier.
    Life and death in the New Testament.

    Translation of: Face à la mort, Jésus et Paul.
    Bibliography: p.
    Includes indexes.
    1. Death—Biblical teaching.   2. Jesus Christ.
3. Bible. N.T. Epistles of Paul—Criticism, interpretation, etc. I. Title.
BS2545.D45L4513   1986   236'.1   84-48211
ISBN 0-06-060194-9

86 87 88 89 90 RRD 10 9 8 7 6 5 4 3 2 1

Sodalibus in Societate Jesu

Contents

Translator's Preface

This translation of *Face à la Mort: Jésus et Paul* is from the corrected edition of 1979. In the case of Biblical citations I have made use chiefly of the Revised Standard Version. Occasionally, punctuation or the translation of one or more words have been modified to take into account an aspect of the biblical original which the author wished to emphasize.

In his account of the ministry of Paul, Father Léon-Dufour describes a paradox often found in the life of Jesus' disciples: that new life and possibilities arise, as God's gift, from amidst misfortunes and setbacks. This experience is my own as this translation project is brought, finally, to its completion; and for that I am grateful.

Thanks are due, in the first instance then, to John Loudon and the other staff members of Harper & Row (Dorian Gossy, Melanie Haage, and Janet Reed, to mention but three who had a prominent part in producing the finished copy); their patience with delays at this end was remarkable. Also, to Moira Hughes and Kathleen Robbins, for their cheerfulness and care in typing the handwritten manuscript. Last, I give thanks to my Jesuit companions in Halifax, Nova Scotia (where the translation was begun) and to those at Regis College, Toronto (where it was completed) for the constant encouragement they gave me in so many ways. To them this translation is affectionately dedicated.

Terrence Prendergast, S. J.

Toronto, Ontario
14 August 1986

Author's Foreword

Another work on death? Isn't the literature on the topic already more than enough? Historical and sociological inquiries on human behavior in the face of death, philosophical essays, testimonies of faith—our generation seems fascinated by the specter that twenty years earlier it fled. It is as if we are trying to renew bonds with ancestors from past ages. We want to tame death.

We even want to change it. This at least is beneficial, for it means alleviating the suffering of those dying. In fact, this effort is aimed more at making the present life more bearable than at understanding death. Death, in and of itself, is beyond us, even though it also remains a permanent question for us.

To the throbbing question of death, many answer "with an icy silence to the deity's eternal silence." Christians, however, want to make more of it. From the outset, let me admit that this book has been written in the light of faith. It presupposes, on my part, that God is *the* living being beyond all others and, as well, that Jesus Christ lives forever. Does this mean that someone who regards himself as an "unbeliever" ought to lose interest in these pages right off the bat? Not at all! For it is quite possible, even probable, that this rejection of God is concerned not with the God who lives, the one whom as a Christian I confess in my faith, but rather with some representation or other which, alas, all too often is given to God.

The living God, whom the Bible reveals, shares nothing in common with the great watchmaker of the universe. According to the philosophers, God is "transcendent" and yet "immanent." Or to put it in more contemporary terms, simultaneously completely within and completely outside, totally other and yet totally near. This hidden God, who is involved in human history, is the living one in the strictest sense, the source and the sustainer of all that is alive.

I believe, too, that Jesus of Nazareth rose from the dead and lives forever. I cannot exactly "imagine" how he lives but I experience his presence. Not like an object set to one side of me, but as that of a personal being who is at work in the universe and in me, enabling me to be present to others in love and to trust in the living God who will bring me even through death.

So far so good! But doesn't this faith stem from a beautiful dream? Isn't it more realistic to be satisfied with the stoic's resignation, which welcomes death in all its starkness, eschewing any attempt to give it meaning? This present work is not the kind that finds a place within apologetic presentations of the Christian faith, nor is it a dogmatic synthesis of what faith represents. Rather, it modestly seeks to examine terms used by the ordinary Christian as well as the terminology of Scripture.

Today's way of speaking, for example, might take the form of a celebrity's question asked on the radio: "How can one accept a religion that depicts God sending his Son to death in order to save us? Can we honestly believe today in such a cruel and barbaric God, whom people dare to claim is prefigured by Abraham sacrificing his beloved son?" Today's way of describing things is also found in the Latin American devotion to the *Cristos de los dolores* (the sorrowful Christ) who displays his bloody wounds to have the poor patiently bear with the oppression that keeps them in misery. Today's approach is also found in the words of the preacher who presents Jesus' suffering as the means by which redemption was effected.

There is no need to belabor this point. More worthwhile is the effort to sketch the outlines of the Christian mind set underlying such depictions. Instead of changing along with the pattern of theological developments in various ages, this mind set survived in varying depth—but always well rooted—in what we call Christian culture. The following are the main characteristics of this view. If death is found in the world, it maintains, this is as a consequence of sin, for the order of justice, once destroyed by sin, could not be reestablished except by a penalty. To redress the offense done to God demanded that God personally make expiation and suffer. So God demanded the death of a Son, who offered himself as a mediator. In fact, Luke seems to say precisely this: "Did not the Christ have to endure these sufferings?" Our death would derive its meaning, then, from the fact that Jesus, God's Son, had welcomed his as the means of human redemption: "By his death he saved us." By his death and the blood that he shed, he appeased God's wrath and reestablished the order of justice. Also, once the human person joins his or her death to Christ's, he or she discovers its meaning. Each person ought, therefore, to welcome suffering and death as graces from God.

To what conclusions did such explanations lead? Doubtless, to heroic dispositions, which deserve to be admired. But also to an unjustifiable submissiveness in the face of this world's injustices. Without wanting to, but with that complicity deriving from the instinct for passivity inherent in humanity, such an understanding went along with an attitude of resignation in the face of the fatalism of evil. And this was the case as truly for the affluent as it was for the poor.

With such consequences, who would not understand the revolt of sensitive people? Room was thereby made for a revolution that would attempt to sweep away everything, not only the unjust social order but also the religion that had made itself the underpinning of that order. How could one not reject this depiction of God who seemed to take pleasure in the suffering of his Son and who seemed to encourage the victims of human greed to cherish their slavery by making a better tomorrow a sparkling attraction? Did this theory not maintain that suffering was meritorious for heaven?

To elaborate fully all the aspects of such a mentality requires long and exacting labors; it means getting rid of the chaff without losing the wheat. Death and suffering in themselves ought never to be magnified, but they should always be situated in relation to the Resurrection, which gives them meaning. This is what the liturgical reform of the Easter Vigil showed and continues to show. This is what spiritual writers express when, desiring to have the believer fix his gaze on the Christ who lives forever, invite him to recognize in people's suffering an enemy to be mercilessly fought against; all the while these same spiritual people know how to welcome death and suffering when they are thrust upon them. All these Christians do not empty out the meaning of Christ's death; they situate it in its proper perspective.

This book moves along the same pathway. Its intention is to address the topic of our death as an aspect of the death of Jesus. More precisely, since it is written by an author who is an exegete, it strives to understand the texts on which our faith is founded. Unfortunately, these texts have often been distorted, even deformed, to justify certain social conditions and, on the rebound, they have been minimized or simply been lost sight of.

Among other things, we are hereby faced with a hermeneutical problem. In these last few years I have tried to expound the meaning of "resurrection" terminology, the meaning of the word *miracle*, and even to specify as explicitly as possible the majority of the terms used in the New Testament. Each time I ran up against philosophical or theological presuppositions. What is the body? Is the human person composed of body and soul? What is time and what is eternity? Finally, underlying all these, who is God and what relation does he have with the created world?

Long past is that time when one could imagine being able to speak of one thing or another with a "commonsense" philosophy. We have to take cognizance of our dependence on the milieu in which we were reared and in which we live; otherwise we run the risk of equating our language with the mystery being looked at.

When I undertook this task, I naively believed that its completion would be swift. But I was quickly brought down a peg or two, my biblical sense constantly being hurtled against the language received from the texts. The usual words were snares: *sacrifice, expiation, shed blood, merit, satisfaction, substitution*, and so on. Let me share with you a discovery that clarified my enterprise. For a long time I had been buffeted by two classical ways of speaking. Theologically, there had been a tendency doubly to isolate Jesus' death from his life, which preceded it and which made it partially intelligible, as well as from the Resurrection, which followed it and gave it meaning. In this way there came about a tendency to preach on the merit of the blood that had been shed and to make of Christ's death a kind of saving act of magic. Existentially, in everyday life, the same mistake was extended by isolating the death and the suffering of human persons, conferring on them meaning in themselves.

It was in order to escape these illusory distortions that I sought to revise my vocabulary and, following the lead of recent theologians but also through examining the texts more carefully, I attempted to develop a terminology that would be intelligible today. The reader is thus invited to look anew; also to grasp how one can communicate the faith he or she is trying to live. May this work to some degree correct the crooked notions about Jesus' death and our own deaths, which lie so close to hand for us today.

I wish to take this opportunity to say how precious to me and how efficient Renza Arrighi's collaboration in this work has been. Also, how much I owe to my audience at Centre Sèvres, who enthusiastically welcomed the first sketch of these pages.

Xavier Léon-Dufour

Paris
Easter 1979

Introduction

It is important in beginning this work to specify what I mean by the word *death,* by the reality that it designates and by its meaning which I am trying to grasp for myself today. First of all, apart from any faith stance, death is the cessation of what we call the "vital" signs: no breathing, no pulse, no more heartbeats—let us leave to the doctors the description of difficulties regarding clinical death and definitive death. For our purposes it is sufficient to say that, for everyone, *to die* means to disappear and to stop living. The word *death* is necessarily defined as an aspect of life.

"Spectators" of death will differ in their appreciation of it according to their understanding of life. If some limit life to that biological existence that can be sensibly grasped, then it is clear that the term *death* can only be used in two ways: either realistically, as I have just done, or metaphorically, as, for example, when one speaks of civic death, the death of trade, the death of a civilization. But if, through my faith, I think that life is not reducible to material existence, if it instead knows a secret origin that is God himself, then I will be brought to discover a new dimension to death, without however leaving the realm of reality. Let us start with the fact that God alone is alive. It follows that to cut oneself off from God is to cut oneself off from life; this would mean to really die, although at a level other than that of biological existence. This is sin in its root meaning, breaking with God and so with life: this is spiritual death. Thus we have the possibility, along with the Bible, of speaking of a "second death," without in any way having to do with a metaphor.

Physical death and spiritual death: these are two uses of the word death. Let us add an important distinction. These two kinds of usage are not properly separable, as if they coexisted one alongside the other. In fact, they enjoy a relationship that is not easy to specify but one that is fundamental. The "spiritual" world is not a world juxtaposed with the physical world; it belongs to another order. Here, then, is the reason why the two realities are "symbolically" linked. With the Bible, and more precisely with Paul and Jesus, we grasp the relationship that fits them together, namely that physical death—without losing any of its phenomenal character—can symbolize spiritual death. In the believer's eye, then, it acquired a dimension that remains concealed for unbelievers, a hidden dimension. I do not take anything away from its common meaning but I can read into it, in its deepest significance, the death that separates from God, "spiritual" death. Put in another way, death in its harshness presents a double visage to me, each and both opposed to life, and yet stirring up in me sentiments of revolt or fear.

Clearly, the believer hopes that God who brought him into being will not go against himself and let him be shipwrecked in nothingness; he is even assured of God's pardon. God does not want the sinner to perish but to live. So, temporal death itself comes to be depicted in various guises to the believer's eyes, sometimes as a sorrowful wrenching away, a separation, a break, at other times as a peaceful passage to "heaven." To the pair of physical death-spiritual death, we need to add the pair of wrenching death-passage death. If the first pair belongs to the symbolic order, linking two distinct realities belonging to different orders, the second describes two versions of the same happening.

Now, to speak of a "passage" is to hint at eternal life, a life that is not identical to earthly life, for words fail to describe something that no eye belonging to this world has ever seen. From this vantage death can appear as a place for the transformation of beings; but how can one reconcile the body's destruction—that is, the total corruption of a living organism—with the continuity in being of "me"—something that necessarily implies the idea of transformation?

For faith, all these uses are concrete: biological death, spiritual death, wrenching death, passage death, destruction death, and transfiguration death. On the other hand, New Testament terminology also presents metaphorical uses of the word *death,* at first glance analogous uses of current terms that we mentioned above. So, we find the maxim that communicates human wisdom: "Unless the grain of wheat dies, it does not bear fruit" and the instance in which Jesus spoke of "losing one's life." In other cases, the metaphorical usage seems obscure and one would have to specify the anchor point in each instance. Thus, for example, "to be baptized into the death of Christ" refers to the historical death of Jesus of Nazareth understood as a salvific act. When Paul says, "Death is at work in us, but life in you," he considers this same death of Jesus to have the effect of a "dying" that is at work in him. We note, moreover, that there are reverse usages: to say that one must "die to sin" is a reversal of terms, because it is sin that causes death and not the contrary. Now, all these metaphorical uses suggest that death, anticipating itself, already exists in life, well before the last encounter happens.

This work intends to clearly state the precise meaning this word takes on in various New Testament texts. I wish to caution the reader against too hasty a judgment. I am not so naive as to think that I can resolve the meaning of death by doing this. Death remains a mystery, just like love.

QUESTIONS OF TERMINOLOGY

To speak of death means to gaze on a mystery, and it means as well to encounter the phrases of a classical catechism—that is, the descriptions through which people tried to communicate it. I would like to enumerate briefly several delicate questions that will necessarily come up in the course of these pages. I do not want in any way thereby to put theology on trial. I will be satisfied to come to grips with the contemporary terminology.

First of all, with regard to *final ends:* what happens to us at death? According to the usual description, the particular judgment takes place at death and determines the lot of each individual: this one goes to hell or to heaven after spending some time in purgatory in order to be rendered fit for heavenly bliss. At the end of time there will be a second judgment, the last and universal one, followed as well by the resurrection of the body. In the meantime, the heavenly existence of the elect is that of "separated souls" who, nonetheless, delight already in the "beatific vision." Moreover, for infants who die without baptism, "limbo" has been imagined—indeed, I would say, quite well "imagined," because there is, strictly speaking, no question of such in the New Testament. Apropos of hell, for a long time it served to frighten because of its punishments, which people did their utmost to describe in detail.

Another imaginative exercise was to locate these destinies. Up until quite recently, heaven, purgatory, and hell were depicted as places where the souls of the departed lived after having left their bodies, the soul being a spiritual substance and by nature immortal. An intermediate time then elapsed before the earthly bodies, after being revivified and leaving their graves, would be retrieved by their souls.

It is quite clear that these depictions all derive from a specific philosophy of time and eternity, from an ancient cosmogony, as well as from an anthropology that we will see is not biblical. However, it was with such images that we were raised in the Christian faith, at any rate those not so young among us. Earth, then, would be the place and the time to prepare for heaven; earth has its value in relation to heaven. If we suffer, this will be the occasion of merit that in paradise will become the source of glory.

Faced with this imaginary understanding of the afterlife, which tends to turn earth into a "valley of tears" and which provokes flight toward heaven and a risk of freezing activity in behalf of men and women, how should we not reckon as legitimate the reproach of those who struggle against a religion that is the "opium of the people"? In addition, ideas of "punishment" can only root in one's spirit a false conception of a God who punishes and avenges the offenses committed against him.

We are now up against a wall, for to speak of Christian death straightaway implies a reference to the *death of Jesus Christ*. In dying on the cross, we have learned, Jesus merited salvation for

us: "by his wounds we were healed." In the *Office of Readings*,
the praying person is invited to recite with the poet:

> O Passover lamb,
> O lamb that saves from exile,
> You came to ransom the lost sheep
> And you paid the price of blood.

What then does "redemption," what does Jesus' "sacrifice"
mean? Was Jesus punished in our place, his sufferings being the
Son's terrible expiation demanded by the Father? The Christian,
in his or her case, is invited to treasure the pains of life within a
perspective of "doing reparation" and to build up the inner spiritual being with a certain kind of "mortification" that is self-
destructive.

Well now, we are going to claim that Jesus did not desire suffering nor the cross insofar as these might be meritorious; he simply accepted them as the inevitable consequence of his mission
and his witness. If this is so, does his death still have salvific significance for all?

When we use the word *sacrifice*, it must be carefully specified,
for in the Christian dispensation sacrifice no longer has anything
to do with suffering as such, because of the break with the former
cultic order that has taken place. And so the whole gamut of
words that have to do with sacrifice is called into question: *expiation, satisfaction, shed blood,* and so on. At this point I would
like to puzzle the reader by asking what, for example, he or she
understands by *expiation.* Let us consult the dictionary definition.
In the *Petit Robert, to expiate* means "to repair by undergoing
an expiation that has been imposed or accepted . . . by extension,
to pay for by suffering a consequence or by a disposition of guilt";
thus one "expiates one's rashness." Expiation is defined there as
"a religious ceremony meant to appease celestial wrath . . . in the
Christian religion, the reparation of sin by penance," the latter
being "an irksome practice which one imposes on oneself to expiate one's sins." It is easy to recognize in these definitions the

echo of a certain type of catechetical teaching or oratory that was typical up until the recent era.

In opposition to this, we shall state that penitential practice, suffering, reparation are not immediately involved in the term *expiation*. To make use today of a word that has radically changed in meaning is to lead people into error, particularly when only the activity of the subject who "expiates" is taken into account. Now, if we take into account the Latin etymology of the word, *to expiate* means to render once again favorably disposed someone who had broken off a relationship with someone else; above all this concerns a relationship between two parties. To put it briefly, despite the evolution the phrase has undergone in the English language, "to expiate sins" does not mean to undergo punishment, whether or not it is proportionate to the fault; it means to let oneself be reconciled to God through faith that is at work.

This quick survey shows that the terminology in use to describe the effectiveness of Jesus Christ's life and death often is conditioned by erroneous understandings of the scriptural text, and this begets further defective descriptions of the mystery. There is then a felt need to rediscover the meaning of the words and figures exployed in the New Testament, a task entrusted to the exegete first of all.

GOAL AND METHOD

The exegete has a task limited to the search for meaning. His field of work, as for the dogmatician, is the Bible. No less than the latter, he or she is bound to the categories of his or her era and to the state of allied disciplines (linguistics, history, archaeology . . .). No less than the Bible, does he pretend to attain an illusory objectivity, of the kind found in what are called the exact sciences.

The exegete's role, however, differs from that of the dogmatician, because tradition does not have the same role in this trade. While the dogmatician has to take into account the multiplication of interpretations given to the Scripture through the ages, the ex-

egete is obliged to eliminate these methodically. Only the dogmatician strives to give the text's meaning in all its fullness,
beginning with the relationship that links Scripture and tradition;
the exegete offers a result limited by reason of his methodological
option. Sometimes also people regard its conclusions as rather ane-
mic, compared with the fruits of dogma or spirituality.

But the exegete's role is necessary, for it illustrates where the
originating point of tradition is located. Again we need to be precise. The exegete must not be confused with the historian, who
concerns himself above all with reaching, behind the interpretation
of the evangelists, the historical essence made up, for example, of
the *ipsissima verba* (the very words) of Jesus or his very own
deeds. The exegete, too, has to take into account the interpretations given in the texts in the New Testament itself. The relationship that joins these interpretations and the historical focal
point is in fact what the exegete is able to produce with the help
of the tools of our epoch.

In his turn, the dogmatician, confronted with the results obtained by the clearing off of later accretions, is invited to understand the relation of tradition with the Scripture itself. These
observations may quite usefully be kept in mind if one is to grasp
the limited scope of this work: on the manner in which Jesus
depicted his own death, for example.

The problems discussed in the following pages, accordingly,
concern the terminology in which the message of the New Testament about death has been communicated. This will require that
special attention be paid to understanding the death of Christ, that
alone gives meaning to every death. Thus, this book extends, in
some fashion, what was written in *The Resurrection of Jesus and
the Message of Easter* (French edition 1971; English translation
1974) about the various terms used to communicate the mystery
of Christ alive after his Passion. To tell of the meaning of death,
we likewise will claim that there is a plurality of terms; this is
crucially important to the faith, for this affects its understanding
and its communication.

To speak of terms means speaking of multiple interpretations of one single and unique event—in this instance, the thought and behavior of Jesus when he faced death. So the exegete in this faces up to historical inquiry. With the outlook of learning what Jesus could say and do, the historian examines texts in two ways: on the one hand, in spite of their particular viewpoint, to establish the words that Jesus actually said or the actions he performed; on the other hand, to note successively the various viewpoints in the texts. It is through this twofold movement that the historian gains the opportunity to discern the attitude of Jesus of Nazareth. He or she is not thereby limited to producing a "historical Jesus," a colorless personality unable to reflect the full reality of the past; he or she also would want to examine the major interpretations of the gospel and compare these with the first treasure trove.

Two fundamental criteria allow for the recognition of an authentic word or deed of Jesus. The first is that of its *difference*: in comparing what has been attributed to Jesus by the evangelists with what we know of the contemporary Jewish world and primitive Christianity we detect similarities and differences. What cannot derive either from the Jewish milieu or early Christianity may be reckoned authentic. Yet this criterion is one-sided: all the same, Jesus could have spoken and acted like a good Jew, for example, in believing that he would one day rise from the dead. As an analytical criterion this one in no way justifies, by toting up its results, a "reconstitution" of Jesus' personality. It needs to be complemented, as well, by a second criterion, that of *coherence*: the various expressions of a personality derive from a unique focal point. One can then cause the global picture obtained elsewhere to cautiously interact with the texts that are less certain analytically. Having worth as a synthesis, since it is obligated to take the personality of Jesus as something whole, this criterion depends, just as the earlier one does, on the exegete's approach. Having said this, it remains for us to note that these criteria are both indispensable in reaching the goal because of their mutual interplay.

When it is a question of the viewpoints of texts that an exegete has to take into account, how is he to treat the synoptic gospels?

All too often, and even recently, works have not avoided offending in this domain. One imagines oneself able to reach the goal by basing oneself on what the most ancient traditions, those called "primitive," say. There are two "foundational sources" Mark and Q (the material common to Matthew and Luke and absent from Mark), from which one could elaborate Jesus' very own thought. And, without wincing, one gives oneself leave to build edifices on the life of Jesus or Christian existence, while showing oneself a slave to the results of one or another school of exegesis. Two criticisms should be voiced in opposition to such a reading. In the first place, one does not strictly speaking get at the event but at a tradition that is thought to be primitive; so why dare to present this outcome as the thing itself? In the second place, it is certain that one has not thereby taken account of the other traditions (that of Luke or that of Matthew, and even that of John) to be able to establish the relationship that, by uniting these various interpretations, better allows for a sighting of the event itself.

I have just referred to the Fourth Gospel. I myself had thought for a long time that an historical study of Jesus' thought had to be limited to the three Synoptics, for they are not as theologically elaborated as the text of John is. Now, the witnesses all have to be examined both on what they state and on the way they state it. John himself comes to us as an evangelist; he intends to educate the community of his day by making one Jesus of Nazareth live again in faith. Hence, there is a pressing demand that we take account of the Fourth Gospel as well as the Synoptics. At every stage of my presentation on Jesus facing death, I forced myself, then, to take into account the Johannine interpretation. Without doubt there will be Christians who will be happy to see me retrieve the Fourth Gospel in this way, but they would be sadly mistaken if they thought that I did this independent of critical methods in the style of the ancient "lives of Jesus." This is not a case of artificially combining the data of John with those of the first three gospels—this kind of harmonizing is intolerable—but of recognizing and locating his tradition. Conversely, there will be exegetes who will reproach me for this intervention of John in a work that in the first instance has an historical objective. Allow me to challenge their outlook. If I have recourse to John, it is to allow him to intervene as an interpreter of the tradition and to show his relationship to the synoptic interpretation. I even dare to mention that the Johannine text is a key to the authenticity of what can be retained from the Synoptics. This then is why in this work I allowed myself to take up anew the interpretation of the Gethsemane episode and that of Jesus' last cry. If the reader wishes to appreciate the method applied here, recourse should be had to these chapters. In any case, the Johannine tradition offers a totally different picture of Christ going to death on the cross, a picture with enormous importance to an understanding of death in general.

To arrive at this New Testament understanding, it seemed to me essential to not be satisfied with looking at the gospel tradition; I judged it indispensable to research as well the way in which Paul related himself to the death of Jesus and to death itself. From all the evidence, this was required by the investigation of terminology that we set in motion. In fact, what Jesus did not make explicit, Paul did; not only under the form of a theory on death, but also as an expression of his own experience. As one aspect of the inquiries of his correspondents, he offered an understanding of the mystery of Christ, without thereby making Jesus of Nazareth live again, as an evangelist would. Not only did he testify to his faith, he also reflected it: Jesus, the crucified, lives; we share in his death and his life. From the outset Paul was seized by the paschal mystery: his theological discourse on the cross went on being clarified and amplified; in addition, he tried to show to the recipients of his letters the meaning that the death of their friends could have. Finally, he himself was faced with suffering and the threat of death. Thus, we can enter into the spirit of a simple believer and the first theologian of Christianity, at the same time grappling with the difficult problem of Paul's language concerning the death of Jesus.

This work does not constitute an exhaustive New Testament theology on death. The Epistle to the Hebrews, on its own, represents a specific reading of Jesus' death and its efficacy for the human race; we can only touch on it in passing. And there is also what Peter and John say in their letters, not to mention the Book of Revelation. This would have required the exegetical study of the viewpoints of all the New Testament writers as well as showing their relationship with the results uncovered in this work. I leave this concern to others, and to the theologian of dogma that of bringing this outcome to bear on the data of the whole dogmatic tradition. Only then would we be able to reckon that we had related thoroughly the meaning of death according to Christian faith—a colossal undertaking!

THE APPROACH TAKEN

Here we are at the beginning of the task. The foregoing options dictate the divisions of this book. Instead of a synthetic exposition, I have chosen the viewpoints of two remarkable men who faced death, Jesus and Paul.

In the first part I will try to enter into the mystery of the person of Jesus both by searching out the firmest historical substrate that underlies the interpretations of the evangelists and by clarifying the result of this through their varied viewpoints. Here too it was necessary to be courageous and limit myself so as not to be crushed by the abundance of material. I divided the inquiry to take into account Jesus' view on death in general and then particularly on the deaths of other people (Part One) and after this on death itself (Parts Two–Four). For this latter section another division allowed for the treatment of Jesus' attitude according to whether death appeared to him as threatening (Chapter 2), imminent (Chapter 3), or being experienced (Chapter 4). This structure has the added advantage of following, as much as possible, a certain chronological order. It runs the risk of misleading anyone who would want to draw conclusions before having read all the chapters, as I will make clear later on.

Many of the questions raised in this section dealing with Jesus, especially that regarding his death as "redemptive," do not receive an answer until we get to the presentation of Paul's theology. As a matter of fact, this work tries to be aware of the gap that separates Paul's theology and Jesus' own existence—not to insinuate wrongly that Paul is unfaithful to Jesus, but to show the difference that there is between the behavior and sayings of a man who expresses himself existentially and the constructs that a theologian elaborates.

The approach taken here will be the following: first of all, Paul the Jew, faced with the death of Jesus, the significance of which was revealed to him by the Damascus Road experience (Chapter 5); then, inquiring about the essence and power of death on one hand (Chapter 6) and, on the other, about suffering which remains in the world after Christ's victory (Chapter 7); and, lastly, Paul faces his own death (Chapter 8).

Despite its two parts, this work forms a whole, in such a way that one ought not to disengage one chapter or another from the statements that are necessarily partial and must be situated within the totality of the book. It is from this approach, patiently pursued, that a Christian vision of death must be distilled. If I state that Jesus did not explicitly characterize his death as a "sacrifice," this does not mean that Paul did not do so; but this statement is useful to stress the sovereign way in which Jesus located himself within his language without ever subjecting himself to some such custom of his time. Thus do we grasp the universality of Jesus, who reigns above every possible language. In the case of Paul, it is equally important not to reduce to a single formulation his expressions of the mystery; I carefully note that sacrificial terminology is not his principal one: it exists but it has to be situated among the other terms used by the same Paul, ones that occupy much more room in his thought and that are more clearly in a direct line with the thought or conduct of Jesus. To repeat myself again, it is not possible in fact to encapsulate the mystery in one set of terms. The issue is all the more important because we are dealing with mind sets geographically and sociologically different from the European mentality proper to a certain theological era and, as a consequence, it would be foolish to impose on them a cultural mode through which not only Paul but particularly later theologians believed it appropriate to embody the gospel message. Moreover, no subsequent interpretation has value unless it firmly maintains a close connection with the foundational event.

The reader is invited to undertake a difficult task. In order not to be discouraged, on a first reading he or she should be content with gleaning bits of information here and there, postponing to a second reading any attempt to master the whole of the analyses, something I tried to do in the conclusion.

Lastly, I repeat, I could not have written this book except for my faith. I do not try to demonstrate the truth of my Christian vision of death; I suppose that, like me, the reader sees in God the one on whom his existence radically depends. To call into question the mystery of God is to refuse to hear the message of Jesus. On the other hand, whoever admits that God is present and alive will surely be able, after a first casting aside of catechetical dispositions, to grasp with greater serenity the mystery of that death to which we are all invited, a mystery that perdures, but nevertheless enlightens our present life.

I. JESUS FACES DEATH

1. Jesus Faces Death in Others

Like the majority of us, Jesus did not first of all face his own death. He experienced it while seeing others disappear. By every likelihood he saw his father Joseph die, and he knew the bloody repression in which, in Year 6 of our era, Varus crucified 2,000 Galilean revolutionaries. This probably happened at Sepphoris, some 4.5 km (almost three miles) from Nazareth[1] when Jesus would have been about twelve years old. The evangelists have not judged these events worth reporting but they can serve us as examples of what his people had to endure. If death was seen and accepted in Israel[2] as every person's normal destiny, still it was reacted against with horror whenever it struck young people or courageous warriors.

Here are aspects of Jesus' personal attitudes toward death that can be gleaned from his sayings and deeds. Receiving Israel's legacy, Jesus did not expressly speak of death except as an aspect of life, because, for a Jew nourished by the Bible,[3] only life itself was judged worthy of interest. And yet, death in its brutal aspects is often alluded to in the gospels. This can be noted through reference to a concordance and its many Greek terms that express the idea of "killing." Though Jesus proclaims peace, he was handed over to a world of brutality.

Postponing to the next chapter the death threats touching Jesus himself, let us sketch the environment surrounding the young prophet. Herod had had John the Baptist killed;[4] the prophets of Israel had been assassinated. God's emissaries had been put to death, and Jesus' disciples would be persecuted in the future.[5] Violent death was so present in his thought that he, the most gentle of all men, was not afraid of recalling the law that condemned anyone who did not honor parents to death.[6] His very parables reflected a cruel world. Brigands left a man journeying from Jerusalem to Jericho by the side of the road half-dead,[7] vineyard workers killed the owner's servants and son,[8] and the king whom they did not want to rule over them[9] himself had the murderers put to death.[10] In such circumstances, what meaning did that commandment have that said, "Thou shalt not kill"? Even though Jesus denounced the anger that was the principle source of homicides,[11] it remains a fact that the world of violence did not acknowledge the message of forgiveness, acceptance, and fraternal love proclaimed by Jesus and it seemed to triumph over him who described himself as gentle and humble of heart.

This was the context for Jesus' thinking. However, one must not reduce his experience of death to violent death only. Every person, including Jesus, is affected in the depth of his being by the loss of those who were dear to him and have been released from their life on earth—the "departed" in the strict sense. But violent death especially shakes our outlook and brings us face to face with the deepest mystery of an existence destined for death.

Here we come to the major points of this chapter. Death coexists with life; death is however, overcome by life; this life transcends and integrates death.

LIFE AND DEATH

In beginning his message, which proclaimed the Kingdom of God, Jesus brought to its completion the authentic Jewish tradition: the living God, from whom all being springs, brought existence to its fulfillment in his envoy; from now on he offers what the Fourth Gospel terms "eternal" life.[12] This was the certainty that characterized Jesus and that clarifies his attitude when he faced others' deaths. On the one hand, death, which is the rupturing of life, is part of the human condition. On the other hand, because it is brutal, death symbolizes another stark reality: everlasting death.

DEATH AND THE HUMAN CONDITION

Unlike philosophers, Jesus did not spell out a theory about death, and the gospels do not hand on his reactions to deaths, which we could call "normal" ones. As well, to grasp the originality of Jesus, we have to try to show what is left unsaid by the gospels.

In Jesus' eyes, as was the case for his Jewish contemporaries, every person would one day "taste death."[13] According to biblical phraseology, one went "to sleep with his fathers," if possible "full of days" and in a "happy old age."[14] This was the way for the whole world.[15] Death in fact, was everyone's ordinary fate.

> O death, how welcome is your sentence
> to one who is in need and is failing in strength
> very old and distracted over everything;
> to one who is contrary, and has lost his patience!

To these down-to-earth reflections, the wise one adds,

Do not fear the sentence of death;
remember those who went ahead of you and those who will come after
this is the decree of the Lord for all flesh
and how can you reject the good pleasure of the Most High?

(Sir 41:2–4)

As a wise man, Jesus did not rebel against the human condition received from the creator; there is no rebellious sentiment before the inescapable nature of death. This peaceful conviction is reflected in the sobriety of his speech, as for example when he says,

The poor man died and was carried by the angels to Abraham's bosom. The rich man also died and was buried.

(Lk 16:22)

The communal experience of death gives rise to symbolic language; for example, in the description of the loss of the prodigal child:

My son was found dead (and he has come back to life).

(Lk 15:32)

However, isn't there room for rebellion against death that strikes someone in the prime of life?

> O death, how bitter is the reminder of you
> to one who lives at peace among his possessions,
> to a man without distractions, who is prosperous in everything
> and who still has the vigor to enjoy his food!
>
> (Sir 41:1)

How can one not even more strongly denounce death when it prematurely seizes on a devout person?

> In my vain life I have seen everything:
> there is a righteous man who perishes in his righteousness,
> and there is a wicked man who prolongs his life in much evil-doing.
>
> (Eccl 7:15)

In answer to this scandal, the psalmist proclaimed well the almighty love of the faithful God,[16] but the sages offered only a theory of retribution.[17] Job also could do no other than cry out his despair, avowing an impenetrable mystery and humbling himself in dust and ashes.[18]

DEATH AND GUILT

This weighty pondering also finds a hearing in the New Testament. Regarding the man born blind, Jesus' disciples ask him,

> Rabbi, who sinned, this man or his parents, that he was born blind?
>
> (Jn 9:2)

According to the teaching of immediate retribution,[19] the scandal of death or sickness striking in some unforeseen and brutal way has to come to articulation: if God truly rewards people here below according to their righteousness, how can one not denounce a sin that lies at the root of the malady or untimely death.

Jesus squarely takes a stand. First of all with a categoric "No": "Neither he nor his parents" sinned, he answers his disciples, refusing to make an intrinsic connection between the sickness and some fault. Well and good, but can this reply calm anxiety?

In another circumstance, Jesus gives the meaning that ought to be taken from two recent misfortunes:

There were some present at that very time who told him of the Galileans whose blood Pilate had mingled with their sacrifices. And he answered them, "Do you think that these Galileans were worse sinners than all the other Galileans, because they suffered thus? I tell you, No; but unless you repent you will all likewise perish [apoleisthe]. Or those eighteen upon whom the tower in Siloam fell and killed [apekteinen] them, do you think that they were worse offenders than all the others who dwelt in Jerusalem? I tell you, No: but unless you repent you will all likewise perish [apoleisthe].

(Lk 13:1–5)

When informed of these two happenings, which we can claim "historical,"[20] Jesus reacted in two ways. He began by taking into account what his contemporaries thought before he himself drew his conclusions. According to the principle of retribution, mentioned above, people deduced a cause-and-effect relationship: there is no misfortune that is not divine punishment come to sanction some fault; if there is misfortune, it is because there was some sin or guilt. Hence, Pilate's victims or those on whom the tower fell had to have been "greater sinners" or "worse offenders"; through the cause-effect relationship their deaths became comprehensible.

But, for Jesus, God's justice cannot be measured according to the norms of human retributive justice.[21] He declares that the Galileans who came to offer sacrifice in Jerusalem had not been greater sinners than their compatriots, nor, moreover, were the victims of the Siloam tower. There is no necessary correlation between a *certain kind of* misfortune and a *certain kind of* sin.

Now, Jesus did not leave the matter only with a negative pronouncement. He changed the perspective and invited his audience to pass on themselves the judgment they laid on others. There is no point in speculating on the responsibility of the unlucky ones and being smug about oneself by saying, for example, "I, at least, was spared." The moral of the story is to put oneself under scrutiny. More specifically, instead of dallying over sundry matters, one should turn one's attention to God's Kingdom, which Jesus proclaimed in his words and actions. Rather than fixate on the accidents, one should discern the moment of the Kingdom of God, which is at hand, the *kairos* as Jesus called it in a statement reported immediately prior to this one:

You hypocrites! You know how to interpret the appearance of earth and sky; but why do you not know how to interpret the present time?

(Lk 12:56)

If the facts are as they are, men and women ought to turn back, "to repent," acknowledging that they are sinners, guilty. To hear the call of God's Kingdom present in Jesus, one ought not reckon oneself more righteous than others: "Unless you repent, you will all likewise perish!"

Now, in concluding in such a fashion, Jesus seems to contradict himself. On one side, he says there is no connection between such a death and such a sin; on the other, he encourages people to leave sin behind so they will not perish. Someone's death is not strictly tied to his sin; and yet, on the other hand, perishing is tied to nonconversion. How to justify such an assertion? The answer to this can be delineated on two levels, one by referring to the universal occurrence of sin and the other by reference to the symbolic significance of death.

By refusing to link misfortune with personal responsibility, Jesus states that misfortune does not necessarily derive from individual sin; but he does not push his explanation further. Moreover, by suggesting that "all" are implicated in the call to conversion, he directs his listeners toward a higher-level reality: sin touches every human person; it is universal.

Theological light will be shed on this reality later by Paul and John who declare war against sin and against the "sin of the world;"[22] that is, the social dimension to the sin of individuals. The universe is a broken world. Consequently, the disasters that afflict men and woman can signify this profound split.[23] Jesus' word, then, serves to interpret this fact: "If you do not rebel against sin's ascendancy in the world, you will be its victims, and disasters will continue."

More immediately, and leaving aside the foregoing theological interpretation, we can more closely approximate Jesus' very word. First of all, we note that there is a difference between the phrases "to be killed" and "to perish." The latter verb can simply designate violent death;[24] however, more often it refers not to the loss of physical life but that definitive fall into Hades, the dwelling place of the dead without hope of return: that is, "perdition."[25] This meaning is even clearer here because it is being distinguished from the term "to be killed." Jesus, then, threatens his questioners not with a violent death but with final death: "If you do not turn back to God, you will go to eternal death." Besides, isn't this a tautology or evidence from a mystical realm for one who knows that God is the only living being, the sole giver of life?

The two catastrophes that happened suggested to Jesus, then, the dramatic human condition that is embroiled in sin. Although he refused to connect sin with a tragic death, this was so as to reveal a secret bond tying sin to final death. Hence, the appeal to conversion that typified his speech. Violent death, accordingly, symbolizes that lost condition (perdition) to which humanity is bound because of the world's sin. That is what a striking declaration by Jesus made clear.

TEMPORAL DEATH AND FINAL DEATH

The precise use of the two terms "to be killed" and "to perish" suggest that Jesus distinguished two kinds of death. This distinction is even more explicit in a saying of Jesus that has been preserved in the source common to Matthew and to Luke (Q).

Mt 10:28	Lk 12:4–5
Do not fear (at all) those who kill (*apoktennontōn*) the body but cannot kill (*apokteinai*) the soul;	Do not fear (at all) those who kill (*apokteinontōn*) the body and after this can do nothing more. I will tell you whom to fear:
fear rather the One who can destroy (*apolesai*) in Gehenna both soul and body!	fear the One who, after having killed, has the power to cast into Gehenna.

An attentive consideration of these two versions introduces our topic. Matthew's text reflects the Semitic tradition more precisely than Luke's. In fact, Luke has modified it by avoiding saying that one could "kill the soul," an expression unintelligible to a Greek, who thought that the soul was immortal by its nature; hence it was sufficient for him to say that one could do no more than kill the body. For his part, Matthew surprises us at first glance: he is the only one in the whole of the New Testament to distinguish body and soul so closely. Generally, the soul was treated as the vital life force given and sustained by God; at other times, the body was regarded as the means by which a person could communicate. In both these instances, soul and body did not designate two elements comprising the human person, but complementary aspects of the one unique person. The human person was not composed of an "immortal" soul and a mortal body. Rather, the human being enjoyed two aspects: that of the soul, by being bound to God the creator for breath; that of the body, which enabled communication with others and with the universe.[26]

When a distinction is made by Matthew between soul and body, this does not imply dependence by him on a new anthropology of a Hellenistic sort. Rather, this points to that facet of life by which the human person is handed over to the power of persons like himself. Human persons can deprive someone of temporal life, but not of eternal life; the first of these referring to the "body," the second, to the "soul." God, the only truly Living One, has power over life in both these aspects, the temporal and the eternal; he can ratify by a person's total perdition that separation that a sinner wants to establish with him. Gehenna is, precisely, the place of a human sinner's punishment in its entirety, soul and body. The text calls for one not to be afraid of a martyr's death, but to be quite afraid of final death. That is the meaning suggested by the presence of the verb "to lose." By using this, instead of the verb "to kill," Jesus indicated the dimension of eternity that impinges on death.

Although final death is alluded to in this way, this is not to frighten, but to draw one to the living God who has all power over soul and body. Men and women, thus, need not fear physical death even when they have to bear witness before courts. This is the meaning highlighted by Jesus in the words reported immediately afterward.

> Are not two sparrows sold for a penny?
> And not one of them will fall to the
> ground without your Father's will.
> But even the hairs of your head are all
> numbered. Fear not, therefore; you are
> of more value than many sparrows.
> (Mt 10:29–31 = Lk 12:6–7)

Encompassed within the paternal embrace of God who is all-powerful, the believer no longer has to be in dread of temporal death, even a violent one.

For Jesus, as for the Bible, physical death participates in the human condition and finds its meaning through its relationship with life.[27] In the case of a violent death, Jesus refused to relate it to any kind of secret culpability on the victim's part, and he did not comment on its source. By contrast, he finds significance in it:

it calls those who witness it to be converted. Furthermore, Jesus sug

gested that it symbolizes the collective risk of perdition brought about by sin in the world; and again, for one bound to God, death is not to be dreaded, for God is the Lord of life beyond death.[28]

LIFE STRONGER THAN DEATH

Although death and life coexist on earth, they do not have the same worth. Only life is worthwhile, death is not. These are the stakes in Israel's faith in the Living God; Jesus is the authentic interpreter of that faith. The Bible accords to death a superhuman power that seems to hold its own even against God.

THE DUEL BETWEEN GOD AND DEATH

Experiences of a death that reaped at random, taking youth and aged, wise and foolish, righteous and wicked, led to the personification of this enemy force under the figure of Death; it was also called the Pit, Sheol.[29] This biblical terminology, sometimes taken up by Jesus, can be described as "mythical"; that is, it attempts to depict in narrative form an existential reality, a reality to which the senses have no access; it tries to account for the mystery of death that man comes up against.

So, a duel between God and death is undertaken. After giving forth a last breath, the human person is "interred," descends into the tomb, into that hole, which, in the end, gets identified as the abyss, hell, the dwelling place of the dead, Hades.[30] He or she then enters the region of darkness and shadow,[31] the place of loss,[32] the country of the forgotten;[33] considering oneself there to be dwelling among the "Shades,"[34] asleep, deprived of all,[35] reckoning oneself excluded from God's memory, cut off from his hand,[36] finding oneself unable of praise or hope.[37] Is this still life? It is rather a nonexistence.[38] A monster with a gaping and insatiable mouth,[39] Sheol lies in wait for its prey and carries it off with full vigor.[40] Thus did Hezekiah in the mid-time of his life see the "gates[41] of Sheol"[42] open. Men and women, God's creation, are so in the grips of an evil power that they appear, from the beginning, to be doomed to death.

Cast as the trophy in this duel between God and death, the human believer knows that God comes out the victor. All the powers, even of Sheol, are dependent on God, who is creator and almighty.[43] God can rescue from sickness and danger[44] and can even bring back from the pit.[45] Without doubt, the wicked are destined to Sheol forever, since they are the flock that Death pastures,[46] but the wise and the righteous are to hold out hope:

But God will ransom my soul from the power of Sheol, for he will receive me.

(Ps 49:15)

Life is promised to the one who remains faithful. A day will come when the very power of Death will be destroyed:

He will swallow up Death forever.

(Is 25:8)

God will come out of it the victor. Let it be so! But how? This hope that the Jews hoped for at the end of time the Christian knows to have been achieved already in Jesus' resurrection from the dead. For his part, Jesus did not wait to be raised before proclaiming in what sense death had already been vanquished in his view. He did so implicitly on the occasion of Jewish burial and mourning practices; he illustrated it symbolically by his gestures of "resurrection."

JESUS AND BURIALS

In the Jewish view, burial seems to have had a twofold purpose. It indicated the final aspect of the decease, so that often the tomb gets identified with Sheol.[47] On the other hand, unlike the corpse, which decayed, it ensured a permanent reminder to those who survived; finally it preserved the identity of the departed. This is why the worst fate that can happen to someone is to be deprived of burial, to be left to the mercy of voracious predators. Of the woman whose bones were scattered, people could no longer say, "That's Jezebel!"[48]

Jesus did not criticize these customs, but he manifested his profound thinking on several occasions. He stressed the two sides of these memorials:

graves which signify nothing, and men walk on them without knowing it;

(Lk 11:44)

white-washed sepulchers, which outwardly appear beautiful, but within are full of dead men's bones and all uncleanness.

(Mt 23:27)

Far from admiring these monuments to the dead or stressing the traditional presence of the prophets in the tombs,[49] Jesus denounced formalistic practices of piety that make use of these tombs to conceal their wicked desires, even murderous ones:

Woe to you *who build the tombs of the prophets, when it was your fathers who killed them!* And you say, "If we had lived in the days of our fathers, we would not have taken part with them in shedding the blood of the prophets." Thus you witness against yourselves that you are sons of those who murdered the prophets! Fill up, then, the measure of your fathers!

(Lk 11:47; and see also Mt 23:29–32)

Finally, without condemning the practice of performing the final duties for one's parents, Jesus refused to make of it an absolute:

To another he said, "Follow me." But he said, "Lord, let me first go and bury my father." But he said to him, "Leave the dead to bury their own dead; but as for you, go and proclaim the kingdom of God."

(Lk 9:59–60; see also Mt 8:21–22)

This saying, apparently harsh, locates human rites in relationship to the arrival of God's Kingdom. The "dead" in this instance refer to those who want "to assure themselves,"[50] of their life, those who imagine that they will live in men's memories, although God is the God of the living and the dead.[51] It is not the memory held by one's descendants that assures one of life after death, because the reality Jesus proclaims is totally other. This he foreshadows in his action.

JESUS AND THE RESUSCITATIONS OF THE DEAD

Several gospel narratives report what are ordinarily referred to as "resurrections" but what we prefer to call "resuscitations"; in fact, in New Testament terminology, "resurrection" designates the passing from death to a life that never ends—something that is not the case with Jairus's daughter, the son of the widow of Nain or Lazarus, any more than it was the case with the children restored to life by Elijah and Elisha.[52]

In three instances, Jesus had contact with people who had just died. His interaction with death appears so startling that it is initially appropriate to examine briefly the historical problem presented by these accounts: how, then, were they handed on?

The historian observes a development from one account to the next. When one considers the editorial redactions of the same episode, the resuscitation of Jairus's daughter, one notes that Jesus' power over death continues to be magnified. According to Mk 5:23, the father said to Jesus, "My daughter is at death's door," and it is during the course of the story that Jairus is informed, "Your daughter is dead, why trouble the Master any further?"[53] In Matthew, the father himself, at the outset, tells Jesus, "My little girl has died just now";[54] Jesus' action immediately and clearly becomes a raising of the dead. That there has been a development in the tradition is confirmed by two details in the narrative, in every regard similar to what occurs in an ordinary healing story: Jairus's request for the "laying on of hands" and Jesus' gesture: "He took the child's hand."[55] Thus, the tradition's tendency was to assimilate this return to earthly life to a resurrection of the dead and, in this, to symbolize Jesus' Resurrection.

The development that we have just described allows us to appreciate the two other episodes of the resuscitation of the dead. While Jairus's little girl was still in the house, the son of the widow of Nain was laid out on a bier[56] and was being carried to the graveside by his mother and a crowd of people. As is still the custom in the East, the interment took place on the very day itself, some eight hours after death.[57] Doubtlessly, then, it was a case of a recent death, one that elsewhere the Jews thought not irrevocable: after the decease, according to their belief, for three days the soul fluttered around the corpse, struggling to enter into it again.[58] All of this argues for the historicity of the account being related.[59]

In the case of the third story, the difficulty has been compounded. Lazarus already has been in the tomb for three days. Ought we to take this precise detail literally? Clearly, according to Jewish belief, after three days the soul can no longer re-enter the body that it has left lifeless.[60] Consequently, it is either a simple detail (but how can we judge historically?) or else it is a feature that John has deliberately stressed; this second hypothesis would be supported by the scholarly advancement of Jesus' dialogue with his disciples or with the Jews.[61] The historian is led to conclude that John wanted to prefigure in a most explicit way Jesus' resurrection.[62] This narrative, whose basis, seemingly, is historical, has been profoundly reworked by the Johannine theology of Jesus' glory, anticipated even during the earthly life, to such an extent that it is scarcely possible to get at the event itself in its details.

In conclusion, Jesus certainly found himself faced with several cases of death, although we do not dare assert that they were "actual" cases of death. So the historian is wont to classify these narratives among the healing stories as borderline cases. But, whatever the historical kernel, Jesus' gesture has been interpreted as heralding his own triumph over death.[63] The best reading that one can make of these accounts is to discover in these actions a delicate prefiguring of God's victory over death. Why could Jesus himself not have conceived of it in the same way?

The symbolic dimension of this narrative has been supported by the terms used by Jesus, as well for ordinary healings as for the resuscitations of the dead.[64] For the former as well as for the latter, Jesus said, for example, "Get up!" The Greek word *egeirein* means "to get up" or "to wake up." Sometimes, when a man goes "to sleep with his fathers," he rejoins horizontally the people of the earth; when Israel has been defeated, prostrate on the ground, a prophet sees an immense army stand up, "and the dead shall rise."[65] At other times, "to die" means to enter into the rest of sleep. After a day, a life filled with days and labors, one "goes to sleep with one's fathers."[66] Hence, the metaphor of the "cemetery" (*koimētērion*), the place where one lies down (*koimaō*); thence, also, the hope of "awakening" foretold by a prophet:

Many of those who sleep in the dust of life earth shall awake, some to everlasting life, and some to shame and everlasting contempt.

(Dn 12:2)[67]

Similarly, for Lazarus as for the daughter of Jairus, Jesus' terminology passes, without transmission, from "he is asleep" to "he is dead." Such is also the terminology of several primitive confessions of faith:

> Awake, O Sleeper, and arise from the dead,
> and Christ shall give you light.
>
> (Eph 5:14)

Whether it is through his terminology or by his gestures, Jesus was depicted as the one who symbolized the Resurrection to come; that is, the victory of life over death.

JESUS AND MOURNING RITUALS

Along with the majority of its neighboring peoples, Israel was familiar with quite complex mourning rituals: fasting, torn clothing, prostrations on the ground, and so on. Through these the friends of the departed come to show their grief at being separated from one dear to them.[68] These rituals, as elsewhere in the East, went to excess, and the Old Testament already struggled against their deviations,[69] perhaps because Yahwist faith and worship was opposed to any worship of the dead. It is a fact that the gospel stories reported the turmoil that went on around the deceased. Jesus, for his part, manifested great calm and tried to make the tumult stop:

He saw a tumult and people weeping and wailing loudly. And when he entered, he said to them, "Why do you make a tumult and weep? The child is not dead, but sleeping." And they laughed at him. But he put them all outside.

(Mk 5:38–40)

Why this calm, if not to suggest that the grieving with its noisy manifestations ought to stop once he arrived, he the one who was unafraid of death and who was convinced that life would win out? This is why Jesus could say to the tearful widow, "Don't cry" or rather, "Stop crying," for he will console her by restoring to her her son.[70]

In the Fourth Gospel, the interpretation becomes even more profound. If the contrast between death and sleep continues from Mark through John, the contrast between weeping and not weeping has been transformed by John. Jesus is seized by the death of his friend. He no longer sovereignly holds in check that deep emotion that comes over those who have just lost a loved one. Clearly, as we have said before, it is difficult to disentangle from this narrative what is strictly historical; nonetheless, as in other cases, it is inappropriate to be content with the historian's bare residue, but one has to take into account the privileged interpretation that is given to it.

When Jesus saw her weeping, and the Jews who came with her also weeping, he was deeply moved in spirit and troubled; and he said, "Where have you laid him?" They said to him, "Lord, come and see." Jesus wept. So the Jews said, "See how he loved him!" But some of them said, "Could not he who opened the eyes of the blind man have kept this man from dying?" Then Jesus, deeply moved again, came to the tomb.

(Jn 11:33–38)

The nuances in the text allow us to be more precise about the situation. Jesus was deeply moved in two ways: by the crowd's sobbing and by the unbelief it manifested. The term connotes a certain irritation when faced with some behavior.[71] Here, since before the second mention John adds "again," Jesus' irritation may be due in both cases to the same motive, namely the absence of true faith. The matter is clear in the repetition. How can they fail to recognize Jesus' omnipotence over death? How also, then, can they also give themselves over to these quasi-spontaneous tears (laments, groaning, sobs) ordinarily directed to draw others' attention, all while they are in the presence of Jesus, the one who proclaims himself personally to be the Resurrection?

Now, this is Johannine paradox. The man whose irritation signifies knowledge of life's mystery, this one is "troubled." According to John's interpretation, this is because "trouble" must normally precede mastery over death. Thus Jesus must pass through troubling before he gives thanks to the Father who always hears his prayer,[72] before asking the Father to glorify his name,[73] before glorifying God who lets him fall into his traitor's hands.[74] Death, present in the corpse, is thus the source of Jesus' trouble, as for everyone, as it will be for the disciples whom Jesus will leave behind.[75]

And this dead man was his friend. Jesus begins to weep, to shed tears, a reaction less calculated and more personal than the sobs.[76] Quite probably, for John, these tears express not only the grief caused by the loss of his dear friend, since the love with which Jesus loved Lazarus came from the Father;[77] these tears of Jesus also symbolize God's own tears, faced with death, which separates persons.

While the Synoptics seem to depict a Jesus who is more serene when facing others' deaths, because of his mastery over death itself, John has us enter more deeply into the mystery of Jesus.[78] The dominion that he wields over death's power does not spare him the feeling of sadness that touches him at the most intimate level of himself. Thus, he is troubled when confronted with death, which decomposes a man's body; when confronted as well with men and women crushed by the destiny and fate, which the tomb symbolizes; confronted lastly by what foretells his death for him.

And yet, Jesus the person who suffers in seeing humanity handed over to the infernal power is the same one who, through his union with the Father, feels in himself a surge of life's force, which is stronger than death.

LIFE AFTER DEATH

By the weight of human sadness it creates, as well as by its representation of the break between God and men that it symbolizes, the death of others surely troubled Jesus, without thereby calling into question his certainty that the living God would conquer death. This fact clearly stands out in a unique and strange controversy that Jesus engages in with the Sadducees in the case of the woman who had married seven husbands.

And as for the resurrection of the dead, have you not read what was said to you by God, "I am the God of Abraham, the God of Isaac and the God of Jacob?" He is not the God of the dead, but of the living.

(Mt 22:31–32p)

Luke is more precise: "for him all (the dead) live"; they all share in his glory. So, for Jesus, God revealed himself to Moses as the God of the patriarchs; that is, the living God who directs the history of those who live. Such is the shining evidence that clarifies Jesus' terminology.

In fact, Jesus often used his contemporaries' representation to tell of what had to be after death, but he constantly transformed them out of his personal experience. This way of doing things ought to be emphasized because in our day any language that attempts to address a reality beyond our experience spontaneously meets with skepticism. The Risen One himself did not confide anything on the topic. So, it is important to recall what terms Jesus used and what function he attributed to them in his proclamation of God's Kingdom.

In order to describe, if possible, the realities of the afterlife, Jesus took up images and conceptions from his era. Thus, recompense would be made to the Twelve "when all things are made new."[79] Or again, "when the Son of man comes in his glory, escorted by all the angels, . . . all nations will be assembled before him,"[80] and "he will render to everyone according to his behavior,"[81] that is, final damnation or eternal life.[82] Let us begin our reflection by recalling what Jesus said about these last things: the wonderful festival celebrated in joy and communion or else a definitive separation in exterior darkness, what we call heaven and hell.

HEAVEN OR HELL

"Heaven" is depicted with the help of several symbolic realities: it is God's throne,[83] it is the Kingdom into which human persons are invited to enter.[84] Above all, it is the wedding banquet celebrated by God and humanity, an image that tells of the joy in the communitarian happiness of all the elect, the "Master's joy" shared with women and men.[85] Jesus scarcely held on to any of the traditional statements, except that of the Resurrection,[86] but he added to it that of his own presence: he will serve at table those who have proven faithful to the end.[87] When one tries to bring these diverse images together in relation to their symbolic value, we find a quite simple statement: heaven is the joy of always being with God, with Jesus and his brethren or else a statement that picks up the intuition of a Jewish tradition that called God "heaven."[88] Heaven is God himself.

Conversely, hell is existing "without God," separated from God

and Jesus: "Depart from me! I don't know you!"[89] In trying to
lay hold of this condition of "final death," various representations
were proposed, more numerous than those of heaven—as if the
reality was even more difficult to specify. So we find Gehenna,
the place of punishment by fire,[90] the fire that does not die,[91] the
worm that consumed everything,[92] weeping and grinding of
teeth,[93] the exterior darkness that shrouds those who are outside
the banquet hall.[94] All these images attempt to paint one single
reality in all its honor: to be separated from the living God,[95] to
be cut off from the source of life, to die ceaselessly.

Stripped in this way of the glitter with which it has been
adorned in the course of time, hell can be thought about by those
who truly believe that God is God and the human person is a
being joined to him by his breath. Let us immediately note that
this hell was not created by God to punish the wicked, but that
it has been produced by men and women who fail to appreciate
the unique source of life: God cannot constrain the one who wants
to withdraw himself definitively from his love. Let us remark, in
addition, that we cannot speak of hell except as Christians, and
the consequences are measured: my faith affirms the possibility of
hell, my hope rejects it for myself, and my love repudiates it for
anyone. For how can one admit the possibility of a definitive separation from God and from one or another of my sisters and
brothers?

JUDGMENT

If heaven and hell truly ratify the option taken in the course of
one's earthly life for or against God, why go on then to speak of
"judgment"? Will God on the last day come to sanction outwardly
human behavior? This question deserves to be squarely put, for
it preoccupies many minds, even though there have disappeared
the traces left behind by the "horrors" of the Last Judgment, ones
that terrified so many little children, innocent victims of the struggle for power by preachers who had little eloquence. The question
remains a pressing one, for the Last Judgment is one of the most
widely attested of the biblical data and an article of faith: "He will

come one day to judge the living and the dead." What, then, are we to understand by the reality of the judgment?

In a general sense, judgment is an activity of the spirit whereby the relationship in truth between two terms comes to expression; to get at this, we proceed by way of inquiries, verifications, and so on. However, judgment essentially consists in the sentence that is brought to bear on a state of unclarity, of the nonevident, or of obscurity. Solomon, for example, determined between two women, discerning which was the true mother of a child.[96] So Jesus, according to John, declared that judgment consists in the division between light and darkness,[97] something that presupposes a state of conflict. Judgment, then, does not amount to a ratification; it is at one and the same time a discernment and a division, as the Greek word *krisis* neatly expresses it.[98]

When applied to the Last Judgment, the word presumes that humanity is in a condition that requires clarification and alleviation. Someone may well say, "My conscience does not accuse me of anything," yet all the same at the core of his being he knows there is an area of obscurity that escapes him. Furthermore, men and women do not need to be persuaded that among themselves at various levels a more of less open warfare is carried on, with the fatal consequence of disagreements and misunderstandings. Is it necessary to demonstrate that all people long to leave this state of injustice and to clarify the last recesses of existence? Certainly not. The problem is finding the means to attain this light and this peace.

It is here that faith in God intervenes. All men and women are dependent on the Creator, on the one who alone knows the human heart. It is to him, then, that judgment hearkens back; namely, God's revelation of the depths of hearts, God's re-establishment of truth and justice, and, by means of these, God's making evident the marvellous operation of grace in each person. Conceived in this way, judgment belongs to God, to a God who, according to Jesus' message, is infinitely good. But we can also say that it is the human person who, in a definitive way, judges himself in God's light: his works manifested in full daylight, revealing that deepest choice either to be with or against the Lord. The perspective of the judgment is also an invitation to improve human existence here below; it prompts a transformation of the present state of this earth.

Here, then, it seems to me, it is appropriate to hear of this through the terrifying terms of the Old and even sometimes the New Testament,[99] at least if we agree not to take these images as a material description of the coming reality. It will take great lengths to show this. Let us be content with focusing our attention on the allegory of the Last Judgment: in it we can vividly grasp the originality of Jesus' message.

The initial setting reflects a biblical flourish, with a pastoral tone typical of Jesus:

When the Son of man comes in his glory, and all the angels with him, then he will sit on his glorious throne.

Before him will be gathered all the nations, and he will separate them one from another as a shepherd separates the sheep from the goats, and he will place the sheep at his right hand, but the goats at the left.

(Mt 25:31–33)

We note as we go that the judgment is attributed to the Son of man, who becomes the glorious "King." He "separates," a task proper to royal judgment. Then comes the verdict:

Then the King will say to those at his right hand, "Come, O blessed of my Father, inherit the kingdom prepared for you from the foundation of the world; for I was hungry and you gave me food, I was thirsty and you gave me drink, I was a stranger and you welcomed me, I was naked and you clothed me, I was in prison and you came to me." Then the righteous will answer hiim, "Lord, when did we see thee hungry and feed thee, or thirsty and give thee drink? And when did we see thee a stranger and welcome thee, or naked and clothe thee? And when did we see thee sick or in prison and visit thee?"

And the King will answer then, "Truly I say to you, as you did it to one of the least of these my brethren, you did it to me." Then he will say to those at his left hand, "Depart from me, you cursed, into the eternal fire prepared for the devil and his angels; for I was hungry and you gave me no food, I was thirsty and you gave me no drink, I was a stranger and you did not welcome me, naked and you did not clothe me, sick and in prison and you did not visit me."

Then they also will answer, "Lord, when did we see thee hungry or thirsty or a stranger or naked or sick or in prison, and did not minister to thee?"

Then he will answer then, "Truly, I say to you, as you did it not to one of the least of these, you did it not to me."

And they will go away into eternal punishment, but the righteous into eternal life.[100]

(Mt 25:34–46)

The judgment takes place at the end of time and concerns all men and women without distinction and not uniquely the people of Israel or only those faithful to Christ. Each individual, then, is involved in this unique judgment: in the Bible there is not the issue of the "particular judgment,"[101] for the individual is always present within the bosom of the entire humanity.

The "lesson" that the reader draws from this text is ordinarily an invitation to attentively meet "the least ones."[102] And it is well that this is so, for the judgment given prompts one to act better in the present. Nonetheless, it is not strictly in this point that we find the original teaching of the allegory; the whole Bible already summoned one to be concerned with the poor, the widow, and the orphan, indicating that such is the existing order of creation. To this point, the text offers but a reminder, certainly opportune, of one's "natural" duty to men and women,[103] the one advocated by Judaism.

The message proper to this prophetic description of the Last Judgment is the following: it reveals the hidden dimension of charity practiced on earth. All were surprised to learn that the Son of man had been "present" in the littlest ones; some discovered this presence with joy; other recognized that they had been absent from Jesus since they had been absent from the little ones. Here again, as we pointed out above in the case of heaven and hell, it is an issue of presence or absence, but here the issue is of one's presence or absence to Jesus Christ in this world. When the elect enter into the joy of the Kingdom and when the others depart far from him to the fire that does not die out, this is merely the expression of their behavior in the course of earthly life. Without knowing it, some lived in companionship with Jesus, while others did not recognize his presence; Jesus says it will ever be thus.

So, the judgment does not consist in a detailed accounting of good actions or bad; it operates on two levels. First of all, it is a separation of those who fell in with the little ones and those who did not fall in with them; this judgment recapitulates the teaching of the entire Bible, the teacher of humanity. On a second level, the judgment reveals the mysterious presence of Jesus Christ in the faces of the little ones. The division is effected either in view of the "works" or between the symbolizing and the symbolized. Both are the clear manifestation of what was mysteriously lived out here below.

Anticipated within time, this revelation does not mean that one must necessarily be able to recognize Jesus in the littlest ones, but it gives worth to the human activity of being present to others. Henceforth, once could conclude, "I encounter Jesus in the little ones, or I so dispose myself as not to meet them: heaven or hell already exist here on earth."

TERMINOLOGY OF THE AFTERLIFE

Considering this profound understanding of judgment, heaven, and hell, we can justify the diverse terms used by Jesus to talk about them. From the outset, let us put aside a false way of posing the question. Jesus never distinguished a "particular judgment" from the "general judgment." In his view, as in Israel's, the individual has no importance except within the people and within the whole of humanity. On the other hand, there are, without doubt, two headings under which we can address the topic of the Last Judgment, not by distinguishing the individual from the collectivity, but by being specific about the moment when the judgment takes place. For Jesus, in fact, the judgment will take place "at the end of time"; however, judgment also takes place not only at the moment of death but also "from now on." These are the two sets of terms in which Jesus proclaimed judgment.

Jesus spoke in accord with the long, prophetic tradition that had been relayed by the Jewish tradition of his time. The prophets had focused the gaze of their contemporaries on the coming Day, the day on which all would be reestablished, when

> the wolf shall dwell with the lamb,
> the leopard shall lie down with the kid . . .
> the suckling child shall play over the hole of the asp,
> and the weaned child shall put his hand on the adder's den.
>
> (Is 11:6,8)

And the rabbinic tradition readily distinguished two worlds, "this world" (*ha 'ōlam hazeh*) and "the world to come" (*ha 'ōlam habba*). In polarizing the faithful toward the perfect world to which they aspired, Jewish revelation gave a foundation to hope and to fear which, far from paralyzing action, rather stimulated it. The future makes the present fruitful. This is the language of "eschatology," a language that places the consummation and fulfillment of history at "the end of time."

Jesus was heir to the prophets when he made the coming of the Son of man or the vantage point of retribution sparkle in the eyes of his contemporaries. Although he has his eyes constantly peering toward the future, this is not to turn his listeners aside from the present; quite to the contrary, it is to give worth to the present. If one is to await the God who is coming and if one must carefully keep watch to greet the return of the Son of man, of which we know neither the day nor the hour,[104] this is to make our concrete existence more just. To gather appreciation for the quality of one's conduct on earth, Jesus alludes to the recompense awaiting us: "Your Father will reward you."[105] If Gehenna or the inextinguishable fire looms large on the horizon of his message, this is to strongly shape up his listeners, who seem oblivious to the gravity of the decisive engagement. Always this way of speaking has as its purpose that of bringing people back to the present moment, for this latter does not find its meaningful fulfilment except with reference to the future. The future gives discretion to the present.[106] In comparison with the biblical language of the Old Testament, Jesus adds a specifying note: he identifies the Day of the Lord with his own Parousia.[107] Thus, heaven is no longer simply God himself, it is also Christ in person; the reward promised is Jesus Christ. With regard to hell, it is no longer simply separation from God, it is also breaking with Jesus himself: "I do not know you!" In this way, biblical language continues to be ours: hope animates our life in this world.

TERMINOLOGY OF THE ETERNAL WITHIN TIME

Jesus used a language other than that concerning the afterlife and the end of time, and in this he departs from the prophetic tradition. The prophets had heralded the day on which the covenant would be made with each of the believers, one on which the Law would be written on hearts and when God would dwell among men and women.[108] For Jesus, this day had already come. Satan fell from heaven like lightning;[109] the Strong One has been bound, overwhelmed, and despoiled by a "stronger" one than he.[110] The Evil One recognizes the presence of the End in the actions of Jesus.[111] The Kingdom of God is not only a coming reality, "it is among you."[112] Not tomorrow nor in years far off will the fate of the Good Thief be decided, but "today."[113]

What had already been suggested in the Synoptics became perfectly clear in The Fourth Gospel. Judgment becomes realized in one's attitude of acceptance or refusal of Jesus as he speaks. It is not only at the end of time that "the resurrection on the last day" will be granted; already from this very moment the believer "has passed from death to life."[114] Judgment happens today through the word of Christ, who is ever alive.

The fact that the Day has come and that judgment has taken place is a radically new affirmation. But the terminology in which it is expressed is rooted in another biblical tradition, the "apocalyptic."[115] Succeeding to the position of the prophet, when the latter no longer was manifest in Israel, the apocalyptic writer did not announce a world "to come." From the outset he situated himself in the end times in such a way that he could no longer speak of a world that would come "after" our age; having already placed himself at history's term, he strikes against its end. Henceforth, in designating the "other world" and while respecting its total otherness, he cannot speak of the "world to come." Rather, he proclaims the "world above," a "heavenly world" that stands over against the "world below" and the "earthly world." Doing this, the apocalyptic author without doubt maintains the difference between the two worlds, but he does not make any more use of the categories of before and after; his categories are those of above and below or else those of the inferior, which is terrestrial, and the superior, which is celestial. In applying these categories to the occurrence of the Day, which has already arrived, the heavenly already now exists within the earthly, the world below has been transfigured by the presence of Jesus of Nazareth.

While eschatological language stirs up hope, apocalyptic language requires a vision of faith. The former is directed toward an unseen goal, the latter hopes to catch sight of this goal already in the present; it discovers the reality of the other world through its manifestation in this world. This language offers great advantages, and contemporary minds find themselves at ease when they hear it. In effect, it immediately gives value to the present, precluding flight into a dream of a world that is perfect though absent. It calls for the transformation of the present world, which has already been worked on by the heavenly world; the present is the chief part of the future, the earth the bearer of heaven.

Well and good. But this terminology also carries along with itself the risk of a grand illusion, that of confusing the heavenly world with the earthly. In fact, if heaven is already "on" earth, only the keen regard of faith is able to not confuse the two worlds. If terminology about the end of time encourages flight beyond the present, the terminology of apocalypse easily leads to an "activism" that scarcely has any relation to the gospel proclamation.

TWO LANGUAGES: LIFE BEFORE AND AFTER DEATH

To remain faithful to the gospel data, one has to admit the existence and the worth of two sets of terms apparently opposed if not contradictory. Eternal is fully given *after* death, yet it is already given *before* death. This is the paradox of Christian faith, of the "already" and the "not yet," a paradox rooted in the conviction that in Jesus Christ all has been given and that, notwithstanding this, we shall have to await the ultimate end.

Moreover, as we have said, Jesus made use of both. Since he was a true prophet everything was present to him at once, but at various levels and depths. Simultaneously, he lived the present and the future of God's Kingdom. Thus, in speaking of universal judgment, Jesus included judgment of the individual. This is why texts sometimes explicitly eschatological ("the Kingdom is near at hand" and "the Kindgom must come") and sometimes radically "mystical" ("the Kingdom is among you") are found side by side. It is useless to divide these logia into immediate and distant or between universal and particular; they are both one and the other even though their perspectives are different. We cannot harmonize these two ways of speaking by locating the former type as referring to the death of the world and the second to the instant of an individual's death.

There are different ways of being unfaithful to this paradox. Some eliminate one of the two languages at the expense of the other, according to their own preference.[116] Others have thought it possible to reconcile them by locating them respectively on a single time line: "the individual judgment at each person's death and the Parousia are seen as the extension of one another."[117] But to proceed in this fashion means inventing the existence of a "particular judgment," of which, we have seen, Jesus never spoke (even if it is presupposed in the general judgment). The two languages cannot be sustained except by both being respected in their respective originality.

This originality rests on the radical difference between the "not yet" of the Judeo-Christian eschatology and the "already" of its realization in Jesus Christ, which are irreducible one to another. The first language places the end at history's term, the second anticipates the end in the time of Jesus Christ. One magnetizes the present as an aspect of the future it hopes for; the other transfigures the present by a faith that is lived. The tension between the two languages reflects the tension that should animate the believer's being, namely hope and faith.

If the reader finds himself or herself in difficulty about accepting the two languages to speak about the end of time, he or she should closely study the Fourth Gospel. Not to divide the texts that seem incompatible between a putative John 1 and John 2, but to hear the text as it has been trasmitted to us. For example, in Chapter 5, Jesus declares,

> **24** Truly, truly, I say to you, he who hears my word and believes him who sent me, has eternal life; he does not come into judgment, but has passed from death to life. **25** Truly, truly, I say to you, the hour is coming, and now is, when the dead will hear the voice of the Son of God, and those who hear will live . . . **28** Do not marvel at this; for the hour is coming when all who are in the tombs will hear his voice **29** and come forth, those who have done good, to the resurrection of life, and those who have done evil, to the resurrection of judgment.
>
> (Jn 5:24–25, 28–29)

If the author of the Fourth Gospel did not perceive an incompatibility between these two successive languages, it is because he understands them on two different levels, in the prophetic perspective of the before-after and within the apocalyptic perspective of the already. In John's view, time is not simply a succession of days until they run out; time has acquired, since Christ's coming to earth, a new dimension, that of eternity.

Once we admit this, the Johannine presentation can help to harmonize the two languages. If it's true that the symbolic operation of faith leads from one world to another world by transforming the former, one can say that the earth, quite real and distinct, symbolizes heaven. According to the language of the end of time, heaven is not earth and the resurrection of the dead will take place at history's end. According to the language of the eternal in time, the earth is and is not heaven itself, Jesus' word "anticipates" the judgment in act. Neither one affirmation nor the other appear contradictory except to someone who does not know the nature of the symbolic operation that is at the basis of their association or of the symbol that is and is not what it symbolizes.[118]

There is another consequence from the fact of these two languages, namely that a new understanding of death underlies this duality. In Jesus' eyes, as he maintains by using the verb "to perish" beside or in place of the phrase "to be killed",[119] death is not simply the end of earthly life; it can become final death, although this latter is merely a possibility to be avoided.

Factually, life "continues after" death under a form that it is inappropriate to imagine through a reduction to earthly experiences. But it is appropriate to "symbolize"[120] life with the help of realities of this world brought to perfection, such as a banquet, the joy of being together with God and with those one loves. What eye has not seen is certainly not on this side of all that we experience as the fullness of relationships and life, and certainly is beyond every limited representation that we can give of it; it truly is the fullness of God himself. Underlying this symbolism is an experiential certitude. By means of my faith and my love, I am united with God and so I have already passed from death to life, already now, and this by reason of my encounter with the Lord Jesus. Hence, death is behind me, insofar as it is separation from God, the Father of Jesus; and yet it is still ahead of me, insofar as it has to put an end to the deficient life here below.

To accept these two languages means accepting my condition as a creature who at one and the same time already possesses and does not yet fully possess God's life. Certainly, the earthly life that my existence knows here below remains in a relationship with temporal death, but it coexists as well with eternal life, which has begun, overtaking death and leaving it in the darkness of the past. It is only eternal life that gives meaning to earthly existence. And yet it is not attained except through that existence. How this is to be so is what still must be asked of the gospel and of Jesus.

LIFE THROUGH DEATH

As we have just seen, according to Jesus a human person's existence is not just the breath of life provisionally committed to him at the moment of the first creation: true life, one without end, has also been sown within him, and hence it is already at work. This life has to be affirmed and affirmed absolutely, and to this end clear a passage for itself through the concrete human experience. How will this happen?

Jesus reveals how by means of paradox: it is through death that existence is definitively asserted. This paradox certainly belongs substantially to the authentic words of Jesus. Now it is a fact that the gospel tradition has reflected it back six times in exceptional fashion; this shows the importance it enjoys. Behind the various versions of the paradox, scholars think that we can, for the most part, reconstruct the following original saying:

> The one who wants to save his *psychē* will lose it
> the one who loses his *psychē* will save it.

Before attempting an interpretation of this saying on the level of its context and of its level in the text, it is necessary to specify the meaning of the main terms, while taking into account the various interpretations set forth by the evangelists.

Mt 16:25 = Mk 8:35 = Lk 9:24	Mt 10:39	Lk 17:33	Jn 12:25
The one who wants to save[a]	The one who finds	The one who seeks to gain	The one who is attached to[a1]
his existence[b]	his existence[b]	his existence[b]	his existence[b]
will lose it[c]	will lose it[c]	will lose it[c]	loses it[c1]
but the one who will lose[d]	and whoever loses	and the one who will lose[d]	and the one who is not attached[d1]
his existence[b]	his existence[b]		to his existence[b]
on my account	on my account		
(+Mk) and the gospel's			in this world
(Mk/Lk) will save it[c]		will keep it	will keep it
(Mt) will find it.[f]	will find it.[f]	alive.[g]	unto eternal life.[h]

a. *sōsai*   c1. *appoleusei*   f. *heirēsei*
a1. *ho philōn*   d. *hos d'an apolesei*   g. *zoogonēsei*
b. *psychē*   d1. *ho misōn*   h. *eis zoēn . . . phylaxei*
c. *apolesei*   e. *sōsei*

THE MEANING OF THE TERMS

The paradox bursts forth from the opposition between the terms *sōsai* and *apolesei*. The first verb means "to save" from some grave or mortal peril; it also means "to keep safe" from danger. Since this text does not specify from which peril one's snatched,[121] it seemingly has to do here with preserving oneself from imminent danger, a probable loss, and hence with keeping a hold on or assuring oneself of some good that one already has at one's disposal. The second verb, *apollumi,* has already been met earlier on.[122] These verbs, "to save" and "to lose," both have a double dimension. In the earthly sense, they signify the maintenance or the loss of existence; in the eschatological sense, they can designate salvation or final damnation. The meaning slips from one meaning to the other; in the first part of the sentence, final perdition corresponds to the desire to maintain one's earthly life; in the second it is the reverse: eschatological salvation is the answer to temporal loss. In actual fact, the human person has power only over temporal life, not over eternal life. In the earthly sense, "to save" means to attach oneself to life, "to lose" means to detach oneself from, to relinquish, not to hold on greedily to, to surrender, to leave, everything. Ultimately, the paradox keeps distinct what separates the temporal from the eternal; to hold onto is to lose, to lose is to save.

The two opposed verbs have as their object one and the same reality, the *psychē*. Most Bibles translate this word by "life," a translation advised by the biblical tradition.[123] Only, it is useful not to confuse this word with the general and abstract one, *zoē,* which means "life" plain and simple. *Psychē,* however, designates the very human person, insofar as he or she is the one who has received and continues ceaselessly to receive from God the spirit (*rua'h*) and vital breath (*n'chama*) and thereby is constituted as a living being, an existing individual. Hence, it is the whole, concrete being that is envisaged by the term *psychē,* even in the most ordinary of its vital manifestations.[124] This meaning of *psychē* scarcely has anything to do with the Hellenistic concept of a soul, as distinguished from the body and its functions. It has reference to the existence of a specific individual, something that is stressed by the possessive pronoun that always accompanies the word.

A confirmation of the biblical meaning for *psychē* is found in the parallel text of the Fourth Gospel. John distinguishes there "this world" from "eternal life" (*zoē*), two opposed worlds within which the *psychē* by turns can be either loved or hated (that is, not loved). It is clear that *psychē* is not to be confused with *zoē*. While the latter can be qualified as temporal or eternal, *psychē* is one and can either live or "die" in the world to come.[125] The best translation of the logion, then, would be

> The one who would save his existence will lose it,
> the one who loses his existence will save it.

From this text, taken in itself, we can deduce only the following: *psychē* is not reduced to what we see of it; existence thus presupposes an other on whom it depends. To discover the meaning of such a paradox, it is indispensable to closely examine the various contexts in which it is enshrined.

THE PARADOX IN ITS "HISTORICAL" CONTEXT

The gospel tradition, including the Johannine recension, locates Jesus' word in a persecution context. Jesus was convinced that he would be killed by his opponents: he had just told his disciples that he would be mistreated and put to death and that he would rise again.[126] Immediately afterward, he challenged those who wanted to be his disciples to follow him on the road to glory, which went by way of the cross.[127] To be Jesus' disciple means to follow him in the direction he has undertaken. The Fourth Gospel presents Jesus' word in a slightly different setting: it was on the occasion of some Greeks[128] coming to him that Jesus made his declaration about his fate.

Located in a historical core, the word calls for one to give up one's very own existence, in the same way Jesus intends to be faithful to his mission; that of untiringly proclaiming the Kingdom of the God of love, and to do so in gentleness and peace. The disciples have been associated with this great undertaking by Jesus, while his opponents have been provoked to empty out their violence on him personally.[129] This is what the early Church made explicit not only by locating his word in this context, but by adding the specification "on my account."[130]

Thus the paradoxical formulation undergoes a specific clarification. The disciple discovers himself or herself under a threat of death that requires fidelity to the gospel: one has to be able to put one's very own existence at risk, rather than want to save it in betraying the cause of the gospel mission. To be disposed to risk one's life in this way means to realize that it is dependent on Another. Received from him, it is not my property and I do not keep it safe except by being faithful to the demands of the Other. I am only the trustee of this existence; if necessary, then, I have to give it up rather than betray the gospel, for I know in faith that the Lord can preserve me in life and so free me from death, provided that, if I undergo this, it is in order to remain faithful for him.

The paradox receives light from the word that precedes it in the Synoptics:

If anyone would come after me, let him deny himself and take up his cross [+ every day = Lk] and follow me.

(Mt 16:24 = Mk 8:34 = Lk 9:23)

The versions are the same, except for Luke's addition, and present a text that, without doubt, is older than the negative form preserved in Q.[131] To be Jesus' disciple a condition has been set, expressed in two ways: denying oneself and taking up one's cross.

The verb "to deny" (Gk. *[ap]arnēsasthai*) in the first place has a juridical meaning, which may be grasped by its opposite, "to confess" (Gk. *homologein*). So it was that John the Baptist, in replying to the representatives of the Pharisees, "confessed and did not deny, and he confessed: 'I am not the Christ.' "[132] On the contrary, Peter denied Jesus,[133] though he had been invited like every disciple "not to deny Jesus before men."[134] It seems that the expression "to deny oneself" is not semitic; it would translate into Greek the Palestinian expression "to hate one's *psychē*" and would thus signify the same reality as the saying studied earlier. Thus, it would correspond to the saying in which Jesus declared that his disciple ought to "prefer" him to one's own family,[135] given precisely before the negative form of it concerning "carrying one's cross." To deny oneself is to state that one no longer belongs to oneself, that "if I live, it is now no longer I who live, but Christ who lives in me."[136] At the origin of my being I recognize that it is no longer I but Jesus the Christ. Such is the radical (and elementary) conversion that Jesus demands of his disciple and that touches the core of one's being by showing that God is unique.[137]

The demand to "deny oneself" is specified immediately by another expression, no less delicate to interpret: "to take up one's cross." Classically, the exhortation has been bound up with Jesus' Crucifixion, and all the more readily so since Jesus shortly before this foretold his own fate: he had to take up the cross as he himself did in going up to Calvary. Yet numerous difficulties are against Jesus' having spoken in this way. First of all, in the proclamation of his destiny precisely there is no mention of the cross on his part. Also, it has not proven possible to find a similar expression in the semitic world and, moreover, one cannot suggest that it could have come from the popular expressions deriving from revolutionary circles. Finally, in this text of ours the matter concerns not Jesus' cross but that of a disciple's cross. Hence the conclusion is overwhelming: the sentence was a construct of the early Church.

That is, unless one accepts a recently proposed interpretation.[138] In it, the word *cross* would translate the Hebrew letter *TAW* (or the Greek *TAU*), both of them being symbolized by a sign analogous to a cross († or X). Taking up the cross would be to take up the distinctive sign of belonging to the Lord, as Ezekiel put it:

4 "Go through the city, through Jerusalem, and put the mark of the *Taw* upon the foreheads of the men who sigh and groan over all the abominations that are committed in it." **5** . . ."Pass through the city and smite! . . . **6** . . . but touch no one upon whom is the mark *of the Taw* . . . ."

Clearly this prophecy is a transposition of the activity of the Angel of the Lord, who spared the Hebrews marked with the blood of the lamb;[139] its meaning is that those who have opted for the one God will be spared. To take (or to wear) the *Taw* (Gk. *sēmeion*) is to "signify" one's belonging to the Lord. In the gospel, "to take up one's cross" would be to positively declare one's adherence to Jesus, the Christ, and to follow him even to death.[140]

This saying would thus be appropriate on Jesus' lips, not immediately signifying suffering but, based on renunciation of one's self, the courage to witness one's belonging to Jesus of Nazareth, especially in persecution.[141]

THE PARADOX IN AN ESCHATOLOGICAL CONTEXT

In addition to the preceding historical setting, this saying of Jesus has been placed in the Q tradition in a context of judgment at the end of time. Thus, it would acquire a universal weight going beyond the historical situation of martyrdom in which it had been presented.

The nuance which, in Matthew, characterized the formulation of the paradox in its historical context (that of losing/finding) is found again in the Matthean logion of the Q tradition:

The one who finds his life will lose it, and *the one* who loses his life for my sake will find it.

(Mt 10:39)

Instead of "saving" we read "finding." In the passages proper to Matthew, this word always has a meaning related to the end of time: it concerns the path of life, rest, the Kingdom under its aspect of the treasure or the pearl.[142] On the last day, it is God who will give what one does not have or, in the present case, what one no longer has. Thus, the verb "losing" is quite strongly the opposite to "finding," just as "leaving behind" is to "receiving." To leave one's existence behind means to receive God at the final judgment.

The saying has been inserted into the "mission discourse,"

which, in Matthew, was completed[143] with the help of sayings drawn for the most part from the "eschatological discourse." Doubtlessly, there is still a question in Matthew's tenth chapter of a persecution with which the disciples will be faced in their apostolic mission; but this persecution is described there in terms that derive from the eschatological: at the end of days they will undergo a new outbreak of it. The context of persecution, which is localized in time and space, has been transposed into an eschatological context; touching the end of time, it may be qualified as "a-temporal."

In Luke, the eschatological transposition is more evident:

Whoever seeks to gain his life will lose it, but whoever loses his life will preserve it *alive*.

(Lk 17:33)

The context does not speak of persecution but of the Day of the Son of man. The issue is one of vigilance, which neither the contemporaries of Noah nor those of Lot had, a vigilance that men and women ought to have in their daily tasks under threat of seeing themselves surprised by the Day.[144] Sharply, in the midst of this, our paradox intrudes. We note, first of all, the absence of any mention of "on my account." Then, it is a question of "seeking" to gain one's life, as one "seeks" out the Kingdom of God.[145] What one intensively seeks after here is to "obtain" one's existence, of procuring it for oneself, of acquiring it.[146] On the opposite side, the one who loses it, and, so, does not seek after it, "will preserve" it (*zoogonēsei*). This last verb has a definite meaning of "to beget a living being," "to come to life," "to let live," as the Egyptians let the Hebrew girls live in Moses' time,[147] as God gives life to everything.[148] Here it is not a human person who "gives back life" to himself; rather it is God who, by allowing him to be reborn to a new life, keeps him alive.

The transposition of the historical context into an eschatological one is full of meaning. Renunciation of self at the moment of persecution becomes abnegation pure and simple; the option of martyrdom becomes a firm disposition constantly to opt for the

Lord. It is this which Luke, elsewhere, tends to stress when he says that one has to take up the cross anew "every day."[149] If fact, this is the Church's condition. The eschatological condition universalizes the contingent assertion of history. We have our eyes set here on a truth that is valid for all and at all times.

THE PARADOX OF LIFE THROUGH DEATH

It is with the Fourth Gospel that the paradox of Jesus reveals its full capacity for universalization. Without doubt, as we have said previously, the context of Jesus' death and, hence, of persecution, is still perceptible, but the Johannine formulation retains nothing of the historical dimension of the Synoptics and the relationship to Jesus of Nazareth is no longer expressly stated:

The one who loves his life loses it, and *the one* who hates his life in this world will keep it for eternal life.

(Jn 12:25)

Henceforth it is a fact that life is lost (the verb is in the present tense), a feature that corresponds to the Johannine realization of the Last Judgment.[150] Or else, it will be maintained in eternal life.[151] The phrase pair "be bound to"-"not be bound to" (= to love-to hate) once again generalizes the situation, for it indicates a disposition fundamental for every disciple, one that chooses between loving and hating. The martyr is, without doubt, implicated by this word, but it is every aspect of existence that is envisioned in this principle.

Beginning with this hermeneutical principle of John's, we can cause Jesus' paradox to become real for us. It is not only for the period of Jesus of Nazareth, nor only to face an eventual martyrdom nor only because of the final eschatological tension that his principle holds true; rather, it is for every age and from the core of one's being that the disciple of Jesus is challenged to choose for or against a certain way of carrying on one's life.

Life cannot be reduced merely to the period of time that preceded physical death; it is from elsewhere that life draws its origin and finds its goal and meaning. Clearly it can also be considered as "mine" and I can become attached to it, cherish it, maintain it, preserve it as if it found fulfillment in itself, as if it were a good that I should defend at any cost or were a possession depending only on myself. But, just so, it slips away from me, the water that I greedily want to keep hold of in my hands although I cannot lay hold of its source and although it flows without stopping. On the contrary, if I do not grab onto this life, if I accept its loss, if I leave it behind, if I welcome the law of death, which is nothing other than "ecstasy," life remains a good and symbolizes eternal life, which, in fact, it inaugurates. So, to return to the saying that was uttered just before, the grain of wheat that falls onto the ground and dies will bear much fruit.

In a definitive sense, then, my life is not my own, but that of Another. It began long before I became conscious that it dwelt in me, and it continues after my course in this world, for the One from whom I received it is the Lord.

CONCLUSION

At the end of this brief inquiry on Jesus of Nazareth faced with others' deaths, that is, death in general (excluding its reference to himself), it would be naive to believe that we have penetrated the deepest recesses of Jesus' thought on the subject. The gospel documents, our only source, were directed toward a specific end and from the start we had to question them, despite their viewpoint, to reach the bare facts and only then to take into account their various interpretations. So the text did not become a pretext for getting at something outside the text (the happening itself), but the text suggested reference to the context, which did offer meaning.

No detail could be furnished to answer our curiosity about the afterlife, except for a single assertion: life is not limited to existence on earth, since the Kingdom of God precedes and follows on this latter, as well as penetrates it and surrounds it. There is no real specification of the relationship that Paul seems to envisage, between death and sin; unforeseen and brutal death doubtlessly summons to conversion, but nothing is said about any causal connection between the two.

In Jesus there is no stoic behavior that might tend to scorn the fact of death. Clearly Jesus did not at all appreciate the noisy shows of grief, but he seems himself to have yielded to emotion, an emotion no less appropriate than was David's weeping over his friend Jonathan or his son Absalom.[152] This emotion, nonetheless, takes its origin, which is more profound than mere feeling, in the very fount of life, God himself. And Jesus ably revealed his startling mastery over death by both his words and his actions.

To try to unify the gospel data is to find a single reality: *God is there.* Jesus was present on earth. Whether he loves intensely or, through his parables, reveals himself to be a poet of creation, this does not mean that he dreams of an ideal earth, ignoring death and suffering. But it does mean his awareness of the constant breaking in of life and of God's Kingdom into the present time.

In the face of the various factors involved in violent death, Jesus did not bemoan the fate of humans nor the future of humanity; he called for a much closer attention to the present moment. In his eyes, there was no room for fear, not even fear of nature or fear of the wicked: only one thing counted: faithfulness to God, who is the source and keeper of life. Faced with the affliction of men and women touched by death, Jesus let a glimpse of the sovereign power of life be seen, either by healings or by extraordinary resuscitations: all these symbolized the Kingdom of God already now at work on earth.

If Jesus inherited biblical depictions of retribution, this was to reveal their contemporary dimension: with or against God, such are the stakes of life today.

Even more profoundly, Jesus showed that the present moment of life is fruitful because of an aspect of its conduct that relates it to death: this is the paradox of life. The human present is "ecstasy," a continued going-out of oneself. Therefore, I acknowledge that my life is not so much mine as his; it is an endless gift.

Finally, at the secret core of this experience of a present to which everything is directed, it is appropriate to situate the One whom

Jesus called "Abba." The present has value through God's presence. Death ceases to be a pure end for anyone who is in communion with God who lives and gives life, ever present, even in his absence.

NOTES

1. Josephus reports that Varus seized the city of Sepphoris, which was the starting point for the insurrection of Judas (he had raided the munitions storehouse in the city), Varus burned it and took its inhabitants as slaves (*War* 2:5, No. 68). Afterward, 2,000 rebels were crucified, although the exact place of the execution is not given (*ibid.*, 2:5, No. 75).
2. Besides theologies of the Old Testament, the reader may consult R. Martin-Achard, *From Death to Life: A Study of the Development of the Doctrine of the Resurrection in the Old Testament* (Edinburgh: Oliver and Boyd, 1960); and P. Grelot, *De la mort à la vie eternelle* (Paris: Cerf, 1971).
3. Thus, the promises of life in the prophets, as in Ez 18 and 37. R. Martin-Achard begins his work with a whole chapter on "Life" (pp. 3–15).
4. Mt 14:1–2p; cf. Lk 3:19f; Mt 17:12p.
5. Mt 10:21f; Mk 13:12; Mt 23:30–35 = Lk 11:47–51.
6. Mt 15:5 p = Ex 21:17.
7. Lk 10:30–37.
8. Mt 21:35–39 p.
9. Lk 19:27.
10. Mt 22:6f.
11. Mt 5:21f; 19:18; cf. Ex 20:13; Dt 5:17.
12. Jn 3:15,36; 5:24; 6:47,68; 10:28; 17:3.
13. Mt 16:28.
14. Gn 25:8; cf. 35:29; 49:29.
15. 1 Kgs 2:2.
16. Ps 18:1–4; 27:1–2; 73:23–26.
17. Sir 1:13; 11:18–28.
18. Jb 42:6.
19. Billerbeck, II, 193–197.
20. Pilate's brutality was infamous. In the Year 35, he had pilgrims who had gone up on Mount Gerizim killed (*Ant.*, XVIII, 4:1, No. 85–87). In the present instance, during a sacrifice at the Temple, Pilate had the faithful who had come to offer gifts massacred, and added to this a double profanation: of the Temple, where the murder took place, and of the blood of the offerings, which belonged to God. With regard to the collapse of the Siloam tower, it is not mentioned elsewhere; we know, however, that Jerusalem's southern wall extended as far as Siloam (*Ant.*, XVIII, 3:2, No. 60–62; *War*, II, 9:4, No. 175). In all likelihood, a true occurrence underlies the gospel text.
21. Cf. Mt 20:13–15.
22. Rom 5:12–21; 2 Cor 5:21. Jn 1:29; 12:31f; 16:11–33.

23. Cf. G. Marcel, *Le Monde cassé* (Paris: Desclée de Brouwer, 1933). How can a critic as sensible as W. Grundmann attribute to Jesus the thought of a "substitutive expiatory action" (*"ein stellvertretendes Ereignis"*), in *Das Evangelium nach Lukas* (Berlin: Evangelische Verlagsanstalt, 1964), p. 276? The influence of theology possibly.

24. With the meaning of violent death: Mt 2:13; 8:25p; 12:14p; 21:41p; 27:20; Mk 9:22; 11:18p; Lk 11:51; 13:33; 15:17; 17:27,29.

25. With the meaning of perdition: Mt 10:39; 16:25; 18:14; Mk 8:35; Lk 9:24f; 17:33; 19:10; cf. Mt 11:23.

26. Cf. G. Dautzenberg, *Sein Leben bewahren: Psychē in der Herrenworten der Evangelien* (Munich: Kösel-Verlag, 1966), 13–48; E. Schweizer, *"Psychē,"* *TDNT* 9 (1974), 608–656. [*Editor's Note*: See appendix for abbreviations of journal titles and other pertinent bibliographic abbreviaticus.]

27. We do not present here a development of terminology concerned with life after death (see pp. 19–31 and 282–298).

28. Dt. 32:39; 1 Sm 2:6.

29. Ps 18:5f; Is 38:18.

30. Nm 16:33; Is 14:15; Ez 32:29; Mt 11:23 = Lk 16:22. The lower regions underground tended to become "Hell," the place of God's absence, the place where the worm did not die and where the fire did not go out (cf. J. Guillet, "Hell," *DBT*, 2nd ed., 1973, pp. 233–235).

31. Ps 88:7; Jb 10:21f.

32. Ps 88:12; Jb 26:6; 28:22.

33. Ps 88:13.

34. Is 26:19; Ps 88:11.

35. Ps 13:4; 49:18; Jb 14:12.

36. Ps 88:6.

37. Ps 38:18; Ps 6:6; 88:12.

38. Ps 39:14; Jb 14:10.

39. Prv 27:20; 35:15f; Is 5:14; Hb 2:5.

40. Ps 55:16.

41. The "gates" were typical of the closed space of subterranean Sheol.

42. Is 38:10.

43. I Sm 2:6; Hos 13:14.

44. Ps 30:3f; Is 38:17–19.

45. Jon 2:7; Hos 6:1f.

46. Ps 49:15.

47. Ps 88:12. "The Ur-grave we might call Sheol . . . Where there is a grave, there is Sheol, and where there is Sheol, there is grave," L. Pedersen, *Israel*, Parts I–II (London: Geoffrey Cumberlege, 1926), p. 462.

48. 2 Kgs 9:37; cf. Jer 8:14; Ez 29:5.

49. J. Jeremias, *Die Heiligengräber in Jesu Umwelt* (Göttingen: Vandenhoeck und Ruprecht, 1958) has masterfully described the popular religion that venerated the tombs of the prophets and saints in Schechem (Joseph), Jerusalem (the necropolis, Hulda, Isaiah, Zachariah ben Johoida), Bethlehem (Rachel, Bilhah, Zilpah, Dinah, David's descendants) at Hebron (the patriarchs). Their presence in the tombs was manifested by miracles and by intercessory power. In Herod the Great's time, monuments to the prophets were built to gain from this some expiatory merit (p. 121).

50. "To ensure for oneself" is the meaning that can be given to Mt 16:25 (cf. pp. 33–34).
51. Mt 22:32 = Mk 12:27 = Lk 20:38.
52. 1 Kgs 17:17–24; 2 Kgs 4:31–37; cf. X. Léon-Dufour, *Les Miracles de Jésus selon le Nouveau Testament* (Paris: Seuil, 1977), p. 306.
53. Mk 5:35 = Lk 8:49.
54. Mt 9:18.
55. Mk 5:23,41. The gesture is a typical one in healings.
56. Lk 7:14. The coffin was unknown in Palestine: 2 Sm 3:31; 2 Kgs 13:21; cf. Mk 15:44; Lk 8:49; Jn 19:33; Acts 14:19; 1 Tim 5:6.
57. Cf. J. Nélis, *Dictionnaire encyclopédique de la Bible* (Brepols, 1960,) p. 706. According to Josephus, *Against Apion*, II, 26 (Trans. H. St. J. Thackeray [Harvard: Harvard University Press, 1961], p. 375), from the time of Moses it was a duty to join a funeral cortege that one encountered on one's journey: those who passed in front of a funeral procession had to join the family and mourn with them. ("All who pass while a burial is proceeding must join the procession and share the mourning of the family").
58. According to *Jerusalem Talmud*, Yebamot XVI, quoted by J. Schmitt, *Jésus resuscité dans la prédication apostolique* (Paris: Gabalda, 1949), p. 171.
59. However, several verses later, Jesus says to those sent from John: "The dead are raised" (Lk 7:22) although the reanimation of Jairus's daughter is not reported until further on (8:40–56); so Luke acted properly, then, in relating a narrative of reanimation earlier on.
60. Billerbeck, II, 544.
61. This sickness was not unto death (Jn 11:4), he is asleep (11:11); Jesus spoke of Lazarus's death (11:13), he said clearly that he was dead (11:14). Then came the conversation with Martha on the resurrection at the end of time (11:23f).
62. Cf. R. E. Brown, *The Gospel According to John I–XII, Anchor Bible*, Vol. 29 (Garden City, N.Y.: Doubleday, 1966), pp. 429–430.
63. While Lazarus came forth from the tomb bound hand and foot with linens, Jesus left the linens behind in the tomb; the disciples saw them abandoned there. John wants us to understand that Lazarus is still subject to death, whereas Jesus can no longer die.
64. Thus, both in the case of Jesus' words at the time of raising the dead up (Mk 5:41 = Lk 8:54; Lk 7:14) and at the time of healings (Mt 9:5f p) the resulting action is described with the same verb: Mt 8:15; 9:7,25; Mk 1:31; 2:12; 9:27; Jn 12:1,9,17. More often the verb *anistanai* is found (Mk 5:42; 9:27; Lk 4:39; 5:25; 8:55; Acts 9:40).
65. Is 26:19; cf. Ez 37:1–14.
66. Gn 47:30; Dt 31:16; 2 Sm 7:12.
67. Is 66:24 describes Sheol in this way. The image of awakening is quite ancient (Is 51:17–52:11), as is the sleep of death (Ps 13:4).
68. Gn 37:34; 50:1; Lv 10:6; 1 Sm 4:12; 31:13; 2 Sm 1:2; 3:31; 2 Kgs 20:3; Jer 6:26; Lk 23:28; Jn 16:20; 20:11.
69. Dt 14:1; cf. Lv 19:28.
70. Lk 7:13,15.
71. Mk 1:43; 14:5.
72. Jn 11:41f.

73. Jn 12:27f.
74. Jn 13:21,31f.
75. Jn 14:1,27.
76. Jn 11:35; cf. Mk 5:38f; Lk 7:38,44.
77. Jn 15:9.
78. Cf. Jn 12:27; cf. pp. 111–113.
79. Mt 19:28.
80. Mt 25:31f.
81. Mt 16:27.
82. Mt 25:46. Note that Jesus never speaks of limbo or purgatory.
83. Mt 5:34; 23:22.
84. Mt 5:20; 7:21; 18:3p; 19:23f, p.
85. Mt 8:11; 25:21, 23; Lk 13:29.
86. Lk 14:14; cf. Mt 22:31 = Mk 12:26 = Lk 20:37.
87. Lk 12:37.
88. Mt 21:25p; Lk 15:18,21.
89. Mt 7:23; cf. 25:12,41; Lk 13:26.
90. Mt 5:22, 29f; 10:28 (= Lk 12:5); 18:8f (= Mk 9:43,45,47); 23:15,33; cf. 2 Kgs 23:10; Is 66:24; Jer 7:31f.
91. Mt 7:19; 13:42,50; 25:41; cf. Mt 3:12; Mk 9:43.
92. Mt 6:19f; Mk 9:48; cf. Is 14:11; 66:24.
93. Mt 13:42,50; 24:51; Lk 13:28.
94. Mt 8:12; 22:13; 25:30.
95. This is what the particle *apo* (= "far from") indicates: Mt 7:23 (= Ps 6:9); 25:41. Note that Jesus does not speak of "punishments" endured by the damned.
96. 1 Kgs 3:28: "All Israel heard of the judgment (*krima*) given by the King."
97. Jn 3:17–21; 9:39; 12:31–47.
98. In Greek, the word *krisis* first of all means to sort, to sift, to separate, to discern (Mt 16:3; Lk 12:57), to appraise (Lk 7:43; 19:22; Jn 7:24), to examine (1 Cor 11:31). There came to be grafted onto this original meaning the juridical aspect of law or of justice and decision.
99. Cf. R. Pautrel and D. Mollat, "Jugement," *SDB* 4 (1949), 1321–1394. The Day of the Lord is terrible and no one escapes it; it is the day of darkness, wrath, vengeance . . . , but, at the same time, a day of glory for the elect. His verdict is sharp: shame, confusion, fire, and death for some, victory and joy for others.
100. In Greek, the word *aiōnios* is ordinarily translated by "eternal." This translation is perfectly appropriate to describe God and whatever shares in his fullness. In this case, eternity is not the exclusion or prolongation of time, but the fullness of being, the absolute. If the realities opposed to God are sometimes described as eternal, this is not to say that they are "without end" but that they are absolutely definitive—so, sin (Mk 3:19), the consuming fire (Mt 18:8; 25:41; Jude 7), perdition (2 Thess 1:19), punishment (Mt 25:46). Cf. X. Léon-Dufour, *Dictionary of the New Testament*, trans. Terrence Prendergast (San Francisco: Harper & Row, 1980) p. 181.
101. It was only after the fifteenth century that the notion of the particular judgment was developed, without sufficient ground in the Bible or in the patristic writings or in the Church's councils; it is not found in the Council of Florence

(1438), which did, however, deal explicitly with the last things. And the term is not found in the decrees of Vatican II; cf. P. Adnès, "Jugement," *Dictionnaire de spiritualté* 8 (1974), 1581–85. At the root of this notion is the fact that at death a person is fixed in his lot and is destined to receive, according to his former life, either the beatific vision or hell; but in no way is this a "judgment." There are not two judgments, but two terms to lay hold of the one general judgment. The New Testament texts (the rich fool, Lazarus and Dives, paradise for the good thief) affirm only that death confirms the individual's state: at death each one knows his lot. It follows that the temporal distinction of the two judgments in no way justifies the idea of "souls separated" from their bodies while they await the Last Judgment.

102. Recently certain authors have thought that the "least of the brethren" were Jesus' disciples. But all of the texts of Mt that are cited to support this interpretation add a qualification ; they are "little ones in virtue of being disciples" (Mt 10:42), "little ones who believe in me" (18:6, which controls vv. 10 and 14). In fact, Jesus extends to all who were most wretched what he had said to the disciples alone, whom he describes here as "my brothers."

103. Judaism extolled certain works of piety, which are likewise mentioned in the New Testament: to feed the hungry, to clothe the naked, to show forth hospitality, to visit the sick—to which Jesus added prisoners and he neglects the education of orphans and the burial of the dead, which they had mentioned. Cf. J. Jeremias, "Die Salbungsgeschichte Mk 14:3–9," *ZNW* 35 (1936), 75–82 (= *Abba Studien* . . . , [Göttingen: Vandenhoeck and Ruprecht, 1966], pp. 107–155).

104. Mt 24:42p; 25:13; Mk 13:33,35; Lk 12:37,39.

105. Mt 6:4,6,18; cf. 16:27.

106. How can one regard the irony of unbelievers who suggest that to speak of heaven or of judgment at the end of time is tantamount to administering to weak spirits a dose of opium that turns them aside from their present action and encourages flight from this world? Without doubt people have corrupted this terminology by letting people dream of a better world where the sorrows endured here below in this "valley of tears" will be compensated for, without, however, inviting them to struggle to lessen human suffering. But such is not Jesus' language nor that of the Bible.

107. "The Day of the Lord": Mt 24:30f; Lk 17:24; "The Parousia": Mt 24:3,27,37,39.

108. Jer 31:31–33; 32:39–41; Ez 11:19f; 36:26–28.

109. Lk 10:18.

110. Lk 11:22.

111. Mt 8:29p; Mk 1:24.

112. Lk 17:21.

113. Lk 23:43.

114. Jn 5:24.

115. Cf. X. Léon-Dufour, "Quel langage tenir sur Jésus ressuscité?" *Esprit* 41 (1973), 886–890.

116. This is what the majority of interpreters are doing, without reasonable justification.

117. D. Mollat, "Jugement," *SDB* 4 (1949), 1358–59.

118. Cf. G. Fessard, "Symbole symbolisant, Signes, Symbole symbolisé," in *Le*

Langage: Actes du XIIIe Congrès des Sociétés de Philosophie de langue française (Neuchatel: À la Baconnière, 1967), pp. 291–295.
119. Cf. pp. 6–9.
120. Cf. p. 222, n. 23.
121. Cf. X. Léon-Dufour, "Père, fais-moi passer sain et sauf à travers cette heure (Jn 12:27)," in H. Baltensweiler and B. Reiche, eds., *Neues Testament und Geschichte*: Festschrift for O. Cullman (Zurich: Theologischer Verlag, 1972), pp. 162–163.
122. Cf. p. 9.
123. Cf. G. Dautzenberg, *Sein Leben bewahren*, (above, n. 26) 68–82; E. Schweizer, *TDNT* 9 (1974), 642.
124. The Bible speaks of a soul that is parched (Ps 63:2), famished (Ps 107:9), filled with joy (Ps 86:4), finally relieved (Phil 2:19). "I will say to my soul: 'My soul, take your ease, eat, drink, be merry.' And God says: 'Fool! This very night they will demand your soul of you' " (Luke 12:19f).
125. There is no opposition between earthly life and eternal life, without devaluing earthly life entirely, something that is biblically impossible.
126. Mt 16:21–23 = Mk 9:31–33 = Lk 9:22.
127. Mt 16:24–26 = Mk 8:34–37 = Lk 9:23–25.
128. Jn 12:20–22; cf. pp. 111–113.
129. Raymond Schwager has recently tried to apply to the redemption the inquiry into the scapegoat proposed by R. Girard, *Brauchen wir einen Sündenbock?* (Munich: Kösel, 1978), especially pp. 205–219. Cf. G. R. Girard, *La Violence et le Sacré* (Paris: Grasset, 1972) and *Des choses cachées depuis le commencement du monde* (Paris: Grasset, 1978). Cf pp. 261–262.
130. By not observing this precise detail, Luke and John remove this logion from its historical context.
131.

Mt 10:38	*Lk 14:27*
The one who does not take up the cross and does not follow me is not worthy of me.	The one who does not carry his cross and does not walk behind me cannot be my disciple.

132. Jn 1:20.
133. Mt 26:34,35,70,75p.
134. Lk 12:9 = Mt 10:33.
135. Such may be the Semitic meaning of the verb "to hate"; cf. Gn 29:31; Dt 21:15f; Mal 1:2–4; Mt 10:34 = Lk 14:26.
136. Gal 2:20.
137. It is regrettable that the majority of translations render the text by "renounce his very self," as if such a thing were possible. One can renounce something other than oneself; for example, one's goods, which can be "left behind" (Gk. *aphiēmi*: Mt 4:20,22p; 19:29p) or which can be left aside (Gk. *apotassesthai*: Lk 9:61; 14:33). "Renunciation" is the application to having what "abnegation" is to being (cf. I. Hausherr, "Abnégation, renoncement, mortification," *Christus* 22 (1959), 182–195).
138. E. Dinkler, "Jesu Wort vom Kreuztragen," in W. Eltester, ed., *Neutestamentliche Studien für R. Bultmann* (Berlin: A. Töpelman, 1954), pp. 110–129.
139. Ex 12:7.

140. Cf. the sign of the faithful belonging to the Lamb in Rv 7:3f; 13:16; 14:1.
141. Cf. also J. Schneider, "Stauros," *TDNT* 7 (1971), 577–579; and R. Pesch, *Markuskommentar*, Vol. 2 (Freiburg-im-B.: Herder, 1977), p. 60.
142. Mt 7:14; 11:29; 13:44–46.
143. Beginning with Mt 10:17.
144. Lk 17:22–25; 17:26–32,34–37.
145. Lk 12:31.
146. *Peripoiēsasthai*, the only occurrence in the gospels; cf. Acts 20:28: "The Church which he acquired by his own blood"; 1 Tim 3:13: "to gain a good standing for oneself."
147. Acts 7:19; cf. Ex 1:17f,22: "to keep alive" or "to kill."
148. 1 Tim 6:13; cf. 1 Sm 2:6: "to bring to life."
149. Cf. pp. 35–36 and Lk 11:3; Is 50:4.
150. Jn 5:24.
151. Unlike the instances in which eternal life is introduced by the verbs "to have" (3:15,16,36; 5:24,39; 6:40,47,54 [68]) or "to give" (10:28; 17:2), it is sometimes introduced by a verb of motion followed by the preposition *eis*: welling up to (4:14), gather fruit (4:36), abiding in (6:27); here "to keep for" (*phylaxei eis zoēn aiōnion*). It is not just a case of "preserving" but of "transforming while preserving."
152. 2 Sm 1:26; 19:1; cf. 12:15–23.

2. Jesus Before Threatening Death

To talk about others' death is relatively easy, at least as long as one allows oneself, as Jesus was, to be permeated through one's ancestral culture with the presence of a God who is stronger than death. To frontally meet a personal threat of death is another thing, especially when the very beautiful dream of a heavenly kingdom established on the earth seems to disappear with it. Death threatened Jesus. What was his reaction?

The answer to this is a delicate one. If I declare, after examining the texts, that Jesus not only foresaw but even sought out his death for the sake of the Kingdom, I tend to make him out to be a supranormal being who, as the romantic puts it, "passes through the battles of life with a rose in this hands." If, on the contrary, I concede, equally according to the texts, that Jesus did not wish his death but underwent it to the best of his ability, is this not to withdraw from Jesus' consciousness an element fundamental to his mission as Savior? This, then, is what Bultmann was not afraid of asserting: Jesus' death would be, "historically speaking, a stupid destiny;"[1] it would have been caused exclusively by a political interpretation of his activity. Faced with this excess of a historicizing criticism, believers have always continued to declare with the first Christians that "God handed over his Son" to death, that Jesus willingly went to the cross, that by taking on himself the sin of men and women, Jesus knew he was reconciling human persons with God. Jesus would, therefore, have conferred a redemptive worth on his death. He was the Redeemer, and he knew he was.

Very well! But does this language carry the same meaning today that it did formerly? Let us listen to a self-proclaimed unbeliever:

"If I thought myself, over a period of two years, capable of healing the sick by a simple laying-on of hands and of going so far as to resuscitate the dead at the cost of a few words, perhaps I would not face the last judgment with the same dispositions, let us say, as a simple client of Mr. Hitler's gas chambers."[2] This amounts to the innocent reply that a child gave to his catechist, who asked what Jesus could have said on the cross between the two brigands: "I'm laughing . . . ! In three days, I'll rise again." In reacting this way, the child and the "unbeliever" are dreaming, as is the case in the old myths, of a superman, of a god wrapped up in a bit of flesh, who came to take on a human appearance to console human beings, but who, because of this very fact, is incapable of taking death seriously.

To answer the question formulated in this way we will try to ascend from the dogmatic language to the very language of Jesus, found in his sayings and in his deeds. The difficulty is that the gospel texts have been composed in the light of Easter and they attribute to Christ sayings that often go beyond what Jesus in fact articulated. This difficulty can be overcome by reference to the two criteria of difference and of coherence,[3] which we will try to put into practice.

At the lowest level, the most elementary, it is fitting to ask oneself whether, historically, one can assert that Jesus in fact expected a violent death. On this base, we will try to show how Jesus gave meaning to this death, either by locating it within the divine economy or by conferring on it a universal significance. These latter two developments will allow us to grasp how the primitive Church, in turn, manifested the meaning it gave to Jesus' death, by inserting it into God's plan and by recognizing in it a "redemptive" value for all.[4]

THE OCCURRENCE LOCATED IN THE CONTEXT OF JESUS' SAYINGS

It is in beginning with Jesus' authentic sayings that we can, historically speaking, specify two points: Jesus' behavior led to death threats; Jesus foretold that he would die a violent death.

Jesus claimed to be the herald of God's Kingdom, a Kingdom at hand for everyone—especially for the poor—and one that demanded an immediate change of outlook (conversion). Radical as it was, such a proclamation could not but stir up confrontations with the ruling leaders of the period.

With regards to the law, Jesus appeared to be simultaneously a good, practicing Jew and a revolutionary. Jesus turned the attention of the rich young men back to the Law that leads to life;[5] he stated that the Law and the prophets were sufficiently clear for the relatives of the rich man undergoing torments;[6] he loved the Temple where he regularly went on pilgrimage and he stood in the way of its being used as a short-cut for hard-pressed housewives;[7] he sent the cleansed leper to show himself to the priest;[8] he respected what the scribes and Pharisees taught[9] and did not always criticize their more stringent applications of the Law's demands.[10] But this same Jesus showed no regard for the ritual impurity he contracted from lepers or the woman with the issue of blood, and he deliberately violated the sabbath prescriptions.[11]

For example, the material gathered in Mark 2:23–3:5 reports two typical incidents: the plucked ears of corn and the healing of a man with a withered right arm. Now, according to the Jewish law of that time, the accused had to be found guilty of premeditation by a warning given in front of witnesses.[12] So, in the presence of his disciples who were gleaning on a sabbath day, the Pharisees told Jesus, "Look! They are doing something not permitted on the sabbath." Jesus had been officially warned. And he replied that the sabbath was made for men, not men for the sabbath.[13] He rose up against an interpretation of sabbath rest that he thought damnable. Damnable? Yes, but it was he, Jesus, who could suffer death,[14] and even an immediate one, for in Galilee—unlike in Judea and Samaria, which were directly accountable to the Roman authority—the Jews had not lost their right to stone a guilty person without prior leave from the Romans. Mark, moreover, notes that some kind of inquisition was being conducted: "They kept their eyes on him" and, he concluded, "they took a decision to put him to death."[15]

This sketch can be completed by reference to two other sabbath healings[16] and by recalling the accusations brought against Jesus in the matter of ritual prescriptions; for example, the strict injunction to wash one's hands before a meal.[17] How could such behavior fail to rouse the indignation of religious leaders? But for new wine, new wineskins are needed!

On another point, that of the universality of the Kingdom, Jesus entered into open conflict with the leadership. He was the friend of tax collectors and sinners,[18] not afraid to share their table, something that, a long time afterward, Peter did not dare do.[19] This was because God loves sinners and calls them to repent;[20] they were the ones whom Jesus came to call, not the virtuous.[21] Finally, and primarily, Jesus went to the "poor," those whom God preferred,[22] while the official custodians of the Law despised and rejected them.[23] It is not with impurity that one turns to the outcasts of the land, defending them against the sustainers of the established order.

These "officials" belonged equally to the religious and political worlds, and Jesus' gestures involved all of them. To proclaim that the Kingdom of God was at hand for the poor was to unleash a hard-to-control enthusiasm among the masses who hoped for liberation of the territory occupied by the Romans.[24] Jesus was not understood by the crowds as we will make clear below. His conduct was not accepted by the religious authorities, for example on the occasion of his "Cleansing of the Temple," a scandalous action that unleashed a decisive reaction from the Sadducees. Undoubtedly, Jesus intended by his "eschatological" sign a declaration of the in-breaking of God's Kingdom, but he could have been taken to be a violent revolutionary. Clearly, the motivation for his condemnation cannot be reduced to simply that of a political stir, but this interpretation could find some basis in his outlook. Luke has summarized well the thought of his contemporaries who wanted to suppress this dangerous man: Jesus disturbs, he "troubles" the established order.[25] Seen from the outside, he was a suspect person, a fomenter of rebellion.[26]

Why did Jesus act this way? The answer is clear: because of his message, especially because of the knowledge he had of God. His radicalism could not abide any compromises. Against legalism, he proclaimed the absolute mercy of God toward sinners, knocking over the barriers set up by a tradition that the religious authorities guarded jealously.

Jesus had total trust in God and did not shrink from the eventuality of martyrdom; because of his conduct, he sensed an impending violent death. He said so in a veiled way:

The days will come when the bridegroom is taken away from them, and they will fast in that day.

(Mk 2:19–20)

This saying is probably authentic.[27] It is quite circumspect about the occurrence, unlike the prophecies edited after the fact; it could not be invoked to justify the penitential practices of the early Church (the nature of which we know very little). No doubt, it describes the Messiah as the "bridegroom," a designation that the Old Testament does not attribute to anyone but God himself, but that the Targum (an Aramaic interpretation of) to Psalm 45 applies to the Messiah and that Jesus seems to have used in one or another parable.[28]

THE FORETELLING OF HIS DEATH IN THE COURSE OF JESUS' LIFE

If Jesus could have anticipated his violent death, did he speak of it? This is the second point that a historian has to specify. In it he encounters a thorny issue—was there an evolution, not in Jesus' consciousness, but in the presentation of his message? A reply can be obtained from the Synoptics and from historical data; what is necessary is to get behind the historical substrate in the gospel arrangement of Jesus' ministry.

The synoptic tradition distinguishes two stages in the life of Jesus. The first took place in Galilee; the second, after a split between Jesus and the Galileans, on the way to and in Jerusalem. Now this arrangement was not taken up by the Fourth Gospel; so we have to ask whether it also reflects historical facts very well. As a matter of fact, despite the general overview of the Synoptics,

Jesus went up to Jerusalem several times, as John says explicitly and as several sayings of Jesus reported in the Synoptics themselves elsewhere testify.[29] However, this does not allow us to conclude that there was not a dispute between Jesus and Galilee. What, then, is the import of dividing Jesus' ministry into two phases?

The break with Galilee ordinarily has been justified in the following way. After an initial success in this region, Jesus suffered a triple setback. The religious leadership did not favorably receive his preaching; then, the crowds misjudged him by interpreting his activity as that of a politician who intended to stir up the people against the Roman occupier; finally, Herod tried to kill Jesus. Of these three aspects, we should qualify the last.

About Herod's eventual persecution: when, in effect, he sought "to see Jesus," it was in order to reckon him John the Baptist's equal and to imprison him; but this "to see" explicitly concerned only his miracles, as Luke is later at pains to point out.[30] Luke also reports that the Pharisees ran afoul of Jesus and counseled him, "Flee from here, for Herod wants to kill you." It is possible that this text is a Lukan composition: the Pharisees are hypocritical, always described in a poor light by Luke, never in league with the Herodians, imputing to Herod a murderous intent in order to get Jesus to go away on his own, something that would favor their own designs.[31] Also, to state that Herod definitely wanted to put an end to Jesus' ministry requires a reference to the global context: as we have said, the proclamation of God's Kingdom by Jesus could have been associated with the revolutionary harangues that sought to stir up the people against the Romans; and the putting down of these had been numerous and awful ones.[32]

However, there remains the fact that Jesus ran up against two fundamental experiences of opposition: on the part of the crowd and on the part of the religious leaders.[33] These could explain the desire he had of leaving Galilee and looking for a more authentic acceptance elsewhere.

F. Mussner has taken up this matter[34] and has concluded that the pre-Easter depiction of Christ by the gospel tradition knew two stages. Doubtless, this was not a case of a true "biography" of Jesus, but several literary features require such a division.

The first six chapters of Mark describe a veritable "Galilean spring time." Jesus proclaimed the Kingdom and his fame spread throughout Galilee; he healed, he exorcized demons, he traveled to every locale. People came to him from everywhere, praising God; and this went on and on.[35] In addition, references to these doings were handed on in "summary statements" whose purpose was to generalize and group together traditions on this topic. But, beginning with Chapter 7, these indicators began to diminish[36] and they cannot be associated with the earlier summaries.

The ancient details of the non-Markan tradition corroborate the presentation of the Second Gospel. It is historically certain that the proclamation of God's Kingdom, after a brief success, was not received favorably by the Galilean crowds, although Jesus did not for that reason stop proclaiming.[37] Thus, the Markan view of the course of Jesus' ministry in Galilee is confirmed.

There is a second literary feature: Mark distinguishes two periods in the role of the disciples. In the first stage, they spread the Good News;[38] then, after the Galilean ministry, they seem to be reduced to the small circle of the Twelve, with the new function of being the nucleus of the future community of salvation, which would take the name of Church. Does this modification not signify the existence of two periods, separated by the reversal in Galilee?

Finally, as we will point out shortly,[39] a historical basis underlies the ascent to Jerusalem and the prophecies of the Passion. After having wandered about in Galilee to proclaim the Kindgom, Jesus, after rejection, knew himself threatened by death.

Historically speaking, we can admit that Jesus' ministry was made up of two periods, as the Synoptics propose them. One was the triumphant heralding of the Kingdom of God, which was at hand and demanded conversion; the other revealed that the path to glory passed by way of the cross.

Without doubt, we may not divide success and setback into two blocks that characterize the two periods one after another; but we can, without danger of being mistaken, reserve to the second period the teaching about the Passion. In this sense, it is likely that, to achieve a synthesis, Matthew brought together within the first period sayings that must have been uttered in the second.[40] But, in the essentials, the respective tonalities of the two periods have been respected by the evangelist.

One consequence is unavoidable. Before Peter's confession at Caesarea, Jesus announced that the Kingdom was at hand, he called people to follow him, either in direct fashion or, even, to become fishers of men. A strong wind picked them up and carried them along, even though some remained reticent and the religious leaders were suspicious. Jesus stirred up an irresistible wave of enthusiasm. But after Peter's confession it was no longer the crowds who were invited to conversion, but the disciples who had to deepen their adherence to the young rabbi. If they have been called to follow Jesus, this means to follow him in trial and even to the cross. A striking change has taken place; the setback has intervened. Jesus began to foretell death as inevitable for him and also for his disciples. This is the situation underlying the sayings we have to attend to now.[41]

THE OCCURRENCE IN THE DIVINE PLAN

If there is one characteristic of the Jewish religious mentality, it is the piercing conviction of the history of God, who made a covenant with Israel. Also, every good Jew had to interpret the events he lived through by situating them within God's plan. This is what the early Church did, for example, in stating that "this happened so that Scripture might be fulfilled." This is what Jesus did when he faced imminent death, either by reading his own fate in that of John the Baptist, or by alluding on several occasions to what we can call the law of the mistreated prophet and the law of the persecuted just person: things have always happened this way.

THE TRAGIC FATE OF PROPHETS

In the two most ancient traditions reflected in the gospels, namely Q and Mark, the death of the prophet Jesus is presented as the culmination of a long series of killings inflicted on prophets and God's messengers, and particularly like that of John the Baptist.

Jesus and John the Baptist

It is not impossible to grasp somewhat the experience Jesus might have had at John's death. His beheading is one of the most undisputed historical facts.[42] Josephus gives an account of it closely connected to that of the Synoptics; the latter description possesses a Semitic and Palestinian coloring and derives from the circle of John's disciples. Its literary genre is that of a "martyrdom" interspersed with more or less folkloric details. All this allows us to hold onto a goodly number of points:

- Herod Antipas had John the Baptist imprisioned, condemned and beheaded in the fortress of Machaerus in Transjordan, to the east of the Dead Sea.
- The reason for this imprisonment was his preaching, the success of which became threatening to Herod himself.
- Herod the Great's descendants were known for their banquets, which celebrated their birthdays.
- The disciples of John probably kept watch to see that their teacher received an honorable burial.
- John the Baptist's death confirmed his status as a prophet.

Now, Jesus had been closely linked to John. Baptized by him and having himself baptized with some success,[43] Jesus admired John as "more than a prophet."[44] Without doubt, Jesus was known through his relationship with the Baptist and his disciples had frequent contacts with him.[45] Matthew seems perfectly justified in stating that, with the last imprisonment of John, "Jesus withdrew,[46] he went into seclusion before the threat that Herod brings to the freedom of prophets. A saying of Jesus supports this interpretation:

11 [*The disciples*] asked him, "Why do the scribes say that first Elijah must come?" **12** And he said to them, "Elijah does come first to restore all things; and how is it written of the Son of man, that he should suffer many things and be treated with contempt? **13** But I tell you that Elijah has come, and they did to him whatever they pleased, as it is written of him.

(Mk 9:11–13)

In this saying, there is no commiseration, no sadness at the loss of his friend, but a profound understanding of what has happened and what concerns him. If Elijah has come previously, the disciples implicitly ask, what are its implications for the fate and mission of the Messiah?[47] In reply, Jesus situates the Son of man in relation to Elijah, to show that in John the Baptist one should recognize the prophet Elijah and that, accordingly, John's fate prefigures that of Jesus. Clearly this saying has been edited in the light of Easter, but the relationship between Jesus and John remains historically valid. Jesus claims that John had been mistreated, and he intuits that people will deal with him the same way, following the tradition of the tragic lot of prophets.

A Traditional Outline

Jesus was not only familiar with John the Baptist; he also knew well the prophets of Israel, his people. He referred to the failure of the prophets Elijah and Elisha[48] and even recalled what might have been a popular aphorism:

A prophet is not without honor, except in his own country, and among his own kin, and in his own house.

(Mk 6:4 [Mt 13:57; Lk 4:24; Jn 4:44])

Misunderstanding was the prophet's normal lot. Moreover he is delivered up to hatred, to being cut off from his own family, to outrages, calumnies, the forerunner in this regard of Jesus' future disciples.[49] These sporadic statements come to be situated by Jesus within God's great design, expressed with the help of a traditional outline that remained alive in the Judaism of the first century A.D.[50] Post-Exile Judaism, as the heir of the deuteronomic tradition, produced "resumés" of sacred history, such as the following penitential prayer:

26 Nevertheless they were disobedient and rebelled against thee and cast thy law behind their back and killed thy prophets, who had warned them in order to turn them back to thee, and they committed great blasphemies. **30** Many years thou didst bear with them, and didst warn them by thy Spirit through thy prophets; yet they would not give ear. Therefore, thou didst give them into the hand of the peoples of the lands.

(Neh 9:26,30)

It was in this way that people reflected on the past history of the people, and they made use of an outline to do so:

- A global formulation (prophets in general, mentioned in the plural)
- No scriptural proof, but a polemical tone
- The rejection of the prophets by Israel, stated with verbs such as "kill" and "persecute"

If catastrophes took place over the centuries, this was because people did not heed the prophets. This is the evidence that Jesus, like every Jew of his epoch, had in his head.

Other traditional currents intervened, contributing to the fashioning of Jesus' sayings, such as the sapiential and prophetic currents. And often it is quite difficult to distinguish what is proper to one or the other. The essential matter is that we can recognize at work Jesus' deepest conviction about the tragic fate of prophets. On this point, two sayings of Jesus are typical:[51]

Woe to you! For you build the tombs of the prophets . . . . So you are witnesses *against yourselves*: *You are the children of those who killed the prophets!* *This is why* the Wisdom of God also said, "I will send them wise men and scribes: some of whom they will kill and persecute that the blood of all the prophets, shed from the foundation of the world, may be required of this generation, from the blood of Abel to the blood of Zechariah, who perished between the altar and the sanctuary. Yes, I tell you, it shall be required of this generation."

      (Reconstructed text, based on Lk 11:47–51 = Mt 23:29, 34f)[52]

O Jerusalem, Jerusalem, killing the prophets and stoning those who are sent to you! How often would I have gathered your children together as a hen gathers her brood under her wings, and you would not! Behold, your house will be forsaken . . . .

      (Reconstructed text, based on Lk 13:34f = Mt 23:37–39)[53]

Confronted by threats from the religious leaders, Jesus returns to the past history of Israel; Jesus appeals to God's Wisdom, who guides history. So, wisdom will send missionaries who, in their turn, will be persecuted.[54] To understand his fate, Jesus located himself in the line of prophets, and this is one of the reasons he declared,

For it cannot be that a prophet should perish away from Jerusalem.

      (Lk 13:33)[55]

Jesus: More than a Prophet

    In the death that threatened him, did Jesus perceive only the prophet's destiny? The traditional outline no doubt demanded the invectives that he felt obliged to hurl at his contemporaries. But there was more; namely, what he clearly expressed in the parable of the murderous vineyard workers.[56] To the traditional themes of prophets sent by God to his vine, Jesus added the sending of God's "son," who came to bring to completion the history of God's dealings with his people and to establish a point of nonreturn. The parable, stripped of the specifications added by the early Church in regard to the stone that had been rejected, is completely oriented to the removal of the Kingdom from the chosen people; this is nothing more than the direction given by the meaning of Jesus' death. So also we are entitled to conclude: Jesus, who had seen in John the Baptist "more than a prophet," knew himself to be in a special relationship with God, charged as his Son with the task of crowning the tradition of the tragic fate of the prophets. Therein we link up with another biblical tradition, that of the persecuted Just One.

THE FATE OF THE PERSECUTED JUST ONE

All throughout Israel's history, across a great many vicissitudes, the typical image of a persecuted Just Person took shape.[57] It was normal for the first Christians to cast their gaze on this figure, so striking did resemblances appear to them. Thus, the Passion of Jesus was portrayed in the light of the lamentation psalms:[58] the community, which knew the happy outcome of the drama, was pleased to call to mind the various phases of the trial. To draw a picture of it without losing heart, it made use of Psalm 22 in particular, not afraid to begin the recitation of the opening of the psalm with the tragic cry, "My God, my God, why have you abandoned me?" They knew that the centurion had answered in the name of the community at prayer.[59] In all truth, they were able to look squarely at the humiliations of the one whom they knew to be exalted in God's presence.

For our purpose, the question is one of knowing whether Jesus himself suggested to the Apostles that it was possible to associate his future fate with that of the persecuted Just One. The narrative of the Passion could well be explained as beginning with the primitive community, without thereby stating that Jesus had interpreted his life in the light of the prophecy about the Just One.[60] Moreover, in examining the sayings attributed to Jesus, we can disclose in his thought a tendency to situate his destiny within the divine economy of a Just One who is persecuted and exalted.

The second period of Jesus' ministry was structured by the triple proclamation of Jesus' fate, making out the ascent to Jerusalem.[61] These announcements, closely copying a similar outline, increase in their preciseness so that by the third one we can see in detail what will happen. From the fact of this description, a prophecy *ex eventu* (after the fact) is often discerned in it. Nonetheless, if we can concede this fact for the third Passion prediction, it is not a similar situation with the first two. Underlying the present texts, scholars concur in detecting two pregospel traditions that may be explained in the following way.[62]

The first tradition is impersonal, introduced by the word *must*.

The Son of man must suffer many things and be rejected . . . .
(Mk 8:31; cf. 9:12; Lk 17:25)

In this formulation the designation "Son of man" is unnecessary and could have been added later. Jesus is not the subject of the activity but is the object of the divine decision, of a "must" that from all the evidence is related to God's design and that, in John's gospel, becomes God the Father's commandment, recognized as love.

A personalized formulation is given by the second tradition, wherein Jesus is the subject of the sentence but with the verb in the passive:

The Son of man will be delivered into the hands of men.
(Mk 9:31, 14:41; Lk 24:7)[63]

This formula is still enigmatic, in Jesus' style, analogous to Lk 22:22: "The Son of man goes as it has been determined." It is difficult to conclude to the earlier of one of these traditions in relation to the other; some spontaneously have considered that the two were formed in parallel.[64]

It is not necessary to delay over the problem of the authenticity of the mention of the Resurrection in these predictions, for here we are only concerned with Jesus' death. However, if one wishes to admit that Jesus could have expressed himself thus, it is appropriate to consider as highly probable that in fact he sometimes brought up the Resurrection, something not at all surprising in the case of a good Jew. Nonetheless, it is likely that it was the early community that generalized the mention of the resurrection and that specified the three-day interval.[65]

Treated at this level, the formulations could with some assurance be placed on Jesus' lips. In addition, we note that it is not properly an issue of "prophecy" nor "prediction" but of "revelation," of the manifestation of Jesus' destiny, given to the disciples to strengthen them ahead of time against discouragement and doubt. What could be more normal for Jesus in the circumstances in which he found himself?

The balance sheet of our inquiry is rich. Jesus situated his life within the longstanding tradition of the persecuted Just One whom God comes to save, just as he placed himself at the end of the line of the prophets who suffered a tragic end. Strengthened with this evidence, the reader will be disposed to accept the profound meaning of other sayings of Jesus, despite the critical difficulties that are set up against them. He or she will grasp without turmoil that Jesus spoke by way of images and brief references, stating that he would soon drink the cup of his Passion and would be baptized with the baptism of his death. This was how he replied to the thoughtless request made by the sons of Zebedee:

Are you able to drink the cup that I drink, or to be baptized with the baptism with which I am baptized?

(Mk 10:38)[66]

or else:

I came to cast fire upon the earth; and would that it were already kindled; I have a baptism to be baptized with; and how I am constrained until it is accomplished!

(Lk 12:49–50)[67]

Threatened by death, Jesus showed the secrets of his life: the presence there of the God of love, his Father, who carries out his plan and who will bring it to realization in his own way.

DID JESUS DESCRIBE HIS DEATH AS REDEMPTIVE?

Perhaps the reader has remarked that in the preceding section, when the issue touched on the "divine economy," no mention was made of the two principal institutions of Israel, namely the Law and sacrifices. In fact, we noticed[68] that, though Jesus respected and observed the Law, he was concerned with pointing out its limitations and its excesses when handed over without reserve to narrow scribes and to the deformations brought about by greedy souls. Also he was not afraid of transgressing it when it happened to hinder his liberating mission. In regard to the omission of sacrificial terminology, this is demanded at first glance; in fact, Jesus did not depict his message in terms of cultic practices. On the contrary, following the prophets, he vigorously recalled that "God loves mercy and not sacrifices."[69] It is with difficulty that one would understand that the prophet Jesus used categories of thought deriving from these institutions to give meaning to his death.

However, force of habit is such that numerous are the commentators for whom Jesus himself stated that his death was *the* redemptive occurrence. To give weight to this proposition, one can cite the texts of the eucharistic institution (the study of which will be reserved to the next chapter) and the saying in which Jesus declared he had come to redeem everyone.

If, for my part, I consider that Jesus did not expressly speak these words, it is for reasons that derive from the sphere of scholarship. As for the psychological motives why Jesus, as God, would have had to foretell his future, I am content to make the following observations.

Jesus is an authentic man, and man's alienable nobility is that he can—and even must—freely project the pattern of his life into a future of which he knows nothing. If this man is a believer, the future into which he casts and projects himself is God in his freedom and his immensity. To deprive Jesus of this opportunity and make him advance toward a goal which he already knows and which is distinct only in time, would mean stripping him of his dignity as a man[70] In Jesus' flexibility with regard to events and in his acceptance of the future as it gradually comes upon him, there is something completely different from an avowal of powerlessness and determination to share our weakness; there is also—perhaps we should say "first of all"—the mark of his divine condition. We are the ones who, conscious of our limitations, have to devise plans and schemes to map out our future and protect ourselves from the risks that threaten us. We are the ones who conceive of divine omnipotence as a blueprint unrolled, or a process carried out, second by second, and think of our freedom as the power to throw the whole mechanism out of order. But this omnipotence we bestow on God is only a caricature; and the future which we believe we are placing in his hands is not the future, but only something past which we project before us. . . .

. . . the force of these announcements [by Jesus] does not reside in some divinatory power which might have enabled Jesus to outline beforehand a happening that could not be foreseen humanly. Not one of them derives its weight from this sort of sign; but all of them rest upon Jesus' consciousness of having received from God a unique role in the world, of being obliged to play it till its termination in a bitter and ignominious death, and of scrutinizing events and the people he meets for a gradual disclosure of the future that awaits him.[71]

Having said this, let us first of all examine, independently of the context into which it has been inserted, Jesus' saying

The Son of man came . . . to give his life as a *redemption* for many (*lytron anti pollōn*).

(Mt 20:28 = Mk 10:45)

The word *lytron* has been translated here not as "ransom" but as "redemption." In effect, in the course of centuries, the word no longer referred in Israel to the "price paid in ransom of a prisoner of war or of a slave," nor the price paid to a deity in compensation for or in place of something else."[72] Though Israel's historical experience was one of being delivered from Egypt, the word ended up losing every trace of meaning a "ransom"[73] and, when used as a metaphor, came simply to designate deliverance from some evil or from death.[74] This is why it seemed preferable to me to translate *lytron* by the abstract noun "redemption," to designate the action through which God delivered from a state of oppression.

This metaphorical use is doubly verified in this text of ours. First of all, because there is no reference to "what" the multitude is ransomed from: the term is used absolutely. Then, because the preposition *anti* does not imply here any idea of an exchange or substitution but it is found merely as called for by the noun.[75] Finally, all the scholars agree with Jeremias in translating *pollōn* not as "many" but by the positive "multitude."[76]

The meaning of the saying is clear: by his life given without reserve, Jesus has acquired a new people, the multitude of men and women. To specify the meaning, it is useful to compare it with the institution of the Eucharist:

This is my blood . . . poured out for the *multitude*.

(Mt 26:28 = Mk 14:24)

The "blood poured out" quite probably alludes to the prophecy of the Servant of YHWH:

When you make your life as sacrifice of expiation . . .
He poured out his soul to death . . .
He bore the sin *of the multitude* . . . .

(Is 53:10,12)

We recognize here the same reality as in Mk 10:45: the gift of life (even to blood, the eucharistic text for its part makes clear) and the multitude that benefits from this gift. In Isaiah, the prophecy describes the gift of life as a "sacrifice of expiation" (Heb. *acham*), although in itself, as we have just seen, "redemption" is not a sacrificial term.[77]

Hence, it is difficult to interpret sacrificially Jesus' saying about "redemption" in Mk 10:45. If one admits the (evident) relationship of this saying with that of the Last Supper, an hypothesis can be proposed to justify its tenor.[78] Everything happens as if the redactor of the saying underlying Mk 10:45 had adapted the sacrificial eucharistic saying concerning blood poured out to Jesus' situation during his public life. However, there was then no question of an imminent death (as at the Last Supper) but of a kind of résumé of Jesus' entire life. The saying tells of the gift of self, which has gone to the extreme.

The relationship of the eucharistic saying allows for the addition of an important remark. In fact, within the two instances, there is an "opposition" between Jesus and the multitude, between One and All. Is there not therein the essential aspect of the assertion—independent of terminology, redemptive or sacrificial—used to describe this relationship? Such is the mystery of salvation: it is

accomplished by one, to the benefit of all. This interpretation of
the salvific death of Jesus was widespread in the early Church,
and this saying belongs to one of the most certain sets of terminology. We speak of it again in Chapter 5 with reference to Paul
facing Christ's death.

Can we go still further and say that this saying derives from
Jesus himself? Numerous authors answer in the negative, advanc-
ing arguments of different weight. A first difficulty derives from
the location of the text in the gospel tradition. Although fundamental sayings of Jesus are repeated as many as five or six times
(such as the saying, "The one who loses his life, saves it"), and
sometimes with identical terms, this saying is handed on but once
(by Mark and Matthew, but not by Luke).

The literary context, moreover, does not favor its authenticity.
Clearly, it possesses an Aramaic tone, and it derives from a Palestinian milieu. But, unknown by Luke, it appears to be over-
loaded in its context:

Mk 10:42–45	Lk 22:25–27
42 You know that those who are supposed to rule over the Gentiles lord it over them and their great men exercise authority over them	25 The kings of the Gentiles exercise lordship over them and those in authority over them are called benefactors.
43 But it shall not be so among you; but whoever would be great among you must be your servant!	26 But not so with you! Rather let the greatest among you become as the youngest and the leader as one who serves
44 and whoever would be the first among you, must be slave of all	27 For which is the greater, one who sits at table, or one who serves? Is not the one who sits at table?

45(a) For the Son of man, also came
   not to be served but to serve
   (b) and to give his life as
      redemption for the multitude.

But I am among you
as one who serves.

A glance at this synoptic chart shows immediately that the final saying of Jesus (Mk 10:45) has been added onto a text that in no way requires it. The dominant idea in the passage is that of service, something that Luke has highlighted perfectly by speaking of service at table and by situating Jesus' word in the framework of the Last Supper. In the next chapter we will specify in what sense Jesus' life was recapitulated and his death understood on the basis of a meal.[79] His disposition to service led Jesus to death, a death that crowned all that preceded it. This is the very meaning of the saying in Mark: "The Son of man came not to be served but to serve."

Historically speaking, we can hold as certain that Jesus lived his life as one of service and that he carried it on by breaking down the barriers erected by the narrowness of the Law and of the worship of his era; for example, in his taking meals with tax collectors and sinners, and in addressing his proclamation to the disinherited ones of the land.[80]

Certainly, it is not impossible that Jesus theorized about his activity. But the one who knows Jesus' manner would be shocked to hear in this a proclamation that was not consonant with his customary way. Jesus never declared who he was. He never wanted to encapsulate himself in a title, whatever it might be; he did not define himself as Christ or the Son of God. Jesus explodes all formulas, every plan.[81] He was content to live and stir up questions about his identity, without attempting to fix it into some neat category.[82]

Finally, it would be necessary to show how the early Church, in lending to Jesus' words just such an expression, perfectly transformed his manner of living and his profound thinking. This is what we will strive to do now in reckoning up the conclusions from this entire chapter.

CONCLUSION

We return to the question that set our research into motion. What meaning did Jesus give to the violent death that threatened him? Our reply was limited by the fact that (on the hypothesis of this work) we have not yet considered the totality for Jesus' life, namely his conduct in the face of a death that was imminent and present. We considered it preferable to reserve this study to the next two chapters. But even now it is possible to extract from the data a description the manner in which Jesus saw death approaching him.

As a matter of habit, we project onto Jesus later interpretations made by the primitive community and even those of Paul. This is something quite understandable, especially when we attribute to Jesus the notion that he was living out on earth the propehcey of the Servant of YHWH. Thus, we saw in Mk 10:45 an "admirable synthesis" of the theology of the Son of man in glory and of the Suffering Servant.[83] This presentation, doubtless, is admirable, but did it derive from Jesus? We have just established that the text of MK 10:45, the only one of its kind that precedes the Passion narrative, could not with certitude go back to Jesus himself. On the other hand, wherever Is 53 is explicitly quoted in the New Testament,[84] there is no question of "vicarious expiation."[85] In the course of the narratives of the Passion, no reference is made to the prophecy from this perspective; the sole text that reflects this meaning is found in 1 Peter[86] and one text does not suffice to prove the existence of a "current tradition." Therefore, we cannot seriously invoke such a synthesis to attribute this interpretation to Jesus. It is surer to think that he did not locate his impending death within a sacrificial context.[87]

From the above, it does not follow that Jesus did not give some meaning to it as a part of God's design. We discovered at the end of Chapter 1 that the essential thing in Jesus' eyes was the presence of God in the unfolding of the history of the people of Israel. What, then, touches on death in general holds as well for Jesus' personal death. Threatened with imminent death, Jesus continued to proclaim the message of God's Kingdom. The setback that became evident did not turn him aside from his will faithfully to serve both God and men. This failure, he situated with God's great plan, placing himself at the summit of the prophets' lives, as the Just One above all others. He did not undergo death passively, but consented to die. His trust in God was not shaken; it assured him of the final victory beyond death. In the final analysis, in his eyes, death had no meaning except in terms of his life of faithfulness to the mission it crowned and with reference to God, who vindicated it by the Resurrection.

Violent death, hence, is not fatal, as if God had directly willed it; it is necessary as the inevitable consequence of fidelity to God and human persons: the prophets and the just have always been mistreated. In doing this, Jesus did not resign himself to some "It is written," but he perceived the will of God his Father, who asked him to persevere to the end in the role he entrusted to him. If death seems not to have been "willed," not even "desired" by him, it was clearly regarded as the path of radical faithfulness.

On the other hand, Jesus' death cannot be reduced to that of a prophet like any other, of a just man like any other. Jesus claimed to have a unique relationship with God and a unique relationship with all men and women. In this sense, his personhood is revealed as unique and necessarily raises a question thereby: "Who, then, is this man?" And not only a question but a pressing invitation to give an answer. Already there is emerging a pointer to the interpretation that will see in Jesus' death a deed that has an import for the multitude. Yet the matter has not yet been made explicit, and the historian can decide only after calling on the witnesses to the resurrection, through whom God relays the answer that belongs to him alone.

One consequence is clear. One cannot speak of Jesus' death by isolating this event, on the one side, from what preceded it and provoked it, or on the other, from the Resurrection, which reveals its meaning. It is God alone, who gave Jesus the task of proclaiming without fail the Good News of a love that is infinite and universal. It is God alone who, by means of the resurrection, will reveal the profound significance of Jesus' violent death for all.

What Jesus lived the interpreters of the New Testament echoed while making explicit the riches virtually contained within the conduct and words that we have laboriously discovered underlying the text. The historian has to pursue his task in this way in order to soberly indicate what the principal interpretations of Jesus' thought were. With the Epistle to the Hebrews, we will seek out again the meaning of suffering implied by his death.[88] With Paul, we will take account of the interpretation that sees in Jesus' death the sacrifice of expiation for the multitude.[89] For the moment, we are content, in conformity with our project, to bring a second illumination onto Jesus' death, by confronting the historical results at which we have arrived and the presentation of the Fourth Gospel. The two seem to be contrary, if not contradictory.

For John, apparently, it was with a happy heart that Jesus walked toward death on the Cross, since that was the path to glory, a passage to the Father and to life in its definitive form. Such was the rule of the grain of wheat that has to die in the earth in order to bear fruit, such was the Father's commandment, through which he manifested his love. God so loved the world that he gave his only Son to save it.

However, to comprehend these expressions, one has to keep watch against hearing them through Pauline theology. For John, death is not considered within a sacrificial outlook. It occurs as the crown of a life of service, as the washing of feet expresses it symbolically. When the Good Shepherd gives his life for his sheep, this is to defend them against the wolf, it is to assure them of abundant pastures. There is no greater love than to give one's life for those one loves; and this final gift is significant not only as a gift but as the ultimate gift: it is all of life given in its entirety, which is gift and service. With death, "all is accomplished." Finally, when the Son has been sanctified and sent into the world, this is not on account of some cultic act, but by virtue of a prophetic kind of consecration that sets apart and makes one pass over from what is profane to God himself.[90] Having thus anticipated his glory from the earthly life of Jesus, John can throughout the whole gospel describe his death as a being lifted up toward glory.

Between these two perspectives on Jesus' death, must one choose that of the historian (the crowning of service) or that of John the interpreter (a passing over to glory)? I do not think so, for the remaining is not in either one or the other, but in the relationship that dialectically writes them. In fact, both of them ground the two principal ways in which one can speak about Jesus facing death, and even about every believing person facing death.

In reality, the glory that is anticipated in Jesus' earthly life, expresses the certitude that God is present, guiding the action. On the other hand, the ruggedness of the approaching event prevents the confusion of earth and heaven. So, the fundamental dialectic between the "already now" and the "not yet" is rediscovered. It is this dialectic that clarifies the believer's conduct: He or she is not simply set before death as one might find oneself before a happening to come, but rather he or she already knows life in its definitive form. He or she has "passed" from death to life.[91]

These reflections clarify the disposition of the true faithful one, who sees in death a "passage to the Father." The evidence can be perfectly lived out, without illusion, but it cannot be spoken of in truth except among believers. The flash of glory is such that, sometimes, it absorbs earth's shadows; but the glory is not perceptible except by faith. To the unbeliever it appears as an empty bit of imagination, even a dangerous one in the measure that it encourages flight beyond our world of work and affliction. But this risk does not justify the mistaking of the depth of the believer's experience.

This experience, like that of Jesus, has a two fold dimension: faced with a threatening end, it consents to the occurrence that, by suffering and a tearing away, is needed to fulfill a life of service; on the other side, it awaits from its own death perfect communion with God and with all men and women, a communion that faith has already inaugurated in the secret one's being.

NOTES

1. "Historisch gesproschen—ein sinnloser Schicksal," in *Das Verhältnis der urchristlichen Christusbotschaft zum historischen Jesus*, 3rd ed. (Heidelberg: Universitätsverlag, 1962), p. 12.
2. F. Jeanson, *La Foi d'un incroyant* (Paris: Seuil, 1963), pp. 97–98.
3. Cf. p. xxvi and the development proposed in J. Dupont, ed., *Jésus aux origines de la Christologie* (Louvain: Leuven University Press, 1975), pp. 143–144.
4. Cf. pp. 162–190.
5. Mt 19:18p.
6. Lk 16:29–31.
7. Mk 11:16.
8. Mt 8:4.
9. Mt 23:2f.
10. Mt 23:23.
11. Mk 5:27–32; cf. E. Lohse, "Sabbaton" TDNT 7 (1971), 22, n. 172.
12. J. Jeremias, *New Testament Theology* (New York: Scribner, 1971), p. 279, n. 1.
13. Mk 2:24,27.
14. Cf. *Sanh. VII*, 4.
15. Mk 2:24, 3:2,6. This is what the Fourth Gospel masterfully focused into the incident of the cripple's healing at the Sheep Pool (Jn 5:18).
16. Lk 13:10–16; 14:1–6.
17. Mk 2:14,15–17p; 7:8,9–13,15p. Cf. J. Roloff, *Das Kerygma und der irdischen Jesus* (Göttingen: Vandenhoeck und Ruprecht, 1970), pp. 52–58.
18. Mt 11:19.
19. Mk 2:17p; Lk 7:36–47; 15:4–10,11–32; 19:1–10; Mt 20:1–15; cf. Acts 9:28; Gal 2:12f.
20. Lk 15:1–32.
21. Mk 2:17.
22. Dt 10:17f; Ps 72; 146.
23. Cf. J. Dupont, *Les Béatitudes*, Vol. 2 (Paris: Gabalda, 1969), pp. 88–123; Vol. 3 (1973), pp. 429–450, and *Cahiers "Evangile"*, no. 24 (Paris: Cerf, 1978), p. 17
24. Cf. *Ps. Sol.* 17:23–51; P. Grelot, *L'Espérance juive à l'heure de Jésus* (Paris: Desclée, 1978), pp. 97–100.
25. Lk 23:2; the term *diastrephōn* is the one used by Ahab, King of Israel, to discredit the prophet Elijah's conduct (1 Kgs 18:17f).
26. Let us add to this the fact that he probably brought into his group of disciples men with a suspect past, such as "Simon the Zealot" or the "Iscariot," a word that may signify "hired killer" (Lk 6:15; Acts 1:13). Cf. O. Cullman, *Jesus and the Revolutionaries* (San Francisco: Harper & Row, 1970).
27. Cf. A. George, "Comment Jésus a-t-il perçu sa propre mort?" *LV* 101 (1971), pp. 35–36.
28. Mt 22:2,8,10,11f; 25:1–13.
29. "How often would I have gathered your children together as a hen gathers her brood under her wings, and you would not!" (Lk 13:34 = Mt 23:37). Or else, "Day after day I sat in the temple teaching, and you did not seize me" (Mt 26:55p).

30. Lk 9:9; 23:8; cf. H. Goguel, *Jésus* (Paris: Payot, 1950), p. 287.
31. Lk 13:31; cf. A. Denaux, "L'hypocrisie des pharisiens et le dessein de Dieu-Analyse de Lc XIII, vv. 31–33, in *L'Évangile de Luc*, (Fs. L. Cerfaux; Gembloux: Duculot, 1973), pp. 261–264.
32. For example, Theudas: Acts 5:36; cf. *Ant.* 20:8 = No. 169f; *Ps. Sol.* 17:23–51; *Tg Gn* 49:10; *Ass. Mos.* 10:7; *Ant.* 18:5 = No. 108. In this sense, it would be appropriate to understand a slight variation from what I wrote in *Les Évangiles et l'Histoire de Jésus* (Paris: Seuil, 1963), p. 365. The observation of Mk 3:6, "The Herodians sought to kill Jesus," could reflect an historical fact (cf. R. Pesch, *Markus* [p. 48, n. 141], pp. 195 and 336).
33. The crowds were not converted to the young prophet's call (Lk 10:13–15p) and seemingly they quite saw in him a revolutionary able to liberate the country from Roman oppression (cf. Jn 6:14). On the other hand, Jesus' activity was poorly regarded by the spiritual leaders, particularly the Pharisees (Mt 12:24 = Mk 3:22 = Lk 11:14–16).
34. F. Müssner, "Gab es eine galiläische Krise?" in P. Hoffmann, ed., *Orientierung an Jesus*, Festschrift J. Schmid (Freiburg-im-B.: Herder, 1973), pp. 238–252.
35. Mk 1:14f,28,33f,40; 2:1,12–15; 3:7–11,20; 4:1; 5:21,24; 6:6,12f,33f,44,55f.
36. Mk 7:37; 8:1,4,14; 10:1,46; 11:18.
37. Mt 12:28 = Lk 11:20; Mt 11:20–24 = Lk 10:13–15.
38. The existence of a "pre-Easter mission" seems to be presupposed by passages like Mk 6:11; Lk 10:1,4,6,9,11.
39. Cf. pp. 61–62.
40. So, the beatitude concerning the persecuted (Mt 5:11f = Lk 6:22f) or the prolongation of the mission instructions into predictions of persecution (Mt 10:16–42); cf. J. Dupont, *Les Béatitudes* 3 vol. (Paris: Gabalda, 1969–1973).
41. Cf. pp. xxvii–xxx.
42. Cf. R. Pesch, *Markus*, vol. 1 [p. 48, n. 141], p. 343; H. W. Hoehner, *Herod Antipas* (Cambridge: SNTS, 1972), pp. 110–171; J. Gnilka in P. Hoffmann, ed., *Orientierung an Jesus* [cf. above, n. 34], pp. 78–92; Josephus, *Ant.* 18:5,2 = No. 116–119.
43. Cf. X. Léon-Dufour, "Et là, Jésus baptisait (Jn 3:22)," in *Mélanges E. Tisserant* (Rome: Biblioteca Apostolica Vaticana, 1964), pp. 295–309.
44. Mt 11:9f = Lk 7:26. According to Mt 13:40–42, Jesus seems to criticize the Baptist (Mt 3:12).
45. Mt 9:14; 11:2; Lk 11:1; Jn 3:25; Acts 18:25; 19:1.
46. Mt 14:13.
47. Cf. Mk 8:29,31.
48. Lk 4:25–27.
49. Lk 6:22 = Mt 5:11f. Cf. J. Dupont, *Béatitudes* vol. II, pp. 285–294.
50. This schema has been masterfully treated by O. H. Steck, *Israel und das gewaltsame Geschick der Propheten. Untersuchungen zur Überlieferung des deuteronomistischen Geschichtsbildes im Alten Testament, Spätjudentum und Urchristentum* (Neukirchen: Neukirchener Verlag, 1967). The nuances introduced by P. Hoffman, *Studien zur Theologie der Logienquelle* (Münster: Aschendorff, 1972), pp. 158–190, are quite important. Cf. also M. L. Gubler, *Die frühesten Deutungen des Todes Jesu* (Göttingen: Vandenhoeck und Ruprecht, 1977), pp. 10–94.
51. These two sayings belong to the Q tradition. A remarkable thing is that the

death-resurrection problematic finds no place in this tradition, either because it was evident or because the tradition was oriented to the expectation of the imminent return of the Son of man. Despite the fact that there is thus no mention of Resurrection or soteriology, however, Jesus' death constitutes a definite break in it, and his death is understood in the light of the tragic fate of the prophets. Cf. P. Hoffman, *Studien zur Theologie der Logienquelle*, p. 178.

52. This saying has been fairly unanimously attributed to Jesus himself by scholars, even though it reflects a Jewish tradition earlier than Jesus.
53. This saying seemingly goes back to Jesus. In particular there is within it no question of his death and there no characteristic of the primitive community is found in it. Quite probably, it is not Wisdom, but Jesus, speaking.
54. In another place, Q clearly states that Jesus locates himself within the long prophetic and sapiential tradition: "Wisdom is recognized by all her children" (Lk 7:35).
55. A. George, article cited [above, n. 27], pp. 36–37.
56. Cf. X. Léon-Dufour, "La parabole des vignerons homicides," in *Études d'Évangile* (Paris: Seuil, 1965), pp. 303–344. We hold to our view, despite the qualifications proposed by M. Hubaut, *La Parabole des vignerons homicides* (Paris: Gabalda, 1976 [cf. *RSR* 55 (1978), 118–121]).
57. Cf. L. Ruppert, *Der leidende Gerechte* (Würzburg: Echter, 1972–1973).
58. E. Flesserman-Van Leer, "Die Interpretation der Passionsgeschichte vom Alten Testament aus," in *Die Bedeutung des Todes Jesu*, 2nd ed. (Gütersloh; 1967), pp. 79–96; H. Gese, "Psalm 22 und das Neue Testament: Der älteste Bericht vom Tode Jesu und die Erstehung des Herrenmahles," *ZTK* 65 (1968), 1–22; C. Westermann, "The Role of the Lament in the Theology of the Old Testament," *Interpretation* 28 (1974), 20–38.
59. Cf. pp. 127,130,139–140.
60. Unlike what I wrote in the article "Passion (récits de la)," *SDB* 6 (1960), col. 1482–1483.
61. Mt 16:21 = Mk 8:31 = Lk 9:22; Mt 17:22f = Mk 9:30–32 = Lk 9:43–45; Mt 20:17–19 = Mk 10:32–34 = Lk 18:31–34. Cf. the pertinent remarks of J. Guillet, *The Consciousness of Jesus* (Toronto/New York: Newman Press, 1972).
62. Cf. J. Roloff, "Anfange der soteriologischen Deutung des Todes Jesu (Mk X.45 und Lk XXII.28)," *NTS* 19 (1972–1973), 38–64.
63. J. Jeremias shows very well that one can recognize through the present tense *paradidotai* (cf. Mk 14:21) an Aramaic participle *mitmesar bar'enasha lide benê'*: "God will soon deliver the man to men," *New Testament Theology* [above, n. 12].
64. With J. Roloff, "Anfange" [above, n. 62], pp. 38–42.
65. I suggest that the reader consult what I wrote in the article "Jesus Christ," *DBT* (pp. 265–272) or in *The Resurrection of Jesus and the Message of Easter* (London: Geoffrey Chapman, 1974), pp. 8–9.
66. Cf. Mt 20:22. Cf. A. Feuillet, "La coupe et le baptême de la Passion," *RB* 74 (1967), 356–391; S. Legasse, "Approche de l'épisode pré-évangélique des fils de Zebedée (Marc X. 35–40 par.)," *NTS* 20 (1973–1974), 161–177; E. Arens, *The ELTHON-Sayings in the Synoptic Tradition. A Historicocritical Investigation* (Göttingen: Vandenhoeck und Ruprecht, 1976), pp. 75–78.

67. Cf. E. Arens [above, n. 66], 64–90.

68. Cf. pp. 51–52.

69. Mt 9:13; 12:7; cf. Acts 7:24 = Am 5:25.

70. H. Urs von Balthasar, *La foi du Christ* (Paris: Aubier, 1969), p. 181, quoted by J. Guillet, *Consciousness of Jesus* [above, n. 61], p. 145.

71. J. Guillet, *Consciousness of Jesus* [above, n. 61], pp. 146–148.

72. This is the outcome of the long inquiry by S. Lyonnet, *De peccato et redemptione, Vol. 2: De vocabulario Redemptionis* (Rome: Pontifical Biblical Institute, 1960), pp. 25–48: the word *lytron* is the "means by which we have been freed from sin;" the meaning being the same as that proposed by Philo, namely "any means whatever by which freedom is obtained, especially in the spiritual order" (p. 31, citing Philo, *Her.* 124 and *Sacrif.* 121,126–127). Words from the *lyō-apolyō* family, when applied to the work of Jesus Christ, quite simply connote the idea of deliverance.

73. "He gave himself for us to redeem *(lytrousthai)* us from all iniquity and to purify for himself a people of his own" (Ti 2:14). The allusion to Ex 19:5 is clear: God acquired a people for himself by setting them free and by redeeming them from the condition of slavery.

74. The Hebrew verb *pâdâ*, used to declare Israel's deliverance at the time of the exodus, no longer contained the idea of a ransom (Dt 7:8; 13:6; 1 Sm 6:23; Ps 77:15); by extension, it could designate deliverance from some evil or from death (Ps 26:11; 34:22; 49:7f; 107:2; 130:8). The other Hebrew verb *gâ'al*, had the same meaning (Is 35:9; 41:44; 44:22–24; 52:3); it always had to do with the deed by which God delivered from a state of oppression.

75. This is what is suggested by the transposition into good Greek of the noun *antilytron* (1 Tim 2:6), which expresses the same thing as Mk 10:45.

76. Cf. J. Jeremias, "Polloi," *TDNT* 6 (1968), 536–545.

77. The Hebrew word *acham* is never translated into Greek by the *LXX* as *lytron*.

78. Cf. E. Arens [above, n. 66], pp. 148–150.

79. Cf. p. 87.

80. Cf. pp. 51–53.

81. Cf. E. Schweizer, trans. David Green, *Jesus* (Atlanta: John Knox Press, 1971), especially the chapter, "Jesus: The Man Who Fits No Formula", pp. 13–51.

82. Our interpretation agrees overall with that of H. Schürmann, who developed the happy formula of Jesus' *Pro-Existenz*: "Wie hat Jesus seinen Tod bestanden und verstanden? Eine methodenkritische Besinnung," in P. Hoffman, ed., *Orientierung* [above, n. 34], pp. 325–363 (reprinted in *Comment Jésus a-t-il vécu sa mort?* 1975; French translation, Paris: Cerf, 1977). I myself have published several articles on the subject, to which I refer the reader for a fuller treatment: "Jésus devant sa mort à la lumière des textes de l'institution eucharistique et des discours d'adieu," in *Jésus* [above, n. 3], pp. 141–168 and "La mort rédemptrice du Christ selon le N.T.," in *Mort pour nos péchés* (Brussels, 1976), pp.1–34. With an opposite viewpoint, R. Bultmann's proclamation [above, n. 1] has often been taken up by Protestants such as W. Schrage, "Das Vërstandnis des Todes Christi in N.T.," in F. Viering, ed., *Das Kreuz Jesu Christi als Grund des Heils,* 2nd ed. (Gütersloh, 1968), pp. 49–90, or E. Jüngel, *Tod* (Stuttgart: Kreuz, 1971), p. 133 and by Catholics such as H. Kessler, *Die theologische Bedeutung des Todes Jesu* (Düsseldorf, 1970), doubtless in dependence on A. Vögtle, "Jesus von Nazareth," in R. Kottje and B. Möller,

eds., *Ökumenische Kirchengeschichte*, vol. 1 (Munich, 1970), pp. 21–24. According to these latter, there would be no certitude concerning Jesus' consciousness of the expiatory value of his death for the salvation of men and women.

83. So, O. Cullmann, *The Christology of the New Testament* (Philadelphia: Westminster Press, 1963), pp. 51–82; J. Jeremias, *TDNT* 5 (1967), 700–717 and *The Eucharistic Words of Jesus* (London: SCM Press, 1966), p. 227, n. 2; P. Benoit, "Jésus et le Serviteur de Dieu," in J. Dupont, *Jésus* [above, n. 3], pp. 111–140, especially pp. 121–127, in agreement with A. Feuillet, in *Revue Thomiste* 67 (1967), 533–560 and 68 (1968), 41–74; Cf. M. D. Hooker, *Jesus and the Servant* (London: SPCK, 1959), pp. 6–16.

84. Mt 8:17; Lk 22:37; Jn 12:38; Acts 8:32f; Rom 10:16; 15:21; 1 Pt 2:22.

85. A. George has quite delicately observed that Luke leaves aside the vicarious and expiatory idea to declare Jesus' self-abasement: ("Le sens de la mort de Jésus pour Luc," *RB* 80 (1973), 196–197 (= *Études sur l'oeuvre de Luc*, Paris: Gabalda, 1978, pp. 195–196).

86. 1 Pt 2:21–24.

87. This does not, however, indicate that Jesus' death was reckoned as an ordinary event of his life, its end. But Jesus did not explicitly confer meaning on his suffering; it was the Epistle to the Hebrews that revealed the sorrowful aspect of his passion.

88. Cf. below, p. 150.

89. Cf. below, pp. 184–190.

90. Thus, Jn 17:19. Cf. I. de la Potterie, "Consécration ou sanctification du Chrétien?" in E. Castelli, ed., *Le Sacré* (Rome: Castelli, 1974), pp. 333–349.

91. Jn 5:24.

3. Jesus Faces Imminent Death

The time was at hand when Jesus would be arrested, judged, crucified. It is one thing to talk about the death of others; it is still another to have a premonition of a violent death for oneself. This is what the Passion narratives try to express: Jesus' attitude in his last moments.

According to scholars, these narratives have undergone a quite significant historical process. The original text, which restricted itself to reporting simply Jesus' crucifixion,[1] was first of all enlarged by the episodes of the arrest, trial, and mistreatment.[2] At this stage, the account showed Jesus in the process of almost passively undergoing the enemy's blows. Believers also thought it appropriate to relate additional episodes that introduced the reader to Jesus' sentiments as he welcomed his death. Hence, the narrative of the Passion in secret, which he fought in the company of his disciples;[3] this was made up of two episodes: the sacramental decision[4] and the agony in Gethsemane.[5] Finally the collection was preceded by a historical "introduction" intending to relate the plot hatched against Jesus[6] and the anointing at Bethany.[7]

In the long account of the Passion, some sayings of Jesus are brought in to confirm the indicators pointed out in the last chapter. Here Jesus interprets the gesture of the woman who poured out over his head a costly perfume: "ahead of time, she has perfumed my body for burial."[8] Beforehand Jesus senses the ignominious death that he will endure and, instead of seeing in the attention given him a straightforward homage to a teacher-master, he perceives in it the anointing destined to replace the one that could not be given to a condemned criminal.[9] Two other sayings depict Jesus confronting his fate. He denounces Judas's betrayal,[10] and he foresees the dispersal of the flock gathered under his protection.[11] At the moment of his arrest, he refuses every kind of armed resistance,[12] something that accords with the style of his whole life; at the trial, he is shown testifying to the end to the mission entrusted to him.[13] Yes, Jesus sets his face toward the death that approaches.

His attitude seems to be in characteristic fashion during the course of two episodes of the Passion: in the Upper Room and in Gethsemane. The last meal shows a man who lucidly looks at his nearing death; the agony in the Garden of Olives describes the dejection and the recovery of the one who will be arrested and brought to the gallows of the cross. The figurative proclamation of Jesus' destiny and the real testing of his soul, these, then, are the two scenes on which we will cast our gaze. How did Jesus accept the death that would be inflicted on him, and where was his faithfulness to God tested?

DURING HIS LAST MEAL

The account of the last meal shows in three scenes how Jesus voluntarily confronted a violent death that was at hand: if he was handed over,[14] it was because, as Paul would formulate it later, he "gave himself up."[15] The first scene shows the prophet orchestrating with majesty the last, great act that he will fulfill; he has his disciples prepare a last meal that we can term "paschal": it is Jesus' Passover.[16] In the second scene, Jesus foretells his betrayal by one of the Twelve; by this designation, Jesus willingly fulfills the Scriptures concerning himself.[17] Finally, the third episode, the meal itself, is not simply like the first scene, a proclamation in words (Mt) or some foresight (Mk), each testifying to a superior consciousness; rather, it is a prophecy rendered in a gesture: Jesus fulfills the old Covenant by the New, which afterward will be celebrated "in his blood." Here, as he describes it, is the meaning of his imminent death.[18] Such is the synoptic presentation. It is remarkable that the Fourth Gospel preserves none of this. So, the question of what took place in fact is raised.

THE ACCOUNTS AND THE EVENT

Here[19] I limit myself to recalling the conclusions that are ordinarily recognized to be historical by the whole body of scholars.

1. Jesus took a *last meal* with his disciples. This meal was conducted not according to the Jewish passover ritual, but within a passover setting.[20]

2. Jesus went on to carry out several *actions* over the bread and the cup.[21] First of all, the blessing and the breaking of the bread, which among the Jews of that day inaugurated the fraternal meal on ordinary days; these show that the tradition originates in a Palestinian, not a Hellenistic milieu. Another historical residue: Jesus has them circulate a single cup, although habitually people used individual cups.

3. The *exact tenor of the eucharistic sayings* cannot be determined.[22] From the historical viewpoint, it would not be reasonable to construct a synthesis from them alone. Thus, it would seem, Jesus did not say "This is my body" but "This is my flesh."[23] A consequence should be drawn out: the terms "covenant," "multitude," "forgiveness of sins," "blood poured out for you"—all these expressions cannot be thrown straight away into the historical debate. Nonetheless, we shall claim that they can, at an earlier stage of the inquiry, confirm data deriving from elsewhere.

To these three vestiges testifying to the historical worth of the cultic tradition (the eucharistic institution) a fourth ought, in my opinion, to be added: the existence of a *testamentary tradition*[24] (farewell discourse), according to which Jesus took leave of his disciples. Above all else, it is represented by the Johannine discourse following the Last Supper, but it is found also in Luke in the short address that follows the meal[25] and by traces that appear in Luke[26] before the cultic text and after it in Mark–Matthew.[27] While the cultic narratives do not allow for historical deductions except by way of the emphases of the contexts in which they are enclosed, the testamentary form directly recalls events lived by Jesus of Nazareth.

Several pieces of historical evidence can be disengaged from this testamentary tradition; we will confirm this in taking up below the sayings of the cultic tradition. Here is the synoptic account:

Mk 14:25 (= Mt 26:29)	Lk 22:18
Truly, I say to you	For I tell you that
I shall not drink again	from now on I shall not drink
of [ek] the fruit of the vine	of [apo] the fruit of the vine
until that day when I drink it	until
[with you = Mt] new [wine]	
in the kingdom of God.	the kingdom of God [comes].

FACING DEATH, JESUS DECLARES HIS TRUST IN GOD

This logion allows the secure attainment of Jesus' attitude on the eve of his death. It is authentic, according to the criteria of difference and coherence.[28] Jesus speaks like a good, believing Jew, oriented toward the end of time; he does not concern himself with the eventual actualization of his word (what Christians will try to do later on). On the other hand, he expresses himself in keeping with what we know of him from the most secure historical tradition! No apocalyptic dreaming, but simply the symbol of the meal; in Jesus' teaching, as in the Bible, the joy of the chosen ones is spontaneously symbolized by the banquet.[29] In addition, here the outlook remains general: no Christian precision about what Jesus will accomplish; his Resurrection is not envisaged as a return of forty days' duration. Eschatology is not realized in him; finally, the future is not made more explicit than in the classical predictions of the Old Testament prophets. Except on one very important point: Jesus will certainly participate in the banquet on that day.

Thus, according to its first aspect, the one detailing the vertical relationship with God, Jesus reveals an utterly complete trust in God's triumph as he faces death.

The verses that precede in Luke's account constitute a whole, and corroborate these data.

"15 . . . I have earnestly desired to eat this passover with you before I suffer; 16 for I tell you I shall not eat it until it is fulfilled in the Kingdom of God." **17** And he took a cup, and when he had given thanks, he said, "Take this, and divide it among yourselves; **18** for I tell you that from now on I shall not drink of the fruit of the vine until the Kingdom of God comes."

H. Schürmann[30] thought that these verses were the vestige of the oldest narrative tradition of the Passover meal. In my view, however, they have a totally different origin: they form part of the "testamentary tradition." Before suffering Jesus said his farewell to the disciples, likewise in the context of a Passover meal; and he foretold that the table fellowship among them would cease until God's promises had been fulfilled.

According to a straightforward reading of the text, Jesus declared that he ardently longed to eat the Passover with his disciples; in fact, he could not do so until the end of time, because he was about to die. Similarly, while drinking from the cup one last time, he wanted to associate his disciples with the blessing he had just asked. This was the last evening he would live on earth in community with his own. Thus, Verse 18 reexpresses substantially the same thing as Verse 16, furnishing an excellent parallel to it and thereby revealing an indicator of a quite venerable semitic tradition, which sets us on a solid historical footing. In Verse 16, Jesus confirms the prediction made in Verse 15 ("to eat this Passover meal with you"); in Verse 18 he comments on the gesture of Verse 17, whose memory Luke retained. In this saying Jesus witnesses to his disciples his complete trust in God in the face of his imminent death.[31]

JESUS AND HIS DISCIPLES FACING DEATH

Did Jesus only declare his personal trust in God or did he also foresee the fate of his community? This he also did, if we consider the first saying preserved only by Luke: "I have greatly desired to eat this Passover with you before I suffer." In these words, Jesus not only states that this Passover will be the last he will celebrate; he specifies by the phrase "with you" the communitarian dimension of such a desire. In this Passover, which is that of his Passion, he fulfills his destiny and he wants his disciples to be always associated with him. At the same time, Jesus symbolizes by this last Passover meal the eschatological communion banquet. This throws a special light on Jesus' gestures as he passes around the single cup as a sign of sharing. The gestures of the eucharistic institution narrative, then, are themselves gestures of communion that anticipate the final banquet.

This "with you" is not indicated in the saying of Mk 14:25 = Lk 22:18, but is found only in Mt 26:29. Nonetheless, in all the accounts the communitarian dimension is present, from the fact that it is in every case a meal that is involved. Could Jesus have imagined that the eschatological meal was a single one-to-one meeting with God?

A reunion is thus quite clearly implied by Jesus' words. Why was this not explicitly stated by all the texts? Undoubtedly, the tradition first of all retained what pertained to Jesus and his Father so as to stress that Jesus had a unique role: his person was the very *raison d'être* of the community. Perhaps as well the tradition wanted to recall the problem raised by the cessation of Jesus' earthly existence and the void it left behind. How could the community subsist, then, beyond his death?

The answer is given at length in the "discourse after the Last Supper" in John;[32] but there Jesus expresses himself in so Johannine a manner that the historian has great difficulty in focusing his attention on the sayings taken as they are. This is not the case in the little discourse[33] into which Luke grouped logia that can certainly go back to Jesus of Nazareth. There Jesus asks the community of disciples to live as "servants" of one another, as we have already seen in Chapter 2. Then he gives assurances that the Twelve will sit on thrones in the Kingdom to which he is going, to judge the tribes of Israel with him. Furthermore, he announces that in the time that will come very soon, Peter, after a moment of abandonment and denial, will be strengthened by Jesus, who then personally will be present with him after his own death. At the same time, Jesus shows himself a realist, declaring that the community henceforth will enter the time of the sword. Without doubt, there are traces in this discourse of Lukan adaptations to the audience of the church of Luke's era, but they express clearly what Jesus might have said.

Jesus seems therefore to have said something about the future of the community he had banded about him. Certainly we have to guard against an anachronism and not speak of Jesus' thought concerning the "Church" in the modern sense of that word.[34] But it is a fact that Jesus addressed the reunited Twelve, the Twelve whom he considered not as a group apart but as the Remnant of Israel.[35] To his disciples, who would find themselves alone after his departure, Jesus gave several counsels; through them, according to a constant presupposition of the gospel, he manifestly had in mind the multitude of believers to come.

The historian can thus affirm that Jesus conducted himself as if, during the time of his separation from them, the group of his disciples had to continue to exist through a tie that they would maintain with him. These, then, were the purposes and the outlook of the counsels that Jesus gave to his own before leaving them.

To this global answer of the testamentary tradition, the cultic tradition adds important nuances concerning the union Jesus would maintain with his disciples after his leavetaking.

It is this context that the word *covenant* enters in for the first and last times in the gospel on the very lips of Jesus. In a Jewish context, to say "covenant" was to speak of God's covenant with the whole people. The disciples present, and through them the "multitude," henceforth constitute the new People of the Covenant in Jesus' name. Even if the historian hesitates to attribute the expression to Jesus personally, we are right in seeing in it the best formulation of his thought on the future of the community he formed with his disciples. Did he not say the same thing in the testamentary tradition?

In conclusion, one can think that Jesus, facing an imminent death, did not only affirm that he would share in the eschatological banquet with his loved ones, but he bore himself in such a way as to have it understood that, during the period of separation, the group of disciples had to continue in existence by preserving the indissoluble tie with himself. Doubtless, as we have said, the influence of the cultic tradition of early Church was such that the historian does not dare to take a position on the tenor of Jesus' words; but, whatever they were, these sayings show that, while departing this world, Jesus intended to remain present to the community of disciples and, through them to the multitude of men and women. He goes away, truly, but he does not stop being present in a new way, until the full revelation of God's Kingdom.

DID JESUS ASCRIBE A SACRIFICIAL MEANING TO HIS DEATH?

The answer to this question depends on the meaning one gives to the word *sacrifice*. In truth, its meaning has been quite varied during its use in the history of religions and as it passed through Old and New Testaments. On the other hand, when it refers to Jesus' sacrifice, this action has to possess universal significance: one person obtained for all the reestablishment of the covenant with God. Now, a ritual action, always one that is animated by obedience to the law, can sometimes be a ritual one (the offering of a vegetable or animal victim), and at other times a real one (the offering of one's life of charity).[36]

As we have already said in the last chapter, Jesus located his life squarely in relation to the multitude of people by reason of the unique relationship he experienced with God and all men and women. He never gave forth a theory of his dealings, leaving to God the care of revealing in the Resurrection the value and the significance of his life and his death. The answer to the question raised would thus be affirmative only in the sense of a "real" sacrifice, his self-offering. Contrariwise, we do not find a text that would demand the notion of "ritual sacrifice" as a description of Jesus' death.

But the gospel tradition specified Jesus' existential attitude when, at the time of his death, he expressed his deepest conviction by his words in the eucharistic institution. They have been handed on to us under two types, which we will describe briefly.

The first tradition is preserved in Mark and Matthew:

> This is my blood,
> *the blood* of the covenant,
> which is poured out for the *multitude*.
>
> (Mk 14:24)

We summarize here the results of long study. The expression "the blood of the covenant" surely evokes the sacrifice by which Moses sealed God's covenant with the people;[37] the blood connotes not suffering, but life, and that with a twofold import: when shed unjustly, blood cries out to God to be restored; when shed in sacrifice, it fulfills its purpose, that of uniting the people with God. Hence the context is "sacrificial." At this moment, the blood is Jesus' blood, which is to be shed; that is to say, Jesus is going to die.[38] The reference to the "multitude" universalizes the import of this death. Probably, it depends on the prophecy of the Servant of YHWH.[39] Jesus' death, therefore, enjoys universal significance: this is the very meaning of sacrificial terminology here: one for all. Evidently, this was not understood except with Jesus' Resurrection, and the community very well expressed the basis of Jesus' thinking in this way.

The second tradition is presented by Luke and Paul:

> This cup which is poured out for you
> is the new covenant in my blood.
>
> (Lk 22:20 = 1 Cor 11:25)

This tradition quite properly belongs to that of the Servant of YHWH.[40] The gospel context is without doubt cultic, but the text in another way tells of Jesus' self-offering. His was not that of a "sacrificial victim," but that of a human person who "shed his blood," that is, gave his life for the community that had been entrusted to him, and by that very deed established God's new covenant with his people. Here again, it is one for all. It is another way, not a cultic one, to tell of the universal significance of Jesus' death.

In the preceding chapter we established that, by every likelihood, Jesus did not himself justify his death as a "ransom" for the multitude, but quite simply depicted himself as "one who serves." Precisely this expression is found in the testamentary tradition preserved by Luke.[41]

This means, in fact, that the formula "blood poured out for the multitude" does no more than transpose into sacrificial terminology the existential way in which Jesus considered his life of "service."

His last meal came as the culmination of a long series of meals that the tradition was happy to recount about Jesus in his earthly life, meals shared not only with his own companions but also with tax collectors. Jesus in this way symbolized his will of establishing a perfect union with God and full communion with the participants, with these being extended to all men and women, including sinners. Jesus maintained this symbolic approach to the end by proclaiming that he would be there up to and including the meal at the end of time, and present as one serving:

> Blessed are those servants whom the master finds awake when he comes; truly I say to you, he will gird himself and have them sit at table, and he will come and serve them.
>
> (Lk 12:37)

The community of men and women is established on the foundation of the service rendered by Jesus.

Such is the background on which Luke's testamentary tradition is inscribed. At the time of the Last Supper, Jesus' life was summed up and his death understood as service, and based on a meal. His attitude of service led Jesus to death, a death that took its meaning from all that had gone before. As we have already said, Jesus lived "for others"; he would die "for others," his enemies and sinners included. Jesus died because he lived for. This is the historic anchor point for the sacrificial phrase "blood poured out for the multitude."

The Fourth Gospel, instead of a theoretical transposition like that of Mark (whether it be "ransom for the multitude" or "blood poured out for the multitude") described Jesus' existential outlook through a symbolic action in the scene of the washing of feet. There is no point in looking there for the words "ransom" or "sacrifice" or "blood poured out," not even for the word "service." To "have some share with Jesus," one has to have one's feet washed by him; this is not a rite of purification. Rather, this gesture symbolizes the act through which Jesus establishes the community of his disciples.[42] So John has Jesus act out Jesus' word reported by Luke: "As for myself, I am among you as one who serves."

CONCLUSION

At his Last Supper, Jesus affirmed his complete trust in God and his intention to establish the community of his disciples by his abiding presence. To prove both he summed up his life as one of "service": thus his death, the fruit of his whole life, culminating in his "for you" and "for the multitude," characterized a life perfectly handed over to God and to human persons.

According to the historian's findings, Jesus did not lay hold of sacrificial terms to point this out. The only one who would be astonished by this or regret it would be some who would have wanted Jesus to have used the words that Paul or classical theologians used. In return for this "loss," how can one not see in this omission a sign of perfect harmony with what we know of Jesus of Nazareth? The prophet Jesus does not seem to have been preoccupied with ritual sacrifices except to castigate the abuse of them. Should we, then, have wanted him to have recourse to categories that had no place in his message to describe his life and death?

Jesus' reflected outlook on his life of service is sufficient to make clear to the theologian of the New Testament that the early Church's terminology originates in Jesus; the Church could find in Jesus of Nazareth's disposition the sacrifice with the agreeable aroma awaited from all time by humanity. Moreover, the Church was convinced that her cultic practice made present that past action in which Jesus brought his life of service to perfection.

To call into question in this way the explicit formula that the early Church placed on Jesus' lips in no way diminishes the reality or significance of the gospel tradition. Rather we are kept from indissolubly tying the reality lived by Jesus to one, singular cultic act. We run a great risk of detaching worship from the life that gave it birth and tells its meaning. It was to ward off this danger that the Fourth Gospel set itself the task of giving meaning to worship, not by highlighting it but by situating it in relationship to the life of Jesus of Nazareth: baptism and the Eucharist find their true meaning only in the relationship with the Jesus event that they make present.[43]

Faced with imminent death, Jesus in this way showed how the believer has to and can maintain his or her relationship with the one who went away yet remains alive. The terminology of service tells of the Christian's essential charity; the terminology of sacrifice acts out in time the action of Jesus that grounded and still grounds his life of charity.

IN THE GARDEN OF GETHSEMANE

The episode of Jesus' agony in the Garden of Gethsemane has always fascinated the Christian. For once, the narrator makes Jesus' feelings explicit and brings the listener into the presence of a conflict between his will and the Father's. In the course of this drama, Jesus appears deeply human and perfectly faithful. In a vigorous summation, the Passion is presented as a whole, gathered together in Jesus' interior without our attention being really turned aside to the other actors in the drama. Unfortunately, the "lives of Jesus" were for the most part satisfied to summarily describe this episode or else they dallied over points that were eloquent, certainly, but went beyond the textual details.

The three synoptic gospels locate the episode in the Garden of Olives;[44] this account can be compared with the Johannine account of the Greeks who desired to see Jesus[45] or with the passage in the Epistle to the Hebrews that quickly recalls the Passion.[46] We add several scattered texts, such as Jesus' saying to the sons of Zebedee: "Are you able to drink the cup that I am to drink?"[47] the allusion made at the time of his arrest, "Shall I not drink the

Mt 26 = *Mk 14*	Lk 23
³⁶Then Jesus went with them	⁴⁰And when they came to the place
³⁶*And they went*	
to a place called Gethsemane	
to a place which was called	
Gethsemane	
and he said to the disciples,	he said to them,
and he said to his disciples,	
stay here while	
stay here while	
I go yonder and pray.	Pray that you may not enter
while I pray.	into temptation.

³⁷And taking with him Peter
³³*And he took with him Peter*
and the two sons of Zebedee,
and James and John
he began to be/(to feel)
and began to be/(to feel)
sorrowful and troubled.
greatly distressed and troubled.

³⁸Then he said to them,
³⁴*And he said to them,*
My soul is very sorrowful, even to
death;
My soul is very sorrowful, even to
death;
remain here, and watch with me.
remain here, and watch.

⁴³And there appeared to him an angel from heaven strengthening him. ⁴⁴And being in an agony he prayed more earnestly: and his sweat became like great drops of blood falling down upon the ground.

³⁹And going a little farther
³⁵*And going a little farther*
he fell on his face and prayed
he fell on the ground and prayed

⁴¹And he withdrew from them
about a stone's throw,
and knelt down and prayed,

that, if it were possible,

the hour might pass from him.
and saying "My Father,
And he said, "Abba, Father,
if it be possible, let
all things are possible to you;
this cup pass from me;
remove this cup from me;
nevertheless, not as I will,
Yet not what I will,
but as you (will)."
but what you (will)."

⁴²saying "Father,

if you are willing,

remove this cup from me;
nevertheless, not my will,

but yours, be done." | 43-44 |

⁴⁰And he came to his disciples
³⁶*And he came*
and found them sleeping;
and found them sleeping,

⁴⁵And when he rose from prayer,
he came to the disciples
and found them sleeping
for sorrow,

and he said to Peter,
and he said to Peter,
"Simon, are you asleep?
"So, could you not watch
Could you not watch
one hour with me?
one hour?
⁴¹Watch and pray that you may not
³⁸*Watch and pray that you may not*
enter into temptation;
enter into temptation;
the spirit indeed is willing, but the flesh is weak."
the spirit indeed is willing, but the flesh is weak."

and he said to them,

"Why do you sleep?

Rise and pray that you may not

enter into temptation."

⁴²Again, for the second time, he went away and prayed,
³⁹*And again   he went away and prayed,*
"My Father, if this cannot pass unless I drink it
saying the same words.
your will be done."

⁴³And he came again and found them sleeping,
⁴⁰*And again he came and found them sleeping,*
for their eyes were heavy.
for their eyes were very heavy; and they did not know what to answer him.
⁴⁴So, leaving them again, he went away and prayed for the third time,
saying the same words again.

⁴⁵Then he came to his disciples and said to them,
⁴¹*And he came the third time and said to them,*
Sleep on and take your rest!
Sleep on and take your rest? It is enough;
Behold, the hour is at hand, and the Son of man is betrayed
the hour has come; the Son of man is betrayed
into the hands of sinners.
into the hands of sinners.
⁴⁶Rise! Let us be going! See, at hand is my betrayer.
⁴²*Rise! Let us be going! See, my betrayer is at hand.*

---

²³Jesus answered them, "The hour has come for the Son of man to be glorified. ²⁴Truly, truly, I say to you, unless a grain of wheat falls into the earth and dies, it remains alone; but if it dies, it bears much fruit. Whoever loves his life loses it, and whoever hates his life in this world will keep it for eternal life. ²⁶If anyone serves me, he must follow me; and where I am, there shall my servant be also; if any one serves me, my Father will honor him. ²⁷Now is my soul troubled. And what shall I say? Father, save me from this hour? No, for this purpose I have come to this hour! ²⁸Father, glorify your Name!" Then a voice came from heaven, "I (have) already glorified it, and I will glorify (it) again." ²⁹The crowd standing by heard it and said that it had thundered. Others said, "An angel has spoken to him." ³⁰Jesus answered, "This voice has come for your sake, not for mine. ³¹Now is the judgment of this world, now shall the ruler of this world be cast out; ³² and I, when I am lifted up from the earth, will draw all men to myself."

Jn 12:23–32

cup which the Father has given me?"[48] and the concluding phrase in the first tradition of the Last Supper Discourse: "Rise! Let us go *to the encounter!*"[49]

Drawing on literary critical essays that have been published in the last fifteen years,[50] I would like to offer here a spiritual understanding of this episode, beginning with an authentic exegesis. After this, I will proceed to detail three kinds of approaches to the text: the historic, then the synchronic and, finally, the diachronic.

THE HISTORIC APPROACH: NARRATIVE AND EVENT

Before getting involved in an analysis of the text, it is appropriate to have one's mind set free of preoccupations with the episode's historicity.

For a long time, among Catholics and Protestants alike, people reckoned this episode as one enjoying the historical value of a narrative based on trustworthy eyewitnesses.[51] So, Lietzmann confidently situated this narrative among the four that had been handed on by the apostle Peter (the prediction of the Passion, the betrayal, the arrest, and the denial). On the opposite side, Dibelius rejected every kind of eyewitness value to this and saw in it only a literary construction filled out on an Old Testament base. However, to come down somewhere between these two views, is it enough for us to discuss the quality of the disciples' sleep, whether we reckon it too heavy for them to have followed the event or light enough so that Jesus' words could have been heard? How can we answer this question, since the text tells us nothing about this? Although it is not appropriate, therefore, to appeal to a witness as if to a *deus ex machina*, still one has to guard against summary statements such as R. Bultmann's that it is a "completely legendary narrative" or that of M. Goguel's that it is an "allegorical narrative."

But, as R. Schnackenburg has put it so well, we can find in this text an important piece of work by the early Church:

There can be no question of an eye-witness narrative. It is useless to repeat the attempts made earlier to resolve the question of knowing in what way these sayings of Jesus could have been handed on since, logically, posterity, the Christian community, could not have known them. Could the sleeping disciples even so have been able to hear something of what Jesus said in his prayer? The earliest narrators did not ask this question. They knew that Jesus had undergone the agony, but they also knew Jesus' intimate relationship with his Father; they simply tried to formulate these elements. It is probable that this is a sufficiently late elaboration that they inserted ahead of the arrest scene.[52]

This narrative is not a pure invention. The first Christians knew that Jesus had really undergone the agony on the eve of his Passion without at the same time breaking the bond that united him to the Father. Otherwise, why would they have painted Jesus so differently from the fearless martyrs such as Stephen or Polycarp, for example? Already in the second century, Celsus denied that a God made man could have suffered in this way. How could Jesus have taken his disciples with him to display his sadness to them? On the other hand, the primitive tradition tended manifestly to spare Jesus everything that could have violated his dignity and, what is more, tended to exalt his dignity as Lord. Similarly, it did not try to debase the disciples' role. The account, then, can be said to be "substantially historical" in the sense that people tried to recount Jesus' final confrontation with his destiny before the unrelenting series of events began. Jesus did not flee; he remained strictly faithful to his Father.

As to the essential aspect of the history, the event must have taken place on the night of the eve of the Passion, immediately after the last meal, in the Garden of Gethsemane, on the Mount of Olives. Moreover, numerous details in the narrative agree with what we know of Jesus. Following his custom, Jesus goes apart from his disciples to pray to the Father; he did so at daybreak during his public ministry when he withdrew to the desert: this was at dawn, at the start of the proclamation of God's Kingdom.[53] Now his prayer takes place with night falling, before he enters the darkness of his seemingly total failure. The Passion is Jesus' ultimate test.

Now, though their foundations are substantially identical, the synoptic narratives are quite different. While Matthew and Mark follow a similar outline (division of the disciples into two groups), a threefold prayer, a triple return to the disciples), Luke presents a simpler account and ignores even Jesus' admission of his fear and sadness. If one wanted to be precise about a film on these happenings, one would have to choose between the two depictions, but this would be without a valid reason. In fact, the commentators, with reason, fasten on one or the other version. In opposition, the lives of Jesus often combine the various presentations in the hope of deriving a complete narrative; this mixing is a mistake because each version is the outcome of a particular organizational pattern. Luke frames Jesus' prayer with a twofold invitation to pray that one not fall into temptation's power, thereby indicating the proper object of his narrative. For their part, Matthew and Mark seem to have wanted, by the triple prayer and triple return to the disciples, to systematically convey another message: while Mark seems to find meaning in the disciples' sleep, which Jesus verifies three times, Matthew gives a deliberate meaning to the prayer as it progresses. In any case, one cannot be satisfied with saying—in order to explain the coming and going—that "persons crushed by sadness cannot stay in one place."[54]

John also refers to Jesus' trouble when his hour comes. The four evangelists, then, felt they had to report Jesus' attitude when faced with imminent death. So important are the differences in the accounts that to give an account of these we cannot stay only on the narrative level; also, for the sake of a global overview of the four versions, which aim at giving the episode's meaning, we need to locate the present state of the texts in relation to what is found at their source. Two methods are available to us to clarify this genesis of the texts. Either to search out the sources by beginning with the inconsistencies of the text judged to be the oldest, or else, beginning with the relationships internal to the texts, to uncover a common structure and, from that, to the production of the texts we have. We will carry out these two methods in succession.

THE HISTORY OF THE TRADITION

It is appropriate to begin our study with a reading that has become a classic today.

As the basis to this reading there is a presupposition: Mark's gospel represents the most ancient state of the text. It will be adequate, then, to analyze this text closely to get back to the sources of the Gethsemane tradition. Now, Mark's text seems to be a composite one: there are repetitions, "contrasting pairs," which are striking to a careful reader, both as to their background (v. 32 and vv. 33–34) or their form (vv. 33,35 and 34,36). A chart clearly indicates this.

Source A is characterized by the theme of the hour; Source B by the theme of prayer during temptation. These two themes indicate the orientations of the tradition, one being more "Christological," the other more "parenetic." They would have been rooted in two quite different "life settings."

According to the Christological tendency (A), Jesus withdrew from the disciples who accompanied him to Gethsemane. This is the beginning of the Passion. Jesus fell to the ground and, first of all, prayed a prayer presented by Mark in enigmatic fashion "that the hour might pass him by." The answer was given in the sleep of the disciples who will abandon Jesus. It is finished. But Jesus did not abandon them: "Get up!" he says to symbolize the salvation that is to come. Out of this reading comes awareness of Jesus' admirable attitude as he remains faithful to prayer, that is, to sustaining his relationship with the Father, and this in the face of an imminent and wicked death. It is God's hour. There is a sorrowful acceptance of it in truth.

Source A was rooted in a broad tradition, that of the Just One who must pass through suffering,[55] with trouble and amid loud cries:

	A	B
Two-fold setting	{ [32]the disciples in general [32]stay here!	[33a]the three privileged ones [34b]remain here!
Jesus' trouble is mentioned	[33b]indirectly	[34ac]directly
Jesus' prayer is mentioned	[35]indirectly	[36]directly
Coming to the disciples	[40]to all	[37]to the three (+ Peter)
The arrest	[50]all the disciples	?

[32]And they came to a place which was called Gethsemane; and he said to his disciples, "Stay here, while I pray."
[33b]And he began to be/(to feel) greatly distressed and troubled.

[35]And going a little farther, he fell on the ground and prayed that, if it were possible, the hour might pass from him.

[40]And (*again*) he came and found them sleeping, for their eyes were very heavy; and they did not know what to answer him.
[41]And (*he came for the third time*), and said to them, "Sleep on now and take your rest! It is enough; the hour has come; the Son of man is betrayed into the hands of sinners. Rise! Let us be going! See, my betrayer is at hand."

[33]And he took with him Peter and James and John.

[34]And he said to them, "My soul is very sorrowful, even to death; remain here and watch." *(and he went away and prayed: cf. v. 39)*
[36]And he said, "Abba, Father, all things are possible to you; remove this cup from me; yet not what I will, but what you (will)."
[37]And he came and found them sleeping, and he said to Peter, "Simon, are you sleeping? Could you not watch one hour?
[38]Watch and pray that you may not enter into temptation; the spirit indeed is willing, but the flesh is weak."
([39]And again he went away and prayed, saying the same words.)

Mk 14: 32-42

I had said in my *trouble* [*ekstasis*]: "I am driven far from thy sight."
But thou didst hear my supplications, when I cried to thee for help.

(Ps 31:23)

. . . Give ear to my *cries*,
hold not thy peace at my tears!

(Ps 39:13)

As God's Son, Jesus brings to its fulfillment the lengthy experience of the Just One.

The Epistle to the Hebrews offers an echo of this tradition when it applies the tradition to the High Priest:

7 In the days of his flesh, he offers up prayers and supplications, with loud cries and tears, to the one who was able to save him from death, and he was heard for his godly fear. **8** Although he was a Son, he learned obedience through what he suffered.

(Heb 5:7–8)

The Fourth Gospel also associates itself within this same traditional stream. Behind a typically Johannine portrayal (especially the Son's dignity at the time of the hour, which has come), one easily recognizes the following themes: the hour of the Passion-glorification, Jesus' trouble, the prayer "Father, glorify your Name," the crowd's misunderstanding, Jesus' relationship with his disciples.

According to the parenetic tradition (B), the focus lay on the three privileged disciples who were invited to watch and pray because temptation was about to engulf them. The tradition sought to indicate the conduct that the disciple ought to have, one conformed to Jesus. Also, Jesus' prayer becomes explicit; it is clear that God's will is not that which we would spontaneously wish to fulfill. The true disciple's prayer thus must be joined to Jesus', because what concerns the Master will touch the disciple in the coming Passion.

The Lukan account is exclusively guided by the tendency of the B Source, while the Johannine account takes into consideration only the tendency of Source A. In the case of Matthew and Mark, they have joined the two sources into a single narrative, which they composed with the help of the triple prayer pattern.[56] This is not the place to show how these present texts were produced with the help of the two "sources." The basis for this reconstruction is quite fragile, given the number of hypotheses underlying the excision of a text thought to be "primitive." For example, how justify the threefold coming and going of Jesus in Mark–Matthew? Above all, how explain John's radical transformation? Doubtless, one can consider that there were probably reasons why tradition was interested now in the Christological perspective, at another time in the parenetic approach; but will this really help in a reading of the given text, which is indeed the goal of exegesis? Also, it is a preferable approach to consider the different versions in themselves to try to discover the structure that gave them both.

AN ATTEMPT AT A SYNCHRONIC READING

The reading that we will attempt here can be characterized in the first place over against the preceding reading, which made an effort to reconstruct the text source's origin, a reading that we can label "diachronic" because it follows the evolution of the literary features in the course of time. A synchronic reading, on the contrary, considers the texts in their actual condition as it is delimited by what is before and what comes after. Moreover, it is distinguished from a reading that is tied to the unfolding of the narrative actions in that it examines the elements not in their succession to one another, but in their mutual relationships, striving to uncover those which "structure" the account (for example, the correlative behavior patterns of the diverse personalities, their conjunctive and disjunctive relationship). These correlations can be explicit or implicit; sometimes such an element appears to be "singular," although it finds its proper meaning from the secret relationship it enjoys with another).

The narratives of Jesus' "agony" being four in number (the three Synoptics and the Fourth Gospel), a first reading will determine the structure common to the four texts. It ought, in addition, to show that there is a structure common to the three

Synoptics, for the powerful Johannine resumption must not conceal the outlook of the Gethsemane narrative. It is only afterward, following a diachronic reading, that we will try to show how the structure discovered here gave rise to the texts that we have before our eyes.

THE FIRST RELATIONSHIP: JESUS AND THE DISCIPLES

The central personality is clearly Jesus, but he is always in the company of his disciples. It is as a formed group that "they come," Mark says; the focus is already concentrated on Christ by Matthew and Luke, who say: "Jesus came with them" or "He came . . . and the disciples followed him". In John's case, it is the disciples Andrew and Philip who communicate to the Master the Greeks' desire, and it is the coming fate of the disciples in general that Jesus describes just before dialoguing with the Father. Thus, our episode cannot be read without taking the disciples into account. However, we also note that in this group it is only Jesus who takes the initiative and speaks.

The Jesus-disciples pair is qualified by a relationship of opposition: *together-apart*. This is explicit in the Synoptics. Jesus arrives with his disciples, then he leaves them; then, he returns to them anew and withdraws from them, only to come back to them again. This movement of rejoining and withdrawing is broken by announcements and prayers, by exhortations and reproaches. In John, the disciples, after having fulfilled their deputation to Jesus, are not mentioned again; still less do they speak, so that we can consider them morally separate from Jesus. Jesus, however, does not leave them since he describes the disciples' condition, but he does so as the Master who is alone in facing up to the hour.

A third pair makes the preceding opposing relationship explicit: *going to-remaining there*. In the Synoptics Jesus moves constantly, while the disciples stay without moving. This takes place right up to the time when, after the traitor and the soldiers arrive, Jesus faces the enemy while the disciples, released by Jesus' command, either go away or are about to flee. In John, this opposition is transformed into the teaching given on this occasion: Jesus asks his disciples to follow where he is, something that signifies that they are, in principle, not moving and must begin to follow the Master.

A fourth pair, noted only by the Synoptics, more nearly describes the relationship of Jesus to his disciples: *watching-sleeping.* This fills in the time suspended between the movement from together to apart. Jesus asks his disciples "to watch and pray." The spatial movement is thereby ordered to an attitude of communion in vigilance. Then Jesus establishes that, instead of keeping watch, the disciples sleep. The separation in space corresponds to the disciples' spiritual nonpresence, the solitude in which Jesus finds himself: "What! You're sleeping!" The sleep of the disciples symbolize the disunion Jesus-disciples. Finally, the opposition between watching–praying characterizes not only the attitude of the disciples, it also qualifies Jesus' relationship with them: Jesus watches and prays, while the disciples sleep.

A fifth pair may also be specified, this one likewise found only in the Synoptics: *praying-entering into temptation.* While at first glance "temptation" can seem to be an isolated element in the narrative, it is in reality a correlative to "prayer." In fact, it is mentioned at the moment where Jesus, having prayed himself, asks his disciples to do so (and not merely to keep watch), by enunciating the theme: "lest you enter into temptation." This contrast properly concerns only the disciples, for Jesus is in a state of prayer. Placed in a relationship to prayer, temptation takes on a specific shape.

When Jesus speaks, it is because he has just come into contact with the "cup"; stating that the disciples are not praying since they are not keeping vigil, Jesus warns them that, if they do not pray, they will "fall into temptation's power." This version differs from the official ecumenical translation of the Our Father that has the petition: "Do not put us to the test," a translation rightfully sharply criticized by Carmignac[57] and avoided by the *Traduction oecuménique de la Bible.*[58] Temptation is a power at work, a force that can seize on someone; unlike "scandal" (in the usual, colorless sense), it is not a simple solicitation to evil, but is a power ready to devour. To read the triple temptation Jesus underwent at the beginning of his ministry, is to see that, under a threefold modality—economic, political, messianic—one single goal was aimed at: separating Jesus from God. The tempter is the one who makes efforts to break the bond that joins Jesus to God. Similarly, Christian life appears as a struggle between two powers, between two spirits: the spirit of truth, which is in the believer, and the spirit of evil.[59]

In Gethsemane, Jesus does not enter into temptation because he prays; the disciples, however, will fall into temptation's power because they do not pray. One can visualize this by adverting to the "space" that exists between God the Father and Jesus (or the disciples). Between the Father's will, suggested by the term "cup," and Jesus, there is an interval that distances him from God. This space has no consistency for the one who, at prayer, remains in a relationship with God himself: in order to cross it, to hurdle it, it suffices to ignore it somehow, to wipe it away ahead of time by one's conduct. On the contrary, by not praying the disciple breaks off the relationship with God, creates a distance between himself or herself and God, so that the distance becomes a separation. The realm of temptation is the space stretching between God and the human person made into a solid object, rising up like a wall between the two parties. Once the bond is broken, the disciple finds him- or herself separated from God and thus alone in facing the dangerous condition in which he or she is found. To enter into temptation is to find oneself bound to damnation because communication with the living God has been broken off: this is the deadly result awaiting the one who does not pray.

John leaves aside the invitation to pray lest one enter into temptation's realm, a fact that is not surprising, since the term is not found in his gospel.[60] As a hypothesis, could we not inquire whether in his work there is some equivalent term? In his gospel, Jesus' teaching is infinitely more radical; in it we hear, not an invitation to pray not to enter into temptation, but an ultimate condition: *if you do not accept death, you will not bear fruit; if you remain attached to your own life, you will lose it. And, con-*

versely, if you follow after me, you will be honored by my Father.
There is no command to pray, but to "follow Jesus." The listener
no longer hears talk of temptation, but he or she is confronted
with a radical, definitive choice. In this sense, one can say that
John has transformed the motif of temptation in such a way that
it could be part of the fundamental structure of the Gethsemane
narrative.

Whatever way we turn, the five literary paired opposites converge with the same result: the disciples are apart from their Master; Jesus is alone.

THE SECOND RELATIONSHIP: JESUS AND THE FATHER

Or rather, Jesus is not alone, for another person appears behind
the invocation "Father," according to which Jesus prays in the four
accounts. Jesus is thus separated from the disciples both spiritually
(all the gospels) and even locally (the Synoptics): the relationship
he sustains with his Father stands in contrast with the preceding.
This relationship may be described as "vertical," while the other
is a "horizontal" relationship.

1. The Jesus–Father relationship is clearly expressed in the prayer
that the cup pass by, a prayer that reveals the contrast of two
wills. There we have the cup-prayer pair, which describes the Jesus-Father relationship. Clearly in John this opposition seems to
be resolved from the outset by the welcome accorded the hour,
but the prayer itself presupposes a divergence in perspective. In
the Synoptics, the Father's will manifests itself under the expression "the cup."[61] Jesus encounters the Father through the cup that
is offered him and that he wished to see pass far from him: the
cup is the visage of the invisible Father. The opposition is resolved
by Jesus' submission, a resolution that Matthew artfully describes:
he shades the contents of the two successive prayers he reports,
the second articulating his acceptance in fidelity: "Your will be
done!"

The word *cup* had been translated in some sense by the word
hour in both Mark and John. When this was done, the objectiv-
ization process took a further step: the hour is God's plan for

humanity; this is what the Lord has irrevocably determined and what is about to happen. In the Synoptics, the hour has not yet come;[62] in John it has already arrived; this is why the relationship with the Father appears different. In the Synoptics, Jesus can ask that the inescapable hour pass him by since it has not yet come; in John, the hour cannot be bypassed, not even in a request, not even hypothetically: it must be accepted, and this is why Jesus asks "to pass safely through this hour."[63] The opposition in the two wills is resolved in a positive petition for help and presence in the heart of that very solitude where the awful hour comes upon him.

2. Jesus' relationship to his Father is then expressed through the *cup-trouble* pair: this is the hour of terror. In fact, the cup to be drunk and the hour to be gone through stirs up in Jesus a reaction of dejection, variously translated by the evangelists. If this reaction is mentioned by the Synoptics before the prayer concerning the cup, nevertheless it was the presence of this cup that provoked Jesus' trust and his need to pray.

With the foretaste of the cup, a deep sadness came over Jesus, according to the summary given by Matthew (Gk. *lypeisthai*). What does this mean? This sadness is the opposite not of pleasure but of joy; it stresses the fact that he finds himself without the one good that can fulfill him, that is, God.[64] This biblical term expresses abandonment in this world, the kind experienced by Adam (and Eve) after his sin, the kind whose opposite Noah (= "rest" or "consolation") represented and which is to last until the end of time.[65] This sadness is also that same one which would overcome the disciples through their separation from their Master,[66] until God wipes away "every tear from their eyes."[67] This was Jesus' condition and this, Matthew and Mark make clear, was "even unto death": his sadness leads him to death. Jesus is surrounded with sadness, deeply saddened (Gk. *perilypos*) according to the psalm of the suffering Just One, which Matthew and Mark quote, thereby placing Jesus in the long biblical tradition of the persecuted Just One.

Two other verbs describe this state of abandonment and sad-

ness. *Adēmonein* (Mk-Mt) tells of the effect produced in a soul
that becomes disquieted and tormented: this is the "distress following shock, despondency, loathing."[68] *Ekthambeisthai* was
added by Mark, a term that in his work goes with astonishment
and amazement and leading to disbelief and being beside oneself.[69]
This is the surprise of someone roughly overcome by an emotion
and who remains terrified of it. It is the opposite of self-posses-
sion, signifying a certain interval of disarray, a being crippled,
almost an "ec-stasy."[70] To translate this term, it is preferable not
to talk of "fright" (which connotes fear, a tendency to flee), nor
"dread" nor "shudders" nor "a dazed state." The most apt phrase
would be "to become dismayed" before something that freezes
and immobilizes. The dismay that overcame the disciples when
Jesus predicted to them that he had to suffer[71] now passes to the
Master; Jesus sees opening before him the road that he now no
longer must proclaim but journey on.

Agōnia was chosen by Luke to stress at once a feeling of anguish
and the disposition of a fighter.[72] This is not simply a disquiet,[73]
an entering into combat with an enemy, it is the dynamic anxiety
that enters into a fighter at the moment the fight begins because
the victory has not yet been given. In fact, in Luke, the battle is
won through strength given by an angel.

Finally, John preferred the term "to trouble" (*taraxomai*) to
describe Jesus' reaction. As John had noted earlier, Jesus had been
troubled by Lazarus's death; so the disciples, in their turn, faced
with the coming separation from their Master, were plunged into
a troubled state.[74]

The reader must not be distracted by the multiplicity of terms
used to describe Jesus' abandonment; rather, the reader should
marvel at the groping efforts taken to describe the polarity cor-
responding to the cup offered by the Father: it is the hour of
Christ's dismay.

3. A third contrast in some way incarnates the preceding opposition: *standing-on the ground*. The bodily posture of Jesus expressed the ambiguity of his relationship to the Father. Here he
"falls to the ground," "prostrate with his face to the earth," "on

his knees," in an attitude that contrasts violently with the manner in which he moves about, remains standing, and the way in which, finally, he "rises."

This opposition is highlighted by the Jesus-disciples contrast: while the disciples sleep (stretched out on the ground), Jesus finds himself sometimes prostrate with his face to the earth (in a totally different sense), at other times standing up to reproach the disciples or to tell them to get up.

In the literary arrangement of his text John has transformed this contrasting pair.[75] For the moment, let us merely remark that Jesus' being troubled is mentioned at the lowest point of the grain of wheat's falling into the ground, or, more precisely, between the announcement of the necessity of the fall of the wheat grain and the promise of its final exaltation.[76] To the degree that Verses 24–26 pertain also to Jesus, the contrast between standing and being on the ground is valid to symbolize the relationship of Jesus to his Father, with this difference: that there are two uses of "standing," one before the fall, the other after, in the glory of exaltation.

4. A fourth contrast is found also in the Synoptics: *speaking-silent.* Jesus tells of his dismay; the Father is silent. No more than he does from the disciples, Jesus does not hear the Father answer his prayer, and the cup remains proferred to him. But he remains faithfully turned toward the Father, while the disciples, by their nonprayer and then sleep, signify their separation from God.

A relationship can be established between two silent partners: the noncommunion of the disciples, however, symbolizes and confirms the silence of God, who does not accept Jesus' prayer.

The Fourth Gospel transforms the condition: the hour has already come, and Jesus does not ask that it be kept away from him. He asks only that the Father let him pass safely through this hour. This is why the Father answers this request, for he has never failed to help his Son: "I have glorified [it] and I will glorify [it] again." In a certain sense, one can say that John does not contradict the Synoptics, for the Father's response does not come in regard to the same prayer. The silent-speaking opposition certainly existed in the structure of the narrative; John in his own way transformed it.

THE STRUCTURE OF THE NARRATIVE

Beginning with the two foundational relationships that we have just come to see, it is possible to elaborate the structure that generated the actual narratives. The elements of them have been located within their mutual relationships.

At the starting point, we find the cup presented as the Father's visage that effects Jesus' troubling. This trouble prods Jesus to withdraw from his disciples without thereby losing contact with them. The nonacceptance by the Father of the request Jesus makes becomes enfleshed in the silence and the nonpresence of the disciples, who allow themselves to be overwhelmed by sleep.

The narrative is ordered by a criss-crossing structure incorporating the horizontal Jesus–disciples relationship and the vertical Jesus–Father relationship. The ultimate point of intersection is the ground on which Jesus falls or where he allows himself to fall on his face; this is the midpoint of the grain of wheat's falling into the ground, preceding its rising up again to glory, in John's account. For the Synoptics, the fall to the ground opposes the final "Get up!" symbolizing at once the coming death and Resurrection.

The two relationships interconnect, they even are superimposed on one another, or rather, as we have said, the first reflects and symbolizes the second. So the death that is in view takes on a double aspect.

According to the first dimension, death is the welcoming of the Father's will in naked faith, in God's silence, without an answer except the cup, a cup always proffered by the Father. Also the ultimate test is crossed by the "heroic" affirmation that God is present at the very moment when the Father seems to have abandoned his Son to those who will "hand him over," will betray him. Even if a faithful person declares to the end that God is alive, death remains separation from God, no less so in its appearance.

This appearance figures in the real separation from the disciples and, through them, from the human community: this is death's second dimension. Sleep, the not fighting, the nonvigilance of the disciples symbolizes the refusal by the Father to put away the cup, which henceforth signifies the apparent failure of Jesus' project. Jesus had wanted to constitute a community of disciples; he had reassembled them immediately before, at the last meal, and now it is breaking up at the moment death comes with the one who hands over, the traitor. Jesus has to accept that his own disappearance brings in its wake the dispersal of the community, that he is not the definitive gatherer, that God alone can ensure communion among men and women; in a word, that he did not succeed in inaugurating the Kingdom of God on earth.

Bringing this structure to light shows that, literarily speaking, the relationships among the elements reflect and underscore spiritual tensions, namely the twofold conflict between Jesus and his Father and between Jesus and his disciples.

A paradox ties together these oppositions and the conclusion of the narrative, for Jesus, who began by demanding that his disciples keep watch, closes by saying, "Keep on sleeping and take your rest!" as if in this way they would die until they get up again: "Rise!" But what ought to have announced a glorious "Resurrection" ends up in a shameful flight. This is the symbolism that governs the narrative and that introduces an understanding of the mystery of imminent death.

FROM THE STRUCTURE TO THE TEXTS

The different versions of the narrative of the agony of Jesus interact differently with the fundamental structure that we have just established: the interconnectedness of the two relationships, the one uniting Jesus and the Father, the other uniting Jesus and the disciples. Mark and Matthew transform this very interconnection into a narrative; Luke focuses his account on the Jesus-disciples relationship, John in the Jesus-Father relationship.

THE NARRATIVES OF MARK AND MATTHEW

With the exception of a few minor details, both these accounts represent a narrative integrating into a descriptive sequence a very great number of the structural elements we discovered earlier. At the core of the narrative, despite our propensity for concentrating on the sorrowful aspect of Jesus' prayer, the Jesus-disciples relationship is the most evident.

The first characteristic is the doubling of the group of the disciples, on one side those who must stay behind and on the other, the three privileged ones who, properly speaking, are put to the test of keeping watch. A first explanation of the separation may be found in the fact that these same privileged ones had been the ones invited to go up the Mount of Transfiguration;[77] thus, their cowardice was underlined, so that Jesus' sorrow becomes reinforced. In place of watching they, especially Peter, sleep. What loneliness!

The second characteristic is the threefold movement of Jesus' coming and going. This artifice shows Jesus' desire for communion with his disciples, the frustration of his wish and so his effective separation. D. Daube[78] has related the sleep that fell over the disciples to the sleep that threatens those who observe the Jewish Passover vigil; although dozing is permitted, entering into a deep sleep is not. Deep sleep is apparent when people do not know what to say on being awakened; then, everything has to begin again because there has taken place a separation, a breaking with communion between the participants in the paschal meal. From this issues Daube's hypothesis: Mark saw in the Last Supper the beginning of a *habura*, a "brotherhood" that should have been prolonged into the Passover vigil, and this by means of the Hallel (Psalms 115–118) that had been sung as they left the Upper Room. Sleep thereby signifies the community's division. Put in other words, Jesus perceives that he is alone: the reactions of humans symbolize the Father's refusal of his prayer.

Lastly, the formulation of Jesus' prayer could be better understood if we related it to the Jewish custom[79] that counseled the dying to first declare: (1) "God can do all"; then to add (2) "I would rather not die, Lord"; and finally (3) "but I am ready." Such is in fact the structure within the three periods that breaks up Jesus' prayer. First of all, he declares God's omnipotence: (1) "Everything is possible for you";[80] then he expresses his own specific desire: (2) "Take this cup away from me!" As he faces the setback of imminent death, which appears to him as the fate destined for him by the Father and which derives meaning as a trial to pass through,[81] Jesus expresses his deepest desire that he not die. Finally, he submits his will to the Father's: (3) "Yet, not what I want, but what you [want]."

Beyond these general characteristics, *Mark* has his own distinctiveness. Following his pattern, he duplicates the scene.[82] The avowal of his sadness is preceded in direct speech by a similar indirect statement;[84] Jesus' prayer itself is preceded by a summary in indirect speech, in which the hour is equivalent to the cup.[85] Lastly, Mark stresses the relationship between this scene and the Transfiguration when he notes, "they did not know what to reply to him."[86] The theological tendency is shown by the framing of the narrative by the word *hour*.

Matthew focuses his narrative on the Jesus-Father relationship. The person of Jesus is to the fore, and the disciples tend to disappear.[87] The spatial distance between them and Jesus gets accentuated,[88] and the reproach addressed to them becomes quite general.[89] All is centered on Jesus' progressive prayer by which Jesus little by little enters into acceptance of the cup.[90] The disciples' sleep no longer serves as a point of contrast. The whole episode is properly Christological, revealing the Messiah's perfect obedience. Secondarily, this disposition serves as the model for the disciples' attitude in time of temptation.

LUKE'S NARRATIVE

According to Luke, the episode becomes an exhortation to pray like Jesus in the agony.

Luke seems to be unaware of certain important elements in the tradition concerning the hour: it is not mentioned until after the arrest.[91] The troubling is only alluded to: "And being in an agony, he prayed more earnestly." Although the sadness is mentioned, it is not reported of Jesus, but to indicate how the sleep of the disciples came about. Jesus' prayer, quoted in its entirety, is not mentioned three times but its intensity is indicated by a reference to the bloody sweat and to the intervention of the angel who strengthened the combatant.[92] Hence, the scene is unencumbered to focus all attention on the Master's prayer; Jesus' dismay becomes an anxiety that causes him to pray more earnestly, to such an extent that little drops of blood fall to the ground. Jesus becomes a model for the disciple who faces temptation.

The scene is framed by the double injunction: "Pray that you not fall into temptation's power."[93] In the center, Jesus prays in exemplary fashion. If the disciples have fallen asleep out of sadness, this is because they did not pray as Jesus did: their sleep is not strictly a sign of misunderstanding (Mt-Mk), but one of weakness before temptation. What Jesus advises his disciples is not to keep watch in view of the hour but to pray on account of temptation.

No doubt, Luke did not disregard Jesus' relationship to the Father, but this latter is brought to completion by the Jesus–disciples relationship. This is the type of relationship that the disciples as well ought to have with God. From the fact of this orientation, the same fundamental structure operates differently. According to Luke, there are no privileged disciples, nor any coming from and going to the group. Jesus and his disciples are apart during the prayer, something that clearly denotes their diversity of attitude during temptation. As we have said, the disciple finds in Jesus the kind of prayer that struggles on even to the point of pouring out blood.[94]

Jesus, however, does not enter into temptation, but firmly maintains his relationship to the Father. The intention of the narrative appears even in the formulation of the prayer. Unlike the case in Mark's text, Jesus does not state, "Everything is possible for you," but modestly says, "If you want."

The fundamental structure common to all the accounts is also recognizable in John. The dominant relationship is the Jesus-Father relationship: the cup is designated by the more "objective" one of the "hour." With the approach of the Greeks, which symbolizes the coming accession of the pagans to the Good News, Jesus proclaims, "The hour has come in which the Son of man must be glorified." Two observations on John's terminology follow. The cup is not mentioned here, but only at the time of the arrest, and there it is welcomed without difficulty: "What? Shall I not drink the cup the Father has given to me?."[95] It is replaced with the "hour"; that is, no longer the terrible destiny called to mind by the cross, but God's sovereign plan, which, according to John, allows glory to be transparent through the humiliation of the cross. This hour is the moment that God has determined for the glorification of his Son through his works and through death.[96]

On the other hand, the hour has already come. Unlike the Synoptics, who at most make us feel that the hour draws near but has not yet arrived, John unambiguously declares that "the hour has come." From this fact, in John's account Jesus cannot ask that the hour pass by;[97] he says, "Father, bring me safely through this hour!" In this say, John transforms the synoptic tradition and has Jesus say the opposite, "Yes, it was for this purpose that I have come to this hour," an assertion that precedes the very Johannine petition, "Father, glorify your Name!" in which the profound acceptance of the hour is made explicit.

The hour provoked Jesus' "trouble," similar to the distress about which the Synoptics spoke. But this trouble acknowledged by Jesus himself, is no longer a kind of anxiety before the cross, much less in the anticipation of victory; it is the repercussion of the accepted hour.

Moreover, Jesus hears the voice come from heaven: "I have glorified [it] and I will glorify [it] again." For, unlike in the Synoptics, the Father does not keep silent, but he proclaims the success of

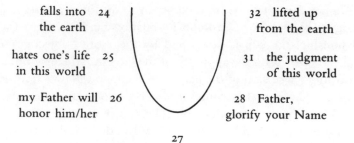

falls into 24
the earth

hates one's life 25
in this world

my Father will 26
honor him/her

32 lifted up
from the earth

31 the judgment
of this world

28 Father,
glorify your Name

27
now
the hour
trouble

Jesus' acceptance of the hour: the exaltation on the cross is the path to glory. The difference stems from the fact that the hour is already at hand. Jesus can now face death on the cross, something that the disciples illustrated when they showed Jesus getting up and going to his disciples.

By concentrating his narrative on Jesus' relationship to the Father, John did not, for all that, eliminate every trace of the disciples. The disciples who led the Greeks to Jesus were there; the crowd itself heard the Father's word, something they took to be a cosmic phenomenon or an angelic communication. However, the disciples were taught by Jesus. A chiastic[98] plotting of the passage illustrates beyond doubt that the disciple has to be identified with the Master.

In fact, prior to the reference to Jesus' trouble, there are in chapter 12 of John three sayings relevant to the disciple:

24 Unless a grain of wheat falls onto the earth and dies, it remains alone; but if it dies, it bears much fruit.

25 The One who loves his life loses it, and the one who hates his life in this world will keep it for eternal life.

26 If anyone serves me, he must follow me; and where I am, there shall my servant be also; if anyone serves me, the Father will honor him.

After Jesus had fallen into the depths of trouble, the general rule of discipleship becomes acceptable by the example Jesus gave. If the Son had to fall into the earth and die, this was so that all might be drawn to the Son: this is the fruitfulness proclaimed (vv. 24 and 32). Because the world is under subjection to its prince, one must not cling to one's life on earth, and this is possible because the judgment has resulted in the expulsion of the Prince of This World (vv. 25 and 31). Finally, since the Father has already glorified the Son, he will honor whoever follows the Son and will be his or her servant; he will bring him or her to the place where the Son already is (vv. 26 and 28). But before that, he or she must pass through the trouble of the hour, knowing the prayer that must be formulated and what the glorious outcome will be (v. 27).

No longer is it a question of being with–being apart nor of keeping watch–sleeping, but only of a general rule that governs the disciple, and this because of the communion uniting the disciple and his or her master.

The wonderful thing in this text is that even his movement reflects Jesus' and the disciple's journey. The proverb about the grain of wheat thrown into the earth, which has to die to bear fruit corresponds to the reference to the descent into trouble and the ascent to glory that completes the chiasm. John is not satisfied with showing Jesus falling to the ground then rising up; he contemplates him already exalted and drawing all men and women to himself.

CONCLUSION

The results of the preceding reading contribute to an interpretation of the totality of the Gethsemane scene. In fact, to conclude does not strictly mean to repeat what was uncovered in the course of the analysis. How did this man, in facing death, suddenly totter on the brink and just as quickly recover? How could this man, whom faith confesses to be God's Son, go so far as to contest the will of his Father? Quite often, people were concerned to fill in the gaps in a text thought to be too sober to be able to answer questions raised by it. Obviously, the answer to these questions must not come from psychology, nor from a specific theology, nor even from Pauline interpretations, but only from the gospel facts themselves.

However, there has been no lack of literary specialists to attribute Jesus' momentary disarray to his having caught cold in crossing the Kedron stream and his being in the grips of a high fever. Although not unlikely, such an explanation does not take into account an extremely complex text, still less Jesus' mysterious disposition.

For their part, certain minds filled with theology have let their dogmatic convictions intervene to account for the event. The God-man knew all in advance and so foresaw that his poured-out blood would not hinder numerous people from damnation and so was cast into a deep sorrow. This is a profound explanation, deriving from a theological method that can be worthwhile and produce interesting results; but it cannot satisfy anyone who strictly adheres to the text and notes that the latter depicts Jesus' total humanity and not the assured disposition of a being who would know ahead of time the history of all ages to come. It seems to me that Jesus would have felt the failure of his mission weighing on him in a totally other way.

In contrast to this, mystics see in Jesus agonizing in Gethsemane the perfect type of those who experience the terrible abandonment by God. We will speak of this explanation in the next chapter devoted to Jesus' words on the cross. Let us simply remark here that this brilliant insight derives not from the text but elsewhere from a specific religious experience.

Finally, there are many interpreters who attribute Jesus' sorrow to the mystery of the condemnation of sin. Sometimes they see the Lamb of God crushed by the "sin of the world," which he has to take away; at other times, the Christ who "was made sin for us." Jesus would have "expiated" for human sins, undergoing the punishment reserved by God for sinners. People invoke Paul's theology as the source for this interpretation, a fact that allows them to add the notion of sin to be printed (although it is missing from the text) and notions of God's wrath or punishment, to which not even an allusion was made. In effect, the "cup" that Jesus wanted to have pass by in no way symbolizes the divine wrath vented against the wicked;[99] properly speaking, it designates the sorrowful fate that Jesus knows to be imminent and which the Father does not turn aside from his Son through some miraculous intervention.

Also, to clarify the Gethsemane scene, one must take the gospel text in its entirety. The man who comes to pray here is the same one who himself proclaimed the advent of God's Kingdom and who revealed its presence through symbolic acts. This man is the same one who hinted at his intimate relationship with God the Father and his tenacious fidelity before his enemies. This man, lastly, dared to proclaim that one must not fear death but "the one who can destroy soul and body in Gehenna." It is the same one who, immediately before this, deliberately entrusted to his disciples the testament of his love and the certitude of seeing them again at the final banquet.

And now this man begins to tremble and to beg that he be spared his fate. Such a change can find an explanation at various levels and depths. Jesus first of all expresses the most profound wish of human nature: that of not dying and, moreover, that of not dying, before the hour, of a cruel death. In revealing a desire contrary to that of the Father who leaves him a victim of his enemies, Jesus allows to come to expression the harsh tearing apart that causes conflict in him between his instinct to live and his will to remain faithful to the end: "Son though he was, he learned obedience through his sufferings."[100] This sorrowful prayer was transformed by John into a positive request to pass safely through the hour, thereby showing another aspect of the prayer that confronts the death on the cross.

At a deeper level, Jesus' sadness is rooted in the mission he received from his Father. Wholeheartedly embracing this mission, Jesus identified himself with it; in curing the sick, in welcoming sinners, Jesus in some way "incarnated" God's Kingdom on earth. He symbolized it in an incomparable way. Clearly, Jesus' agony in a way possesses several similarities with that of the prophet Elijah, who despaired of his own life because he remained the only one who had not bent the knee to Baal;[101] but in this Elijah was mistaken—had not seven thousand remained faithful to God?[102] Jesus, however, truly was the only one to have expressed authentically the Kingdom of God. And now he is on the verge of dying without having been able effectively to establish God's Kingdom on earth. This is undoubtedly what John wished to express when he had Jesus declare, "If I had not come, they would not have sin."[103] Is there not there one of the most profound meanings of Jesus' agony? The one who came to herald reconciliation with God ended up with the opposite result, namely division. The more Jesus had closely linked his life and person to the Kingdom of God, the more sorrowful was its tearing apart: God's will, the cup, was incomprehensible, since it seemed to bring to nothing the Kingdom of God itself. The necessity of the cross as the way to glory, proclaimed in the light of the provisional victory of the "public life," now becomes the reality of his experience. No explanation is possible, except that of apparently blind submission.

Engulfed within a frightful loneliness, through the refusal men and women set up against God's Kingdom, Jesus could read in the behavior of his disciples the seriousness of his failure.[104] All his life he had tried to gather around himself a small group that symbolized the twelve tribes of Israel who had remained faithful to the God of the Covenant. And now among them was a traitor, and the others desert him by their sleeping; incapable of resisting when the trial comes, they will flee and leave him alone. Thus, Jesus who has as his mission the symbolic gathering of the Israel of God, he it is who will precipitate the dispersal of his disciples because he will refuse any form of resistance, by flight or any striking action. The gatherer that he wanted to be becomes the source of disintegration. At this level of the mission, Jesus' agony was infinitely more profound than that of an ordinary person who, at the moment of death, will be separated from his loved ones.

Everyone, indeed, enters into solitude, but there is solitude and solitude.

In the darkest of nights a single ray of light appears: the call "*Abba*, Father,"[105] which explicitly keeps Jesus in a relationship with God without, however, removing him from the experience of abandonment: "Behold, the Son of man is betrayed into the hands of sinners."[106]

Finally, it would be insufficient to limit the reading of these narratives to Jesus' disposition, without also indicating the after-effects on his disciples. In fact, the allusion to the "temptation" that threatened the disciples invites them to go beyond the recommendation to keep watch in the face of imminent death. The same struggle for the Kingdom, for faithfulness, is played out in ordinary life. The disciple must pray when faced with temptation, the power that tends to separate him or her from God. To enter into temptation means already to have discovered a gap that separates the disciple from God, preparing to flee before difficulty.

In his way, John even further enlarges the perspective, showing that death is a constant of life, that it is the rule of a full life.

CONCLUSION

In this chapter we have considered two aspects under which Jesus found himself facing imminent death. First of all, he was the one who, eating his last meal, left his testament to his disciples, affirming his faith in God, who awaited him, and convinced of the survival of a community of his own after his own death. Next, there came the Gethsemane narrative, with a totally different coloration. This event needs to be understood in the light of the diverse gospel interpretations that have been given, lest we find ourselves reduced to proposing hypotheses deriving from piety or modern psychology to fill in the gaps in the reconstructed historical edifice.

In the two narratives, Jesus was shown alone as he faced imminent death. The gestures he performed, the words he spoke, remain without echo. The disciples did not react at the last meal, then they let themselves fall asleep. God did not answer his Son's prayer; or, rather, the disciples' silence heavily corresponded to God's silence. This man who at the Last Supper solemnly proclaimed the meaning of his death was presented with his face prostrate against the ground. This man who predicted the survival of the community he founded was now terribly alone. He lived out the break with his friends, he lived through the silence of God himself. Is there not death in this? In the absolute nakedness of his failure, Jesus continues to utter, *"Abba,"* faithful to his original experience despite the blindness he experiences. Of this kind is the believer's paradox when a terrible death comes: with trust he or she plunges into the infinite mystery of death.

NOTES

1. Mt 27:31–56 = Mk 15:20–41 = Lk 23:25–49 = Jn 19:16–37.
2. Beginning with Mt 26:47 = Mk 14:43 = Lk 22:47 = Jn 18:2; besides, John begins his whole narrative there.
3. Mt 26:17–46 = Mk 14:12–42 = Lk 22:7–46.
4. Mt 26:17–35 = Mk 14:12–31 = Lk 22:7–39.
5. Mt 26:36–42 = Mk 14:32–42 = Lk 22:40–46.
6. Mt 26:1–6 = Mk 14:1–11 = Lk 22:1–6.
7. Mt 26:6–13 = Mk 14:3–9.
8. Mk 14:8.
9. D. Daube, "The Anointing in Bethany," in *New Testament and Rabbinic Judaism* (London, 1956), pp. 312–324.
10. Mt 26:21–25 = Mk 14:18–21 = Lk 22:21–23 = Jn 13:21–30.
11. Mt 26:31–35 = Mk 14:27–31 = Lk 22:31–34 = Jn 16:32.
12. Mt 26:51–54 = Mk 14:47–49 = Lk 22:49–53 = Jn 18:4–11.
13. Mt 26:63f = Mk 14:61f = Lk 22:67–70.
14. Mt 26:2,15f–p, 21p, 23f–p.
15. Gal 2:20; Eph 5:2.
16. Mt 26:17–19 = Mk 14:12–16 = Lk 22:7–13. On the question of the Jewish Passover ritual, cf. below, n. 20.
17. Mt 26:20–25 = Mk 14:17–21 = Lk 22:14,21–23.
18. Mt 26:26–29,30–34 = Mk 14:22–25,26–31 = Lk 22:15–20,24–39.
19. I reserve treatment of the topic for my work, *Le partage du pain eucharistique selon le Nouveau Testament* (Paris: Seuil, 1982). In addition to this work, the reader may consult a variety of contributions on the topic: "Jésus devant sa mort à la lumière des récits de l'institution eucharistique et des discours d'adieu" in J. Dupont, ed., *Jésus* (p. 73, n. 3), pp. 141–168 and "La mort rédemptrice du Christ selon le Nouveau Testament," in *Mort pour nos péchés* (Brussels, 1976), pp. 1–34.
20. The issue is strongly contested. Let us simply note that J. Jeremias, the ardent

defender of the Jewish Passover rite position, closes his study with these words: "It should also be emphasized, however, that the Last Supper would still be surrounded by the atmosphere of the Passover even if it should have occurred on the evening before the feast" (*The Eucharistic Words of Jesus* [p. 77, n. 83], p. 88).

21. Cf. H. Schürmann, *Comment Jésus a-t-il vécu sa mort?*, French trans. (Paris: Cerf, [1972] 1977), pp. 92–97.

22. J. Jeremias, *The Eucharistic Words of Jesus*, p. 164; in agreement with H. Schürmann.

23. J. Bonsirven, *"Hoc est corpus meum.* Recherches sur l'original araméen," *Bib.* 28 (1948), 205–219 = J. Jeremias, *EVT* (1947), 60.

24. Cf. X. Léon-Dufour, "Jésus devant sa mort" (above, no. 19), pp. 150–153.

25. Lk 22:11–38.

26. Lk 22:15–18.

27. Mt 26:29 = Mk 14:25.

28. X. Léon-Dufour, "Jésus devant sa mort," pp. 143–144. Cf. above p. xxvi.

29. Cf. Is 25:6; Mt 8:11; 22:1–19; Rv 3:20.

30. *Le Récit de la dernière Cène*, French trans. (Lyons: [1958] 1966).

31. This interpretation is not based on the doubtful hypothesis, according to which Jesus would have shared in the Jewish Passover meal. It eliminates Jeremias's hypothesis, one in which he attributes a "renunciation declaration" or oath of abstinence; according to him, Verse 15 ought to read: "I would very gladly have eaten this Passover lamb with you before my death" (*Eucharistic Words of Jesus*, p. 208). In fact, says Jeremias, *epithymein* ordinarily means an unfulfilled desire, regret, at least in Lk 15:16; 16:21; 17:22. This meaning is not impossible here, but it is not demanded, especially since Lk 22:15 is a pre-Lukan tradition and since, in Heb 6:11, the word clearly means "desire." Now, Jeremias holds that this is the only way to understand Verse 17. The motivation why Jesus, contrary to Jewish custom, did *not* want to drink the cup was that he wanted to voluntarily renounce the bread and wine of the Passover meal in order to intercede for Israel, in this way laying the foundation of Passover custom of the Quartodecimans. However, Jeremias has not succeeded in proving the validity of this "renunciation declaration" (*Eucharistic Words*, pp. 208, 216).

32. Jn 13–17. These discourses belong to the farewell discourse genre.

33. Lk 22:21–38.

34. So, W. G. Kümmel, "Jesus und die Anfänge der Kirche" (1953), in E. Grässer, et al., ed., *Heilsgeschehen und Geschichte* (Marburg: Elwert Verlag, 1965), pp. 289–309.

35. B. Rigaux, "Die 'Zwölf' in Geschichte und Kerygma," in H. Ristow and K. Matthiae, eds., *Der historische Jesus und der kerygmatische Christus* (Berlin, 1962), pp. 468–486.

36. On the notion of sacrifice, cf. pp. 185–188.

37. Ex 24:8; cf. Heb 9:22.

38. Cf. Gn 9:6; Ez 18:10.

39. Is 53:12.

40. The Luke-Paul tradition is not immediately connected to the prophet Jeremiah (through its reference to the "New Covenant") but to Is 52–53, in which

120 / JESUS FACES DEATH

the Servant, the one who had been constituted by God as "covenant of the people" (Is 49:8), "gives himself."
41. Lk 22:27. Cf. pp. 67–68.
42. Jn 13:1–20; 15:10.
43. Cf. X. Léon-Dufour, *Évangiles* (p. 74, n. 32), pp. 120–124.
44. Mt 26:36–46 = Mk 14:32–42 = Lk 22:40–46.
45. Jn 12:23,27–30.
46. Heb 5:7–10.
47. Mt 20:22f = Mk 10:38f.
48. Jn 18:11.
49. Jn 14:31.
50. M. Dibelius, "Gethsemane," *Botschaft und Geschichte* 1 (1953), 258–271; K. G. Kuhn, "Jesus in Gethsemane," *EvT* 12 (1952–1953), 260–285, T. Lescow, "Jesus in Gethsemane," *EvT* 26 (1966–1967), 141–159; M. Galizzi, *Gesù nel Getsemani* (Rome, 1972); J. W. Holleran, *The Synoptic Gethsemane. A Critical Study* (Rome: Gregorian University Press, 1973); A. Feuillet, *L'Agonie de Gethsémani.* (Paris: Gabalda, 1977).
51. Thus, quite recently also, A. Feuillet, *Agonie*, pp. 42–50.
52. R. Schnackenburg, *L'Évangile selon saint Marc*, French translation (Paris: Desclée, 1973), pp. 271–272. (Cf. X. Léon-Dufour, *RSR* 66 [1978], 115–118).
53. Mk 1:13–35.
54. M. J. Lagrange, *Évangile selon saint Marc* (Paris: Gabalda, 1929), p. 389.
55. Cf. p. 61.
56. The most detailed treatments are those of T. Lescow and J. W. Holleran (above, no. 50). At any rate, a certain rearrangement of texts has to be undertaken in order to get back to the "sources"; thus, according to the proposed schema, it was necessary to glue Verse 39 to Verse 41a, and to move a section of Verse 39 ahead of Verse 36 to obtain the equivalent of Verse 35.
57. On the temptation in general, cf. J. Carmignac, *Recherches sur le Notre Père* (Paris: Letouzey, 1969), pp. 255–268. Temptation here surely does not refer to a "trial" (p. 267) nor to encitement to evil, but to a "snare" in which one is about to become entrapped. Moreover, it would be better to translate "to enter into temptation," which is stronger than "to enter temptation".
58. *Traduction oecuménique de la Bible. Nouveau Testament.* (Paris: Cerf & Mages, 1972), pp. 59–60. I do not particularly like its translation, "Do not expose us to . . . ," because it is too weak.
59. Cf. K. G. Kuhn, "*Peirasmos, amartia sarx* im Neuen Testament und die damit zusammenhängenden Vorstellungen," *ZTK* 49 (1952), 200–222. Cf. *1 QS* 3:24.
60. The term is not found in John except in Jesus' question to Philip where one could buy bread: "This was to test him" (Jn 6:6).
61. Undoubtedly, the Old Testament often used the image of the divine cup held out to sinners (Is 51:17; Jer 25:15; Ez 23:33; Ps 75:9) and the Book of Revelation is located in the same tradition (Rv 14:10; 15:7; 16:19; 18:16). We cannot, however, put the gospel narratives in the same class. In fact, the rare instances of the term in the Synoptics indicate either the sad lot (martyrdom) promised to the sons of Zebedee (Mt 20:22f; Mk 10:38f) or, during Jesus' last meal, the blood of the covenant or the covenant sealed in blood (Mt

26:27f = Mk 14:23f; Lk 22:20 = 1 Cor 11:25). This wider meaning is also found in Ps 16:5 and 23:5, as well as in rabbinic texts.

62. The hour is mentioned by Jesus after the agony, at his arrest, either a little before (Mt 26:45; Mk 14:41) or a little after (Lk 22:53).

63. Usually Jn 12:27 is translated as follows: "Now my soul is troubled and what will I say? Father, save me from this hour? But it was precisely for this hour that I came." However, this translation is in no way demanded by the text. It is more appropriate to render it in the way I have argued for elsewhere: "Now my soul is troubled and I don't know what to say. Father, let me pass safely through this hour. For, indeed, it was for this purpose that I came to this hour." Cf. X. Léon-Dufour "Père, fais-moi passer sain et sauf à travers cette heure (Jn 12:27)," in *Neues Testament und Geschichte*, Festschrift O. Cullman [Zurich: Theologischer Verlag, 1972], pp. 157–165.

64. Cf. Ps 42:6–12; 43:5; Jon 4:9; Kgs 16:16; 1 Kgs 19:4; Sir 37:2.

65. Gn 3:16; 5:29 (which derives the name Noah from the root *nhm*, "to console"); Is 35:10; 51:11.

66. Jn 16:6,20–22; cf. 2 Cor 2:3; 6:10; 7:8f; Heb 12:11.

67. Is 25:8; Rv 7:17; 21:4.

68. According to H. B. Swete, *Mark* (London: MacMillan and Co., 1905). Cf. Ps 116:11 (*Sym., Aq.*); the word is not found except here and in Phil 2:26.

69. Mk 5:42; 9;15; 16:5f.

70. In Ps 31:23, the word "trouble" is translated in Greek by *ekstasis*.

71. Mk 9:32 (*ephobounto*); 10:32 (*ethambounto*).

72. Etymologically, *agōn* means "struggle." Cf. 2 Mc 3:25; 15:26. Cf. M. Galizzi, *Gethsemani* (above, n. 50), pp. 170–176.

73. Thus in 2 Mc 3:14,16.

74. Jn 11:33; 14:1.

75. Jn 12:27. We will read this further on, pp. 111–113; cf. above, no. 63.

76. Jn 12:24,32.

77. Mt 17:1 = Mk 9:2.

78. D. Daube, "Two Incidents after the Last Supper," in *New Testament and Rabbinic Judaism* (above, no. 9), p. 334.

79. D. Daube, "A Prayer Pattern in Judaism," in *Studia Evangelica* (Berlin: Akademie, 1959), pp. 539–545. "The prayer of Jesus follows a fixed Jewish pattern; Jesus has chosen this hour to make the traditional declaration, accepting his death in love" (p. 545).

80. As the Bible readily puts it: Gn 18:14; Jb 42:2; Zec 8:6; Lk 1:37.

81. Cf. Nm 5:12–28.

82. For example, in the account of the woman with the hemorrhage (Mk 5:24–34); cf. X. Léon-Dufour, *Les Miracles de Jésus* (Paris: Seuil, 1977), pp. 318–320.

83. Mk 14:34.

84. Mk 14:33*b*.

85. Mk 14:36 and 14:35*b*.

86. Mk 14:40; cf. 9:6.

87. Thus, Jesus "went" (in the singular: Mt 26:36). Cf. "with me" (Mt 26:38,40), different from "with him" in Mk 14:33. The expression comes back often enough in the Passion: Mt 26:18,20,21,23,29,31,33,35,36,38,40,69,71,73.

88. In succession, Jesus "goes a little farther" (*pro-elthōn*: 39), then he "goes away" (*ap-elthōn*: 42), finally, he "leaves them" (*apheis*: 44).
89. Jesus does not speak only to Peter, but to all (26:40).
90. First of all, "if it is possible" (26:39), then "may your will be done" (26:42), thereby formulating less of an appeal for help, as in Mark, than for an adherence to the Father.
91. Lk 22:53.
92. Lk 22:43f has been considered authentic by a majority of scholars. In Luke's view, Jesus' passion is a struggle; here the angel comes to strengthen him, as of old Elijah was strengthened by an angel (1 Kgs 19:4–8); Jesus struggles to the point where "his sweat became like great drops of blood falling down upon the ground."
93. Lk 22:40 and 22:46.
94. Cf. Heb 12:1–4.
95. Jn 18:11.
96. Jn 13:1; 17:1.
97. This would be the sense of the poor translation of Jn 12:27, going so far as to transpose the request into a question; cf. above, no. 63.
98. X. Léon-Dufour, "Trois chiasmes johanniques," *NTS* 7 (1961–1962), 249–251.
99. On the cup, cf. no. 61 above.
100. Heb 5:8.
101. 1 Kgs 19:10,14.
102. 1 Kgs 19:18.
103. Jn 15:22.
104. Cf. Jerome, *PL* 26:197; Hilary, *PL* 9:1067; Ambrose: "He was sad not on account of his passion, but on account of our dispersion" (*PL* 15:1817).
105. Mk 14:36. An authentic saying of Jesus, because it is not used in the Old Testament or in late Judaism as an address to God; ordinarily one said, "*Abinû*, 'Our Father.'" Cf. J. Jeremias, *The Central Message of the New Testament* (London: SCM Press, 1965), and W. Marchel, *Abba, Père. La prière du Christ et des chrétiens* (Rome: Pontifical Biblical Institute, 1963).
106. Mt 26:45; Mk 14:41.

4. Facing a Death That Has Come: Jesus on the Cross

We are now on the road to Golgotha. Death, which heretofore has been domesticated, culturally and religiously contextualized before becoming imminent—this death was already anticipated in Gethsemane. However, it had not only been accepted into consciousness and confronted in company with the living God, but had also been experienced in the spirit's depth, even in the soul. A first reaction had been violent refusal, one which then gave way to the power of acceptance and love, in a painful but true form of consent. Thus did Gethsemane introduce the reader to an understanding of Jesus' words on Calvary. In the eyes of Jesus, death could not be an event that happened continually, because of God's presence, as if the certainty of the Resurrection or survival could smooth its hardness.

It does not seem useful to our purpose to study each of the sayings which the evangelists reported of Jesus on the cross,[1] just as it would be excessive to have wanted to examine the episodes that preceded Jesus' crucifixion: the arrest, the mistreatments, the trial, the Crucifixion. The last words of Jesus are in some way recapitulated in Jesus' last cry.

The great shout that Jesus gave forth as he died on the cross is known by Christians especially in the version given by the first two evangelists: "My God, my God, why have you abandoned me?" This word of extreme dereliction is presented anew each year in Holy Week; it also resounds in the hearts of believers who are crushed by any cruel trial or overwhelmed by the injustice that ravages the world. So, this horrifying question continually rises up: why does God remain silent? Now, we ask, is it really true that Jesus died with a "Why" on his lips? Doubtless, the text

is clear. But if, trusting Mark, I answer affirmatively, I must conclude that Jesus did not know what he was living through, that
he was unaware of the meaning of his death and that, finally, he
died in the darkest of dark nights.

Uneasy with such a conclusion, I try to reassure myself with
the aid of the sayings that replace this one in the other gospels.
According to Luke, Jesus' prayer on the cross sounded as follows,
"Father, into your hands I commit my spirit"; according to John,
he made a majestic proclamation: *"All has been accomplished."*
Or else, I read with solace in the footnote in my Bible that this
anguished text would simply have been the start of a wonderful
prayer of trust, Psalm 22, alluded to in its entirety by the opening
verse.

This is not only today's difficulty. It is a fact that Luke and John
prepared other, less harsh traditions. And, from the beginning of
the second century, a copyist had modified Mark's text so that it
would read: "My strength, my strength, how you have abandoned
me!"—thereby transforming the question into a flat statement of
fact about the nearness of death. To tackle correctly the correct
perspectives of the various evangelists, it is appropriate to consider
the state of the texts.

As far as the sequence of events is concerned, the episode of
the bitter wine[2] being offered to Jesus by the soldiers takes place,
according to Matthew, Mark, and John immediately prior to Jesus'
death. Luke presents another view, following without doubt another tradition particular to himself, linking the scene to the varied
insults and mockeries: it becomes the occasion of one more decision. For Matthew-Mark, this episode is tied to the coming of
the prophet Elijah, while John links it to the fulfillment of the
Scriptures.

The Synoptics all mention that Jesus died while giving forth a
loud cry, while John, in keeping with his own unique theology,
relates that Jesus simply bowed his head. According to Luke there
is but one cry; according to Matthew, the second cry is explicitly
mentioned by the adverb "anew." According to Mark's account,
it is difficult to choose between two successive cries or only one.

Matthew 27	Mark 15	Luke 23	John 19
45From the sixth hour	33And when the sixth hour had come,	44It was now about the sixth hour	
there was darkness over all the land until the ninth hour.	there was darkness over the whole land until the ninth hour.	and there was darkness over the whole land until the ninth hour, 45while the sun's light failed.	
			28After this Jesus, knowing that all was now finished, said to fulfill the Scripture, "I thirst."
46And about the ninth hour Jesus cried with a loud voice, saying Eli, Eli lema sabachthani? that is, My God, My God, why have you forsaken me? 47And some of the bystanders hearing it said, "This man is calling Elijah!" 48And one of them at once ran and took a sponge, filled it with vinegar, and put it on a reed, and gave it to him to drink. 49But the others said, "Wait, let us see whether Elijah will come to save him."	34And at the ninth hour Jesus cried with a loud voice, Eloi, Eloi lama sabachthani? which means, My God, My God, why have you forsaken me? 35And some of the bystanders hearing it said, "Behold, he is calling Elijah!" 36And one ran and, filling a sponge full of vinegar, put it on a reed and gave him to drink, saying, "Wait, let us see whether Elijah will come to take him down."	36The soldiers also mocked him, coming up and offering him vinegar, and saying "If you are the king of the Jews, save yourself!"	29A bowl full of vinegar stood there; so they put a sponge full of vinegar on hyssop and held it to his mouth. 30When Jesus had received the vinegar,
50And Jesus cried out again with a loud voice and	And Jesus uttered a loud cry, and	46Then Jesus, crying with a loud voice, said, "Father, into your hands I commit my spirit!" And having said this he breathed his last.	he said, "It is finished." And he bowed his head and gave up his spirit.
yielded up his spirit. (51-53)	breathed his last. (38)		
54When the centurion and those who were with him, keeping watch over Jesus, saw the earthquake and what took place, they were filled with awe, and said, "Truly this was the Son of God!"	39And when the centurion, who stood facing him, saw that he thus breathed his last, he said, "Truly this man was the Son of God!"	47Now when the centurion saw what had taken place, he praised God, and said, "Certainly this many was innocent!"	

In fact, the expression "having given forth a loud cry" in Mk 15:37 can be related to the cry mentioned in the preceding verse, Verse 37 rejoining Verse 34 by way of the episode of the sponge with sour wine. So we could reconstruct the pre-Markan text in the following way:

34 And, at the ninth hour, Jesus . . . **37** uttered a loud cry, and breathed his last. . . . **39** The centurion, who stood facing him, saw that he thus breathed his last, said, "Truly this man was [*the*] Son of God."

From the three versions, one sees that two traditions concur in reporting Jesus' last cry: either a wordless cry or a cry with words. One easily understands why John, from his viewpoint, left aside any mention of the cry to observe that Jesus "bowed his head."

Certain writers still ask whether we can create a harmonized reading from these texts. First Jesus would have said, "I thirst," then "My God, why. . .?" Then, regaining his composure, "Father, into your hands . . ." and finally: "All is accomplished." But is it honest deliberately to scarifice the perspectives proper to each of the evangelists in order to hold forth an illusory agreement? It is preferable, rather, to take in succession the points of view of the various authors.

THE LAST WORDS OF JESUS

"MY GOD, MY GOD, WHY HAVE YOU ABANDONED ME?"

Let us start by reading the text as Mark presents it, without delaying over Matthew's presentation, which differs scarcely at all from Mark's except in the Hebraic tone, which he has preserved in reporting Jesus' speech.[3] Jesus declares that he has been "abandoned" by God, that is, according to the biblical use of the term that God did not "come to the aid" of his Son in extreme difficulty. In Scripture, when God's action is being described, the verb is ordinarily employed with a negative turn of phrase: so the Lord promised not to abandon either his wretched people[4] or those who searched for him in their distress: "You will not abandon *your servant* in Hades."[5]

Yet, faced with a violent death, which is at hand, Jesus does not repeat the supplication so dear to the psalmist: "*Do not abandon me, Lord;*"[6] he states that, despite his sorrowful prayer in Gethsemane, God has allowed him to fall into the hands of his enemies, of those enemies who are right in sneering at him, "He *trusted* in God; let God deliver him now, if he *loves* him."[7] Jesus experiences himself as abandoned by God to an ignominious death. The terrible evidence is there.

But other evidence, too, remains. This man, who sees himself handed over without recourse of any kind, calls out in a loud voice, "My God, my God!" For the first and only time in the gospels Jesus calls YHWH not Father, but God. Everything happens as if, in this last hour, the experience of sonship has given way to that of creaturehood. Jesus cries forth his anguish, but in the form of a dialogue: he still proclaims his trust ("*my* God"), his certainty that God carries the play despite all appearances to the contrary.

The paradox is most vivid. The experience of dereliction is simultaneously affirmed (abandonment to enemies) and denied (no abandonment of God): the cry is an appeal proclaiming the presence of the One who seemed absent. The relationship exists, even if God seems to ignore Jesus. In such tension as this resides the mystery of this last word.

In a faith that is tenacious, Jesus dies with a why on his lips. To his question we give no other answer than that of the centurion who, not before but *after* Jesus' death, declared, "Truly, this man was God's Son." One can and one must say that Jesus did not enter death illuminated by some sublime revelation; in faith he did not traverse the silence of God and death without striking up against the wall of a "why," which remains a question.

With some nuances, such was the interpretation of the Fathers of the Church and the great Doctors up to the end of the fourteenth century[8]—Jesus complained about having been abandoned by God to the enemies who put him to death; tortured by his executioners, he tells out his anguish.

We are free to try a psychological investigation of what Jesus could have experienced, by specifying the torments that fell upon him: the sufferings of the Passion, the desertion of his disciples, the rejection by people, the ultimate defeat. Jesus experienced failure to an overwhelming degree; he who had come to proclaim God's love and forgiveness, has become the source of a sin that seems irreparable.[9]

In a similar vein, mystics according to their own experience, have projected onto Jesus the suffering of soul that sees itself "in the winter of abandonment, abandonment by creatures and, more than that, abandonment even by God" (Tauler). While being founded on a theological axiom (Jesus recapitulated in himself the sufferings of all humanity), this interpretation goes beyond the data of the text in suggesting that Jesus not only was abandoned *by* God to his enemies, but was abandoned *from* God. Certainly we would not want to say that God "left" his Son—this, strictly speaking, would be hell—but people translate in this way the feeling, the terrible experience of inner dereliction.[10] "This desertion of God is *in some way* the punishment of the damned."[11] Also, instead of talking of abandonment *from* God, it would be better to speak of abandonment *by* God to a feeling of absolute desertion. Otherwise, how could we maintain the force of the "*my* God" to whom the "Why" is addressed?

Recently, certain interpreters have advanced along a line parallel to the mystical interpretation, but they leave aside the experiential point of view of the man tested in order to take up a properly theo-logical viewpoint.[12] God does not impassively attend the tragedy in which his Son dies, but finds his very self implicated there. Yes, though the Son suffers terribly from the cruelty of men and women, he is not the only one to suffer; the Father also suffers insofar as he does not want to intervene and curb the freedom of creatures to preserve his Son from violence. But he reserves his right to act by raising Jesus; by this deed he signifies that the injustice from which the oppressed suffer has been assumed by Jesus on the cross. And the cross finds meaning in this.

Very well. But does Moltmann, to whom we owe these reflections, not surrender to an imaginary scaffolding, even a mythology, when he delcares that there is "enmity," dissension between the Father and the Son.[13] He has just spoken of "God against God," introducing into God a struggle that we can only with difficulty reconcile with the Father's love and the Son's perfect welcome of the One from whom he ceaselessly receives himself. The share in the truth contained in Moltmann's presentation is that God is "the great celibate of the worlds;" there is from the beginning a dialogue between the Father and the Son. By virtue of the Son's humanity, this exchange of love implies suffering. Since the Son has been handed over to the hardhearted ness of men and women, it follows that the Father, too, but by love, must undergo (not inflict) the suffering that is the result of Sin. If God "made Christ be Sin,"[14] this was not so that he might become the object of the divine wrath, but so that he could suffer with him the sorrowful consequences of the state of sin.

So, profoundly, Jesus' cry on the cross revealed the mystery of a God who suffers with men from sin and its violence against Jesus, his Son.

However, numerous interpreters have been engaged in an opposite orientation: Jesus was not only abandoned to his enemies, but also to the divine wrath because of the horror God has of sin. In fact, St. Paul established a direct link between death and sin; Jesus, he said, "became a curse for our sakes."[15] Calvin believed he could conclude from these Pauline statements that "Jesus suffered the terrible torments that the lost and condemned must experience."[16]

This religious intuition has had repercussions especially among preachers, both Protestant and Catholic. For example, Bourdalone, though afraid people might liken his thinking to Calvin's, similarly thinks,

Strike now, Lord, strike! He is disposed to receive your blows. And, without considering that it is your Christ, cast not your eyes on him except to remember us . . . that is immolating him you will satisfy this divine hatred with which you hate sin.[17]

Some ten years earlier, people heard Bossuet during the Lenten observances held in the Church of the Minims (members of a religious congregation founded by St. Francis of Paola), say on March 26, 1660,

The deity. . . found the means to bring about the closed union between God and man with this extreme desolation, into which the man Jesus Christ was plunged under the many and repeated blows of divine vengeance.[18]

It would serve no purpose to repeat here similar, brilliant pieces of oratory, of which catechisms and sermons have for a long time borne traces. Who would support such views today?

In light of such excesses, one can understand why scholars have striven to find a less terrifying meaning in Jesus' words. So they see a recitation of Psalm 22 in it. The psalmist does not give forth a cry of despair; he merely begins a prayer that culminates in a statement of radical trust:

For he has not despaired or abhorred the affliction of the afflicted; and he has not hid his face from him, but has heard him, when he cried to him.

(Ps 22:25)

The evangelist would have been content with giving the first base, leaving the reader, who was familiar with the Scriptures, to take care to give voice to the entire psalm. Under these circumstances, Jesus' cry would be a "cry of real distress, but not one of despair: this complaint borrowed from the Scriptures was a prayer to God and it was followed in the psalm by the joyous assurance of the final victory."[19]

Clearly, the narrative accounts of the Passion were edited in the light of the psalmic texts of the suffering Just One, and Psalm 22, often alluded to, was particularly apt to support the different episodes. But there is no evidence to prove that the evangelist quoted the psalm here with the intention of implying the contents of the whole psalm. In fact,

1. He does not say explicitly that he is quoting Scripture (unlike Mk 14:27).

2. With the saying being in the original Aramaic, it cannot be a liturgical quotation, which might have been concluded from Matthew's gospel, since it gives the Hebrew version of the text.
3. The context argues against the formulation of a long prayer and rather invites stress on the state of dereliction that Jesus is in.
4. Since the Greek translation is set beside the original by the evangelists, this leads us to surmise that it is an instance of a true saying of Jesus, just like *Talitha qum* ("Little girl, get up!"[20]), which was not a scriptural citation but the very word of Jesus himself.

These themes hinder one from introducing the sentiments of the psalmist into Jesus' cry. The latter needs to be studied on its own, as we have tried to do in the preceding pages. Jesus died alone; he entered into the night of death alone. This is the point that serves as the climax to the Passion.

"FATHER, INTO YOUR HANDS I COMMIT MY SPIRIT."

Most of the time, scholars take into account only Mark, who would have been Luke's source and, so, closer to the historical truth. This prejudgment, though unverified, often unconsciously controls the scholars; so it was that Moltmann brushes aside with the back of his hand the Lukan presentation of Jesus' death. Now, to give pride of place to one evangelist is to commit a grave error in exegetical method, as we shall point out later on. Therefore, it is necessary to give a hearing as well to the saying the Third Gospel reports.

Unlike the text of Mark-Matthew, this saying is not as an isolated moment in the prayer of the Just One, but as its crowning point. Moreover, it is important to show in what sense it brings to fulfillment the glorious combat waged by Jesus against the power of darkness.[21]

Satan, who had left Jesus for a time,[22] re-enters the drama, this time in Judas's heart,[23] and he is ready to tempt Simon;[24] it is, in fact, the hour of the power of darkness, signifying, in the Johannine style, that the battle is waged by dark powers against the light.[25]

On the Mount of Olives, helped by an angel, Jesus triumphed through unceasing prayer, offering a model to all of the battle up to (the shedding of) blood.[26] The ridiculous minor skirmish featuring the disciples is but a caricature of this battle: the battle begins with a word of Jesus,[27] which announces a period of struggle and persecution because of the forthcoming disappearance of the one who had been the defender against these. Following the apostles' misapprehension of the situation, engagement in the skirmish is offered to Jesus,[28] who refuses it and repairs its damage.[29] It is a fact that Jesus appeared not as a Zealot or revolutionary of the kind that Barabbas was,[30] but one whose full power was of the soul and of goodness: welcoming the traitor Judas,[31] healing the wounded man,[32] gazing at Peter after he had denied him,[33] full of composure before the Sanhedrin members,[34] keeping silent in Herod's presence,[35] turning the attention of the women of Jerusalem from him to their fate,[36] praying for his executioners,[37] promising his paradise to the good thief,[38] in the end entrusting his spirit to the Father.[39] Jesus' final prayer came as the crowning point of a battle waged not in the way of the violent, but

with the gentleness of the Just One. Thus, Jesus became not merely an example, but the model type of the suffering just one, accepting in his body the persecution of all times and recalling by his triumph the victory promised to the disciples. The violence of which he was the victim hurled itself against that gentleness that we sometimes refer to as nonviolence and that must have as its effect the dissolution of the hardness of the wicked.

"Father, into your hands I commit my spirit." In introducing it with the familiar address, "*Abba*," Jesus personalized Psalm 31, which had become the evening prayer of the pious Jew.[40] To this request Luke seems to have attached great importance, since he places it later on the lips of Stephen, although this time the prayer is addressed to Jesus himself.

And as they were stoning Stephen, he prayed, "Lord Jesus, receive my spirit." And he knelt down and cried with a loud voice, "Lord, do not hold this sin against them." And when he had said this, he fell asleep.

(Acts 7:59–60)

The first witness to Jesus in his turn takes up the words of Jesus, his request for forgiveness for the executioners and his final prayer.

In the narrative of Jesus' death, the Lukan construction is quite apparent. While Matthew-Mark leave the Crucified's last word open-ended and as a question, Luke intends to show how Jesus brings the "good fight" to its completion by means of the trusting prayer of the Just One who is entirely assured of God's victory. Jesus began his ministry at prayer, and likewise he brought it to a close with prayer.[41] Is not the atmosphere of this death profoundly different from that in which the Markan account is bathed?

"ALL IS ACCOMPLISHED."

If, by means of literary devices that are scarcely justified, the majority of scholars have come to hold in lesser account the Lukan presentation of Jesus' last word, the operating principle is much more general in regard to the Fourth Gospel, which they often reduce to being mere theological speculation elaborated with the help of the synoptic tradition. As if the gospels, even including Mark's, were not, *all of them*, theologies! Clearly the Johannine depiction differs a lot from the synoptic version, but the task consists precisely in uncovering their relatedness at a deep level.

The last episode in Jesus' life, according to John, comprises two sayings: one "I thirst," the other "All is accomplished." The two are referred to the fulfillment of Scripture, as the author of the gospel explicitly says.

The second saying crowns Jesus' life, as if it held the place occupied by Jesus' "cry" at the moment of death. Thus, it is this one that comes to orient the Johannine interpretation. First, however, one must take into account the first saying, since it is tied to the synoptic episode of the sponge dipped in bitter wine offered to the crucified. The difference is that here the proffering of the sponge comes as the answer to Jesus' call, "I thirst" and not to the sentence "*Eli, Eli, lama sabachthani.*" Another difference consists in the statement that Jesus drank the drink that was offered, and only then proclaimed, "All is accomplished."

Let us take John's perspective. The reader of his gospel is not only invited to posit an act of faith (Mk), of adoration (Mt), of participation (Lk), but he is dragged into the powerful, sovereign, triumphal march that leads to the cross, to this throne on which Jesus establishes his Church.[42] From this vantage point, the "I thirst" cannot be reduced to a simple call of a worn-out and impaired man; it must also encompass a mysterious signification, even more profound than the ambiguity one can discern in the request put to the Samaritan woman, "Give me to drink!" which provoked the woman to desire the living water promised by Jesus. There is even more here. Another question surfaces: which Scripture is fulfilled? Often people mention Psalm 69:22, a psalm freely quoted in the early Church, because thirst and bitter wine are mentioned in it. But this is not an instance of physical thrust. The case is similar in regard to Psalm 22:16, which describes the heinous sufferrings of the persecuted Just One. This is why it is more appropriate to allude to passages in which thirst concerns the desire for God which the faithful person experiences. Then comes the weight of the other sayings of Jesus concerning the work he is to accomplish. Thus, Jn 4:34; 5:36; 17:4–5: everywhere Jesus knows himself to be charged with accomplishing the work that the Father has confided to him and that he must bring to a good end; this work consists not only in words but also deeds. These are all "words," of which the Passion may be considered the completion. Jesus thirsts to accomplish the final deed that will bring to its term and to its goal the work entrusted to him by the Father. Just as the Word sent to earth does not return to heaven until it has fulfilled its mission,[43] so is it the case with Jesus.[44]

The "All is accomplished" is thus presented as a declaration of victory: Jesus has succeeded in bringing to good the work confided by the One who had sent him. The commanded "service" has been accomplished.

As this juncture, we might ask whether the psalm referred to is not Psalm 63: "'My soul thirsts for you." John would imply and would recapitulate in this call all the synoptic data according to which Jesus declared that he longed to accomplish his work: fire on the earth, the cup to be drunk, and so on.

In summary, John included (between the two mentions of the fulfillment of Scripture) the last words of Jesus, showing that in some way they were "one": Jesus thirsted to complete the Father's work and through it to bring to its fulfillment all of Scripture.

At the close of this brief analysis of the recensions of Jesus' last word on the cross, is it possible, we ask, to give preference to one or another? I do not think so. And it is an error on the part of a large number of people to incline to favor one more than another, guided only by their secret propensity. In this there is a certain conception of reading the gospel texts. If I am a believer, it is not this text or that which will guide me: neither Mark, nor Luke, nor John separately, but Mark *and* Luke *and* John. The difficulty lies not in adding them to one another on a chronological chart of the type found in a "Life of Jesus," but in situating them in their mutual relationships with one another. This is what we try to do in our researching their meaning.

THE QUEST FOR MEANING

Faced with difficulties in specifying the event, many writers abandon such an enterprise and take refuge in examining only the interpretations to answer the question of meaning. Now what right is there for these people to neglect making an effort to visualize what did take place, to the degree that this is possible? Clearly one will not in this way arrive at the intended goal: even the focal point itself, without which there would not have been interpretations, cannot, by itself, furnish the fulness of meaning. But it is indispensable to look for it and to meet it along with the diverse interpretations.[45]

LOOKING AT THE EVENT

To visualize what took place, the historian proceeds in various ways according to the quality of the facts available to him.

1. Jesus died on a cross; the inscription hung guarantees that fact. Moreover, it is appropriate first of all to recall what Jesus himself thought about death in general.[46] Dying on the cross, Jesus perceived himself given up by God to the enemies who destroyed his earthly mode of a rapport with men and women; but right to the end he maintained a relationship with "his" God. And it was God who accomplished the rest; that is, he caused his Son to "rise up again" from the dead and gave him anew this body of his, which he needs to express himself. Between these two, even if absolutely one cannot properly speak of a space of time, there is for the one who meets death a black hole, a void, a kind of annihilation: no one, not even Jesus, can see himself despoiled of his actual body without experiencing the dread of radical separation from his brothers and sisters. It is only from God that he awaits the recovery of communion with them.

2. Another given seems to be imposed on the historian: Jesus died crying in a loud voice, as the three synoptic gospels variously attest. Surely, it is John who omits mention of it because it is scarcely fitting in the mouth of God's Word, who is seated on the cross as on a throne of glory; nonetheless, the fact is historical because such a cry is abnormal in the case of one crucified, who dies by suffocation. Also, it accounts for the centurion's astonishment when he proclaims, "This was God's Son."[47] But, by itself, this cry cannot be interpreted without our having recourse to the apocalyptic context into which it has been inserted: we will be more precise about this in a later development.

3. As has been said previously,[48] there is little difference whether there was one cry or two; what counts is that there also is another tradition extant, of sufficiently good historical worth: Jesus spoke a word as he gave forth his cry, a word that was variously construed by each community.

Did this cry consist in Mark's word, or that of Luke or John? Did Jesus in fact utter such a prayer? A historian is quite shy about choosing between the different versions or even to reply affirmatively. We have already said it: how would a man dying of suffocation on a cross have been able to speak aloud in this way?

Could the phrases he used have been overheard by those who were there and been correctly reported by the "women who looked on from a distance"? Above all, the differences in the recensions of Mark and Luke will not be explained so. As well, scholars as a whole think that the explicit formulation is the result in the evangelists' writings of specifications brought to bear by the early community upon a wordless cry.

And moreover, a better solution has been proposed in a recent hypothesis, one based on the context in which Mark's account is reported. People have often inquired about the misapprehension by those standing by who, on hearing Jesus' words, believed that the Crucified was calling on Elijah the prophet, a misapprehension that one might suppose to be "historical" because people do not see in it an addition seemingly made by the Church. In fact, it is difficult to account for a confusion between *Eli* and *Elijah* in Aramaic or Hebrew. The prophet's name in Hebrew is *Eliyahn* or, in its abbreviated form *Eliya*. How does one get *Eliya* out of Eloï (Mk) or *Eli* (Mt)? No commentator has been able to give a satisfactory answer to that question.

But, in 1946, Harald Sahlin and, in 1963, Thorlief Boman[49] asked themselves what might be the Aramaic retranslation of what those standing by thought they heard, namely "Elijah, come!" And they proposed *Elia' ta'*. Actually, *ta'* is the imperative of the ʿata: "to come," which we know from the expression *Marana ta'* "Our Lord, come!"[50] Could not Jesus, then, have cried out in Hebrew: *Eli 'atta*, that is, "My God, it's you!"? The misunderstanding would in this case be perfectly explainable, a slip being made from *Eli ʿatta* to *Elia' ta'*, which sound the same.

Now, the cry *Eli ʿatta* is only found six times in the Bible. In one case it involves the caricaturing of the prayer of idolators;[51] the five other instances are in Psalms 22, 31, 63, 118, and 140. Psalm 22, the one that begins with "My God, my God, why have you abandoned me?" has the first part of its overflowing climax with "From my Mother's womb, my God, it's you."[52] Psalm 31, which provides Luke with Jesus' prayer, "Into your hands I commit my spirit," declares, as well, in the face of enemies who conspire in the psalmist's death: "But I count on you, Lord; I say: My God, it's you."[53] Psalm 63, which could have inspired the "I thirst" uttered by Jesus, according to Jn 19:28, begins by proclaiming: "Oh God, my God, it's you! From dawn I desire you, my soul thirsts for you."[54] Thus, the cry, "My God, it's you!" is present in precisely those three psalms that, respectively, are the background for Mark, Luke, and John. In regard to the fourth text, this is the Hallel, which is recited after the Passover meal[55] and ends with "My God, it's you! And I celebrate you."[56]

Thus might the event have been. In saying *Eli 'atta*, Jesus would have been expressing his radical, even violent, trust, as this might be conceived at the moment of dying on the cross. Whether he echoes the persecuted Just One or takes up once more the Hallel psalm, Jesus maintains, in spite of evidence to the contrary, that the covenant with his God has not been broken: the dialogue continues right up to the last moment. The *you* is proclaimed by an I that remains hidden in the *my* of "my God." Historically, Jesus' cry might be likened to the saying which Rabbi Aqiba pronounced while he died a martyr in the Jewish uprising of 135: *Adōnai 'ehad* ("The Lord [is] one"), namely the last syllables of the *Shema' Israël*.[57] Jesus, for his part, leaves this earth by proclaiming the Hallel, a psalm singing God's definitive victory over the enemies of the covenant.

This is merely a hypothesis in the technical meaning of that word, and thus, impossible to prove. Nonetheless, because of the many converging indicators, it deserves consideration. To gauge its worth, one must test it at the concrete level of the gospel tradition in its entirety.

THE EVENT AND THE TEXTS

The exegete's task is not over with the establishment of what could have been Jesus' word; one must also reconstruct the genesis of the actual texts we have. Meaning, in fact, is discovered in the relationship uniting interpretations to the event. This event consisted in a cry, and this cry could have been, "My God, it's you!" But, immediately, this event was interpreted in two ways: by inserting it into an apocalyptic literary context or by situating it within an Old Testament lament form.

Jesus' wordless cry finds a meaning in the apocalyptic context in which Mark reports it. We recall the darkness at midday that lasted as long as Jesus was on the cross. This is a sign of the end of time, as Jesus himself had foretold it.[58] Yet this darkness, which remained *before* the death and ceased when Jesus expired, is not here a sign of mourning as it had been for Caesar (according to Virgil[59]); it did not signify the entry into night. Completely to the contrary, by vanishing it showed that at the very moment of Jesus' death night had come to an end, the New Day had begun. Within an apocalyptic context, Jesus' cry evokes the powerful voice of the archangel at the end of time,[60] the voice that destroys the wicked at the Parousia[61] and saves the just,[62] even that one which causes the dead to come forth from their graves for the final judgment of the resurrection.[63] According to Mark's tradition, Jesus' last cry inaugurated a new world; the Roman centurion's confession of faith is its rejoinder.

Another way of understanding Jesus' cry is that it is the making explicit of an Old Testament structure familiar to believers, that of the biblical lament.[64] Laments, whether national or individual, are scattered through the Bible and especially in the psalms. They are not simply complaints, expressions of distress; they always occur within a narrative or an enumeration that celebrates God's victorious interventions. From the time of the Exodus, these liberation events were not recounted without the point of departure being a presentation of the call of the oppressed to the Lord. When the latter intervened, it was because he had given ear to their plight. The savior God revealed himself in the context of a dialogue. The lament was oriented by praise. To bring the deliverance to mind, one first of all pointed out the suffering of the creature who found himself lost but who trusted in his God.[65]

This structure, then, surrounds Jesus' cry. As formerly the Jews at a time of deliverance, so the Christian community gathered together to celebrate God's victory; for the Church this was Jesus' Resurrection, God's triumph over death. They began with a lament, but this was in order to end up in the centurion's praise. Unlike the psalms, clearly, it was not the same person who cried out and praised; this signifies that Jesus of Nazareth in some sense "shook the hand" of the pagan, in the person of the centurion whose voice proclaimed the Resurrection.

The traditions of Mark and Luke both made use of the "lament" form. Basing themselves on Jesus' word, which, according to the hypothesis presented above, is found in Psalms 22 and 31, they chose in these prayers of sorrow and trust the word that best served as a starting point for God's positive response. According to Mark, Jesus shared the sentiments of the persecuted and trusting Just One. Luke did likewise, but with a completely different tone and with the invocation "Father."

A COMPREHENSIVE READING

In order to get at the meaning, a reader who wants to "understand" the event and let it become real for himself or herself will have to let the different interpretations of it stand in a dialectical relationship, both among themselves and with the historical residue arrived at by scholarship. Each of the interpretations no doubt possesses value in its singular characteristics, but these should not be regarded without the compensatory nuances the "historical foundation" and the parallel versions bring. So, we are now brought to a new reading of the event.

The "historical foundation" may be regarded in two ways. Jesus' last cry, inserted into an apocalyptic context, heralds the advent of a new world. On the other hand, in great likelihood, the saying "My God, it's you!" signifies that, as he died, Jesus proclaimed that, despite appearances, God's covenant had not been broken: the Son, in whom God had poured all his love since the baptism humbly accepted at the Jordan, this Son recognized the God of salvation in a definitive way.

As such, the historical foundation invites us to hear in it a shout of victory. This is a key notion, one that will orient the interpretations in their diversity. But does this historical foundation sufficiently typify Jesus' outlook? The evangelists seem not to have judged this so.

Mark while locating the Crucified's cry in an apocalyptic context, showed in Jesus the one who dies entirely alone, abandoned by God to the violence of his enemies, to the cowardice of his disciples without any extraordinary help. Jesus protests with a "why" the tragic state in which he finds himself. This cry, springing up from the depths of night, is, nonetheless, a cry of faithfulness to God. The Christians of the era, handed over defenceless to all kinds of tribulations, could be encouraged by the example of Jesus, who was the first to undergo persecution. And they know that the faithful God had in a definitive way freed his Son from death. Moreover, if separated from the lament-praise context into which it had been inserted, Jesus' word could be understood as a word of despair, and, in fact, it has been. This is why it must be balanced off by another interpretation, which explicitly affirms that Jesus died fully confident in the certitude that the Savior God is stronger than the death into which his Son descended.

Luke, in effect, showed that in Jesus there is the model of the Just One who is a martyr abandoning himself to God. He depicted Stephen the same way, the first martyr to "fall asleep" while "crying out with a loud voice: Lord, do not reckon this sin against them!" Now it is possible to give an exaggeratedly privileged position to the Lukan presentation. I leave aside the case of those who try to combine Luke with Mark. I mean to challenge a reading of Luke that, if absolutized, would tend to fail to appreciate the deep loneliness in which Jesus found himself. People have gone so far as to say that, for Jesus, it was not hard to die. Moreover, the dimensions of the cry of victory could be so overshadowed as to suggest a pietistic kind of serenity.

In *John's* case, he rediscovers the profound meaning of Jesus' last cry, "My God, it's you!" without obscuring thereby his tragic condition. Clearly, as we have said, the Johannine narrative transforms the Passion into a triumphal march crowned with a magnificent "All is accomplished"; but the "I thirst" that precedes expresses, as much as the Crucified's state of anxiety does, his ardent desire of rejoining God and of perfecting the covenant with him. Even more than in Luke's account, the text of John could be badly interpreted so that it would lead to a failure to appreciate the more rugged interpretations of Mark and Matthew.

AN OPENING UP

The gospel is not only a teaching regarding what Jesus thought; it also proposes to open up the reader to an existential outlook wherein he or she would be united to the person of Jesus. Indeed, it is just this way that the first Christians went about things. The reader is immersed in a community that believes in Jesus' Resurrection and commemorates what happened once. Along with the early community, then, I can existentially encounter Jesus' death, for in faith I am certain that, although it was the end and the failure of his earthly life, Jesus' death was also the entry way to the fullness of life, the blooming in all its fullness of a total presence.

Instead, the diverse gospel perspectives, when they are not forcibly reduced to a biography of some sort, mean a rather pluralistic reading of the episodes, which is made possible by the dispositions of one's soul.

So, with Luke, I can contemplate the one who fights to the shedding of his blood and myself hand back my spirit with fidelity into the Father's hands. This presupposes that I am sufficiently detached from myself to contemplate in Jesus the Just Martyr who thinks only of others, forgiving his executioners and promising the good thief paradise in company with him.

But my soul's disposition can be darkened and weigh heavily on me and on my community to the extent that I do not know where to find light. Yet, through the history I have lived out, I know equally that God is God and I know that the stars shine as brightly as ever no matter how overcast the sky gets. Hence, I have no other refuge than to cry aloud to my God the experience that crushes me, "Why have you abandoned me?" And my questioning cry gets louder when joined with the cries echoing from the foundation of the world and reverberating through the whole Bible. In this way I hear Abel's blood crying out for vengeance[66] and that of the victims of Antiochus Epiphanes's persecution;[67] I quiver with workers who in vain await their pay.[68] I suffer in hearing the alien, the widow, and the orphan groan at the injustice of other men and women.[69] All these cries, quite contemporary, resound in me but not with a desire for vengeance. It is with Job that in purest fashion I cry out my distress and with Jesus who forgives, for his blood is more eloquent than Abel's.[70]

Finally, I can unite myself to the cry itself, to the wordless cry that Jesus emitted at the moment of his death, just as he cried when, as a newborn, he came into the world. To the cry at birth, one that seeks to establish a personal relationship with the world of humans,[71] corresponds the cry of the dying person, who seems to lose all communication with the universe. But in Jesus' case, this final cry puts an end to the darkness spread over the earth; he heralds a new universe. In me it becomes the cry of the Spirit, who proclaims in the depths of my being, "*Abba*, Father."[72] This cry of continual rebirth dares to take on death as it approaches, for it is proffered by the one who, first of all, entered the darkness of death to be reborn as God's Day.

May this cry echo even today! As St.Gregory the Great says, Jesus' cry runs the risk of not being heard "if our speech keeps silent about what our soul has believed. But, so that his cry in us not be suffocated, let each one, according to his or her ability, make known to those who come near to them the mystery that makes one live!"[73]

NOTES

1. For the reader's convenience, here are the sayings attributed to Jesus on the day of his death, prior to his last cry:

    28 "Daughters of Jerusalem, do not weep for me, but weep for yourselves and for your children. **29** For behold, the days are coming when they will say, 'Blessed are the barren, and the wombs that never bore, and the breasts that never gave suck!' **30** Then they will begin to say to the mountains, 'Fall on us'; and to the hills, 'Cover us.' **31** For if they do this when the wood is green, what will happen when it is dry?"

(Lk 23:28–31)

"Father, forgive them; for they do not know what they do."

(Lk 23:34)

"Truly, I say to you, today you will be with me in Paradise."

(Lk 23:43)

"Woman, behold your son!"

(Jn 19:26)

"Behold, your mother."

(Jn 19:27)

"I thirst."

(Jn 19:28)

2. Gk. *oxos*. Not what we refer to today as vinegar, but a sour wine mixed with water, a popular drink given to soldiers. Quite bitter, it was not liked very much (Ps 69:22; Prv 10:26).
3. M. Rehm, *BZ* 2(1958), 275–278; J. Gnilka, *BZ* 3(1959), 294–297; H. Schütz-eichel, *Trierer Theologische Zeitschrift* 83 (1974), 1–16.
4. Heb 13:5, quoting Dt 31:6, 8 or Jos 1:5.
5. Acts 2:27, quoting Ps 16:10.
6. Ps 27:9, 38:22; 71:9,18; 119:8; 140:8 (LXX).
7. Mt 27:43.
8. G. Joussard, "L'abandon du Christ d'après saint Augustin," *RSPT* 13 (1924), 310–326; and "L'abandon du Christ dans la tradition grecque des IVᵉ et Vᵉ siècles," *RevSR* 5 (1925), 609–633; L. Mahieu, "L'abandon du Christ sur la croix," *MelSR* 2 (1945), 209–242; B. Carra de Vaux-Saint-Cyr, in *Problèmes actuels de Christologie* (1961) (Bruges: DDB, 1965), pp. 305–316.
9. Jn 15:22; cf. pp. 115–117.
10. Saint Teresa of Avila depicted this state as that of "all the sorrows of death", yet, said she, "this suffering is accompanied by a joy so delightful that I know not what to compare it with. It is simultaneously a martyrdom of sorrows and delights," (*Oeuvres complètes* [Paris: Seuil, 1949,] p. 200). We can perhaps wonder, nonetheless, whether this presentation is not fashioned in the light of Easter; it was only after the fact that Teresa realized that peace had not gone from her. Perhaps Hans Urs von Balthasar conveys the mystical experience most correctly when he states, "Jesus alone suffered for all the *poena damni* (the pain of damnation) . . . in his loss of all the spiritual illuminations of faith, hope, and love" (*La Gloire et la Croix*, Vol. 3 Part 2 [Paris: Aubier, 1975], p. 200). Let us clearly understand the matter: Jesus did not lose the theological virtues, but their lights.
11. Bourdaloue, "1ᵉʳ sermon sur la Passion de Jésus-Christ," in *Oeuvres*, Vol. 3 (Paris: 1846), p. 518.
12. Thus, J. Moltmann, *The Crucified God,* Eng. trans. by R. A. Wilson and John Bowden (San Francisco: Harper & Row, [1972] 1974).
13. Moltmann, p. 171.
14. 2 Cor 5:21.

15. Gal 3:13.
16. *Institutes of the Christian Religion*, Vol. 2, 16, edited by John T. McNeill; (Philadelphia: Westminster Press, 1960), p. 516.
17. Cf. above, n. 11.
18. *Oeuvres*, Vol. 3, edited by M. Lebarq (Paris: *DDB*, 1916), p. 388.
19. *The Jerusalem Bible* (Garden City, N.Y.: Doubleday, 1966), Part 2, 63. Note however, that Osty is more moderate (*Bible Osty* [Paris: Seuil, 1973], p. 2185, n. 34) and that the *TOB* is more refined (*NouveauTestament*, 1972, p. 121). The most recent commentary on Mark (R. Pesch, *Markus* [cf. p. 48, n. 141], Vol. 2 [1977], p. 495).
20. Mk 5:41.
21. The following treatment derives from my article, "Passion (récits de la)," *SDB* 6 (1960), p. 1477.
22. Lk 4:13.
23. Lk 22:3; cf. 4:13.
24. Lk 22:31.
25. Lk 22:53; cf. Jn 3:19.
26. Lk 22:40–46; cf. pp. 109–110.
27. Lk 22:36, 38.
28. Lk 22:49.
29. Lk 22:51.
30. Lk 23:19,25.
31. Lk 22:48.
32. Lk 22:51.
33. Lk 22:61.
34. Lk 22:67,70.
35. Lk 23:9.
36. Lk 23:28–31.
37. Lk 23:34.
38. Lk 23:43.
39. Lk 23:46.
40. *B. Berakhot*: 5a.
41. Lk 3:21; 24:50.
42. Cf. *SDB* 6 (1960), 1479.
43. Is 55:11.
44. Cf. A. Dauer, *Die Passionsgeschichte in Johannesevangelium* (Munich: Kösel, 1972), pp. 212–213, which carefully examines the relationship of the Greek terms among themselves.
45. Cf. X. Léon-Dufour, *Resurrection*, (p. 75, n. 65) pp. 245–249.
46. Cf. pp.4–19.
47. Mk 15:39: "seing that he died *in this way.*"
48. Cf. p. 126.
49. H. Sahlin, *Bib.* 33 (1952), 62–63; T. Boman, "Das letzte Wort Jesu," *Studia Theologica* 17 (1963), 103–119.
50. 1 Cor 16:22.
51. Is 44:17.
52. Ps 22:11.
53. Ps 31:15.
54. Ps 63:2; cf. Ps 22:16.

55. Mk 14:26.
56. Ps 118:28; see French translations under the expression *Eli' atta* in various ways. Thus, "My God, it is you" is kept by the *TOB* (1975) as the translation of Ps. 22:11, 31:15, 63:2, while the *Psautier oecuménique* (1977) keeps it only for Ps 140:7. Elsewhere, it reads, "You are my God." It is up to the translators to justify their choices!
57. Dt 6:4.
58. "The sun will be darkened . . . then, the Son of man . . ." (Mk 13:24).
59. *Georgics*, I: 463ff.
60. 1 Thess 4:16; Rv 1:10.
61. 2 Thess 2:8; Rv 1:16.
62. 4 Ez 13:12F.
63. Jn 5:28; cf. Mt 27:52, which makes it explicit.
64. Cf. C. Westermann, "The Role of the Lament in the Theology of the Old Testament," *Interpretation* 28 (1974), pp. 20–38.
65. First, the lament, ever present in the Old Testament, is never considered to be a weakness (Gn 25:22; 27:46 and so on). Moreover, a special term distinguished the lament addressed to God from that used in mourning; the latter was purely profane. The complaint, being something "normal," was always present in it.

   Second, laments never stopped at an expression of sorrow; their goal was always one of praise, for the man or woman knew that the Lord answered. Thus, in texts wherever the lament appeared, whether for a national disaster or an individual tragedy, it ended on a note of thanksgiving. Psalms of lament reveal a regular form: a cry of distress, trust, praise in its fullness. One can never dissociate its two components: lament-praise.

   Third, generally, the suffering person who expressed himself or herself in psalms of lament did not admit to being a sinner; simply, or above everything else, he or she was put to the test. This is why these prayers are called the psalms of the suffering. Just One who trusts in God. His faithfulness consists not in letting himself be crushed, but in waiting on God for his deliverance. So, in Ps 22, one who had been saved from a misfortune gathers around himself the community at the temple and offers up a cultic meal to congratulate God for the salvation that he had granted. Briefly put, a lament is constitutive of a dialogue with God. A complaint is appropriate, provided that it leads to thanksgiving.
66. Gn 4:10.
67. 2 Mc 8:3.
68. Dt 24:15.
69. Ex 22:22,26.
70. Heb 12:24.
71. D. Vasse, *L'Ombilic et la Voix* (Paris: Seuil, 1974).
72. Rom 8:15.
73. Gregory the Great, *Morals on the Book of Job* XII:23.

Conclusion of Part One

Jesus face-to-face with his own death: this has been the subject of these four chapters. We treated the topic with a historical method, struggling against having it illuminated straightaway by Easter faith. This is the reason why, in some readers' eyes, the results of our inquiry seem meager indeed in comparison with the affirmations of Christian faith. Let us then be more precise about the nature of this difference by returning to the delicate question raised at the beginning of Chapter 2: Did Jesus seek death in order to save the world from its sins?

With the Church, we affirm in faith that by Christ's death the world was redeemed from its sins, that the covenant with God was restored and that we have been saved. In reiterating the conviction of the first Christians, we base our claim, in one sense, on historical grounds. By contrast, when we state that Jesus faced death to save the world, this formulation of ours bears only an appearance of the historical, for it casts onto the Jesus of the past the light of a faith conviction. Clearly this enterprise is legitimate, for faith does allow us to make explicit the thought of Jesus, whose divinity faith confesses. This is what the evangelists consciously did, for example, when they attributed to Jesus precise statements (anachronistic ones, from the historian's point of view) concerning his coming Passion and Resurrection, or when they showed Jesus ardently desiring to suffer and die. Light from faith thus succeeds in clarifying what the full "consciousness" of Jesus of Nazareth was. On the other hand, the historian's reasoning can only turn its attention to certain and authentic statements by the same Jesus on these topics. If such seem to be wanting, as in the present instance, a historian cannot show that Jesus stated that he was going to his death *in order to* save the world.

Thus, a notable difference distinguishes these two kinds of interpretations. However, to highlight this gap does not imply the erasing of the continuity that links the Christ known by faith to the Jesus of Nazareth examined by the historian, because historical inquiry is also obliged to show how Jesus was that grain of wheat planted in the earth from which the great tree of the Church emerged. It also means entering more profoundly into the way in which God reveals himself. Let us then recall the salient aspects of our research.

To enter into the thought of Jesus means that one ought not to be concerned first off with "Christology" (the titles of Jesus, his "consciousness," and so on), but with what, in Jesus' eyes, was the essential thing, namely an experience of the God who there and then exercised his rule by means of the words and deeds of his Envoy. As a matter of fact, Jesus made no explicit declaration concerning his person (Christ, Son of God, and so forth), but restricted himself to surfacing a question in his own regard, through that uncompromising covenant faithfulness of his that united him to the Father. Who was God, for Jesus? In that question we may discover the ground of his activity and the cause of the persecution he underwent.

For Jesus, God brought pardon to all without exception, not merely to the Jewish people he had chosen to be the mediator of his covenant; in this outlook, Jesus overturned the barriers his contemporaries had set up around the Law and religious observance. God loved sinners and even his enemies. Lastly, and above all, God made the "poor" his preference. To proclaim such a God was for Jesus to expose himself immediately to the hostility of those who were maintaining the established order.

Jesus heralded life and forgiveness, but he did not give a discourse on death. When death threatened, he was content not to hold it in awe, for the living God had to win the victory over it one day. Jesus gave no explanation for suffering; instead he set about wrestling against it by healing the sick, symbolizing thereby the fullness of health; that is *the* definitive "salvation" promised by the God who even today exercises his sovereignty. He located his own death, of which he had forebodings, within God's plan, as an aspect of that biblical tradition that narrated the cruel end of prophets and the persecution of the Just One, and situated it as well as in relation to the resurrection and exaltation that had been promised to the fathers in the faith. Never did death in his eyes acquire any meaning in itself, except the meaning that saw it as crowning a life of service and fidelity. When death loomed imminent, he did not "resign" himself to it as if were faced with a fatality, but he did not, for all that, rebel against or resist it with violence; he welcomed it from the hand of God, out of his fidelity to the message entrusted to him. Jesus did not greet death in the way one searches for a means to a worthwhile end; he carried on simply but with tenacity with his proclamation of the Good News at the cost of his very life.

A question now surges up. Without doubt Jesus is an exceptional prophet and a model for religious living, but the Christian faith confesses much more: that Christ is the author of salvation. Since the historian remains silent concerning the authenticity of Jesus' unique word on the ransom he came to bring to the many, one has to find another anchor point for Christian faith in the redemption. How, then, can we say that Jesus saved the world from its sins?

Jesus did not "give" salvation to a world external to himself, as one might, say, administer a remedy to the sick; he saved it by his "self-donation." He was in the world as one perfectly just and radically faithful to the covenant. In him God took on the human condition, thereby sealing a definitive communion with himself. With Jesus and through him, God's grace from now on is to be found buried in that very heart of the world of human beings. Sharing integrally in the human condition, without however consenting to evil, Jesus allowed God's power to set the world free of its sin. For the one who surrendered all into the hands of the living God, only one thing was required: not to make evident what his "intentions" were, but to cling to the end to the covenant with God. "My God, it's you!" he declared in a final cry, after he had struggled against death and defeat, in what was also a final surrender. In so doing, he brought to its fulfillment the mission he received from the Father.

It was up to God to accomplish the rest, that is to cause life to win the victory.

It was also up to God to reveal to certain privileged witnesses, like Saul of Tarsus, this victory of life over death. These witnesses could then recognize the truth of the message of forgiveness and universal love proclaimed by Jesus of Nazareth and discover in this human person the Lord who humbled himself while living as a servant and while dying on a cross. It is only in faith, through the evidence of the Resurrection, that the universal significance of the life and death of Jesus can be affirmed.

In this way, and only in this way, can the believer honestly attribute to Jesus what formerly had been hidden in eternal silence: God is disposed to save all those who unite themselves to the death of his Son. This, then is what Paul, a believer, would make explicit with the symbolic terms of salvation.

A COMPLEMENTARY NOTE ON THE EPISTLE TO THE HEBREWS

Before taking up Paul's view on death it may be useful to indicate briefly the contribution of the Epistle to the Hebrews.[1] In fact, outside of the gospels, it is exceptional for a writing to be specifically concerned with the sufferings of Jesus. In several passages, the author seems to evoke recollections of Gethsemane or Golgotha. However, it is important not to project onto this text our own "psychological" views. If Jesus "offered up prayers and entreaties with loud cries and tears to the One who could deliver him from death," this was chiefly to show that he was fulfilling the destiny of the suffering Just One.[2] For "he was heard because of his submissiveness; Son though he was, he learned obedience through his sufferings"[3]: he was faithful to the end. The sorrowful experience of death brought him to "perfection"; suffering radically transformed him.

Doubtless, the author was inspired by the sacrificial language of the Old Testament and went so far as to designate Jesus the High Priest. But this was not to tie Jesus' deed to sacrifices; it was to declare that henceforth such sacrifices have become meaningless and useless.[4] Sacrifices are not the "categories" within which the death of Christ is to be thought out; they are used by the author merely as a springboard to enhance the utter newness[5] of the deed Jesus performed "once for all."[6] The Epistle to the Hebrew is not the "first sacrificial theology" of Christianity.

On the positive side, Jesus appears in this work as a man of flesh and blood, completely at one with human beings, "his brothers,"[7] even unto death. But he who had been "without sin,"[8] accepted death with perfect obedience.[9] Thus, "by his death he rendered powerless the one who held the power of death . . . , he delivered all those who were held in slavery their whole life long by the fear of death."[10] So it was that "on everyone's behalf he tasted death."[11] The striking consequence of this is that death no longer is what it had been. Its meaning has been changed. It is now the path to glory. Now it is sufficient to heed the new "forerunner" who has gone ahead.[12] That transformation, which rituals proved incapable of achieving, has been effectively procured by the passion of Christ.[13] Thus, without yet having treated the Pauline synthesis, we find ourselves in the Epistle to the Hebrews with a profound understanding of the events of Gethsemane and Golgotha.

NOTES

1. This epistle seemingly dates from shortly before the destruction of the Jerusalem Temple, that is, around the Year 67. On the theology of this epistle, the reader is referred to the excellent work of A. Vanhoye, *Situation du Christ. Hebreux 1–2* (Paris: Cerf, 1969), especially pp. 306–387. Also the notes to this epistle in the *Traduction oecuménique de la Bible* (Paris: Cerf, 1973).
2. Cf. pp. 61–63.
3. Heb 5:7f.
4. Heb 7:11,19; 9:9.
5. Heb 10:12,14.
6. Heb 7:27; 9:12,26,28.
7. Heb 2:11,17.
8. Heb 4:15; cf. 9:14.
9. Heb 5:8; 10:9f.
10. Heb 2:14f.

11. Heb 2:9.
12. Heb 2:10; 5:9.
13. Heb 12:1–3.

II. PAUL FACES DEATH

Introduction

Did Jesus' history end with the death he underwent in perfect fidelity to God and to human persons? Jesus did not think so; he had foretold that his disciples would be faithful like him and with him. In fact, the *Acts of the Apostles* recount the exploits of the first witnesses to faith in Jesus; these narratives, however, only indirectly advert to the personal thought of their heroes. On the other hand, we do have the writings of Paul, which, even if they are occasional, reflect his experience and reveal his deepest longings. As it happens, then, he let his correspondents in on what his attitudes had been both before as well as after the encounter he had had with the Lord Jesus. We overhear him consoling people who had just lost their friends to death. We also witness him reacting to a death that loomed before him personally. These confidences of his help us penetrate the heart of a believer different from Jesus.

Now, this "ordinary" believer named Paul was not satisfied to repeat what Jesus had said nor what he had heard from the primitive community. He knew how to harmonize certain data; and as well, he was able to "invent" metaphors and categories of thought to articulate the mystery. Right away, we see the distance that will come to separate Paul's terminology from that of Jesus. Jesus was satisfied to present his actions, his behavior, and to proclaim the Good News in a specific milieu (for example, he probably did not say that he was the "ransom for the multitude".)[1] But his comportment gave an impetus to all the subsequent interpretations of it. Paul's attitude in his writings is quite different and much more complex: this is because he is simultaneously an adherent of the tradition and a "theologian."

Two principal factors lie at the origin of his terminology. First, we have what Paul received from the primitive Church, something he repeated or elaborated on according to circumstances. Secondly, we are faced with the fact that he invented new categories, partial syntheses into which he poured his gospel message.

We know that, even if on occasion he stated—with an apologetic purpose—that he had received everything directly from God,[2] Paul clearly had been instructed in the faith by the Christians whom he had met. Luke intimated as much as early as his narrative of the conversion of Saul of Tarsus;[3] the writings of Paul himself are laced with notations deriving from some contexts other than the ones in which they have been placed. The literary makeup of these small units is one characteristic of the hymns or faith confessions that one can recognize in other New Testament writings. These snippets handed on by Paul show him to be an inheritor of the primitive Christian faith.[4] Fundamentally, Paul is a man of tradition.

Besides, the Apostle of the Gentiles was replying to specific concerns that went beyond the limited horizon of the primitive Palestinian community and in this he was surely influenced by his own unique thought world, that belonging to the Hellenistic environment of Diaspora Judaism. Moreover, Paul was endowed with a mind inhabited with personifications, mythical figures who played a role in the drama of human life: death, the Law, sin—all were powers at work in the human world, and locked in combat with life, the spirit, grace. In his presentation of the gospel, Paul made use of these as if he considered that they were personal entities who controlled the realms of life and grandiose temporal eras into which human beings had been inserted. Such was the mental universe of Paul, the one through which we will stroll in the coming chapters.[5]

Paul's way of operating presents a problem that revolves around the relationship between this "theology" of his and Jesus of Nazareth's way of speaking. To lay hold of this fact it has often been necessary—by a provisional operation, insufficient to provide the meaning—to filter the gospel narratives in order to eliminate from them the interpretations of the Church. Such interpretations already created a gulf between Jesus and the community. How much more would this be the case now with Paul's creative power!

In our examination, we will have to take into account the tension between the Paul of tradition and the creative Paul. Let us note as well that we will have to take into account the plurality of languages Paul used to give expression to the mystery. Especially is this the case in our first study in this second part, the one dealing with the interpretation of the salvific value of Jesus' death on the cross.

Paul underwent a journey that advanced in tandem with the concerns in which he found himself most implicated. At the start of his evolution we find Jesus on the cross: this was as it were, the door opening out onto the path he followed. The stages in our mapping of it may be specified as follows:

1. Paul, the Jew, faced with Jesus on the cross
2. Paul, the theologian, on death and sin
3. Paul, the person of hope, faced with suffering
4. Paul, the apostle, faced with looming death

In keeping with our method, we will base our assertions on an analysis of the most important texts. The reader is invited to make an effort to enter into the maze of Paul's argumentation. He or she will be rewarded with a penetration into a different universe and with a discovery at the same time of the principles that lie at the base of contemporary dogmatic terminology.

NOTES

1. Cf. pp. 65–68.
2. Gal 1:12.
3. Acts 9:17f; Saul of Tarsus was baptized by Ananias.
4. P. E. Langevin, *Jésus Seigneur et l' Eschatologie*, Exégèse des textes prépauliniens (Montréal: DDB, 1967), especially pp. 31–38, rehearses the criteria that permit the recognition of texts earlier than Paul (cf. *Resurrection* [p. 75, n. 65], p. 26).
5. It is amusing to return to what an author wrote at the beginning of the second century: "Our beloved brother Paul wrote to you according to the wisdom

given him . . . . There are some things in them hard to understand, which the ignorant and unstable twist to their own destruction, as they do the other scriptures" (2 Pt 3:15f).

5. Paul Faces Jesus on the Cross

In the eyes of Paul of Tarsus before his enlightenment on the Damascus Road, Jesus of Nazareth had died cursed of God because he had died on a cross. Jesus had not died a natural death after many days doing good; he had been condemned to a gibbet, an outlaw, as Scripture has it: "Cursed is anyone who hangs on the wood!" This is what Paul recalled as he wrote the Galatians.[1] Yes, for this Jew descended from Abraham, "circumcised on the eighth day, of the race of Israel, a member of Benjamin's tribe, a Hebrew of the Hebrews, according to the Law a Pharisee"[2] the law forcefully states, "The one hung is God's curse"—he has fallen under definitive condemnation.[3]

It is hard for us to grasp the horror Paul must have experienced when he heard it preached that this crucified person was God's Son. As Luke put it, echoing Paul himself, it is clear that Paul showed himself to be

a zealous persecutor of the Church; entering house after house, he dragged off men and women and committed them to prison. . . . Paul, still breathing threats and murder against the disciples of the Lord, went to the high priest and asked him for letters to the synagogues at Damascus, so that if he found any belonging to the Way, men or women, he might bring them bound to Jerusalem.

(Acts 8:3; 9:1–2)[4]

Such fanaticism surprises only those who do not know the fire of religious passion. Burning with zeal for God and the Law, how could Saul not have done all he could to extricate his unfortunate coreligionists from the clutches of a man whom God had cursed by letting him be nailed to a cross?

Such was the logic of the zealous man. But God had other plans.

The drama of the appearance to Paul on the Damascus Road has been recounted three times by Luke and it agrees substantially with what Paul himself says.[5] Suddenly, Paul understood that this crucified Jesus was alive in God's presence and that henceforth he expressed himself through his disciples.

All of a sudden, Paul's mental world was upset. Its point of departure now was a strange one: a man—and, moreover, one who had been crucified—was discovered to be alive after his death. What, then, was the meaning of this death, which had been transformed from a curse into a blessing, and such a blessing that from now on it was to be the source of every blessing for believers? A brilliant insight had overtaken Paul's mind: peace from the definitive reconciliation with God had flooded his heart.

Paul himself had shared with the Philippians the extent of his radical transformation, contrasting the two conditions, the one before and the one after his meeting with the Risen One:

7 But whatever gain I had, I counted as loss for the sake of Christ. 8 Indeed I count everything as loss because of the surpassing worth of knowing Christ Jesus my Lord. For his sake I have suffered the loss of all things, and count them [all] as refuse, in order that I may gain Christ 9 and be found in him, not having a righteousness of my own, based on law, but that which is through faith in Christ, the righteousness from God that depends on faith; 10 that I may know him and the power of his resurrection, and may share his sufferings, becoming like him in his death, 11 that if possible I may attain the resurrection from the dead.

12 Not that I have already obtained this [prize] or *have already finished the race*; but I press on [*with the race*] to make it my own, because Christ Jesus has made me his own. 13 Brethren, I do not consider that I have made it my own; but one thing I do, forgetting what lies behind and straining forward to what lies ahead, 14 I press on toward the goal [to receive] the prize of the upward call of God in Christ Jesus.

(Phil 3:7–14)

Before recounting Paul's reactions to Jesus on the cross, it is useful to specify what he understands by "the language of the cross," an expression he forged quite early, since we find it in the First Epistle to the Corinthians, which, at the latest, dates from the Year 56. Paul proclaims that this language of the cross is "God's power" and that he himself had "decided to know nothing among you, except Jesus Christ and Jesus Christ crucified".[6] To castigate the Galatians for their inconstancy, Paul made use of the same theme as the basis for his argument: "Oh foolish Galatians! Who has bewitched you? You before whose very eyes Jesus was publicly portrayed as crucified?"[7] Also, when he recounted the eucharistic tradition, he adds his own conviction, "You proclaim the Lord's death until he comes."[8] Truly Paul seems to have focused his thought on the death on the cross; what, then, did he understand by "language of the cross?"

It was a fact: Jesus had been condemned to carry his cross; he had been crucified.[9] Already the Church's reflection had led it to make use of this event and to apply it to disciples in the expression "to carry one's cross."[10] Paul could thus base himself on a precedent in the tradition when he made use of the term in an absolute sense and began to refer to the Crucified as the source of salvation.[11] The cross even became a theological category in his thought.[12]

This way of speaking was scandalous for the times; it was the equivalent of the expression "to join the galley slaves." We can appreciate the reasons why, afterward, it was not taken up again even by Ignatius of Antioch,[13] although quite a bit later it was, by John Chrysostom. Paul did not succeed in making this way of speaking normative.

Why such a choice, such an insistence on his part to do so, at a time when the primitive community was filled with enthusiasm by its viewpoint regarding the Parousia and the Resurrection? It seems that the proximate cause came from the polemical condition in which Paul found himself on several occasions and on various levels: against the Jews (against himself in the first place), against the Judaizers (who wanted to add some requirement to the saving cross),[14] against the libertines (on the subject of dietary prescriptions);[15] against the gnostics finally (who thought everything was permitted them).[16] Against all these people Paul quoted his own experience: he knew that one had to deal with the issue of death to preach the gospel. He knew that he bore the cross and Christ's death about with him in his own body.[17]

But, let us note, too, that when Paul speaks of the "cross," he does not simply think of the shameful and sorrowful death; he has in view, as well, the salvation and the glory that occur through it. Paul, then, is not a sad-faced individual who, under the aegis of Jesus' cross, extols suffering and self-destruction. As a realist, he knows that it is through Jesus' death on the cross that his glorious presence is revealed. This shows the depths of the "language of the cross" set forth by Paul.

Paul speaks so often about Jesus' death that it is difficult to present an overall view of the subject. Classically,[18] people try to differentiate what Paul personally added from what the tradition he received said; but the very delicate task of establishing this earlier tradition is fraught with numerous unverifiable hypotheses. In addition, we have to ask ourselves whether it is honest to state that Paul considered the additions he himself made to be more important. As well, it seems preferable to take the texts as they are, with their internal relationships that link the various elements together.

Two factors will guide us in the division of our inquiry, ones offering two perspectives on Paul's thought. These perspectives sometimes are blended together, but nonetheless they can be carefully distinguished. In the first place, the "cross" of Jesus signifies the fruit of Jesus' death, namely salvation and victory over sin. Then, it can be situated within God's plan with regard to the Law and to sacrifies, the two main institutions of the Old Covenant.

JESUS' DEATH AND VICTORY OVER SIN

Paul did not systematically organize his thought into a total and well-articulated view. He offered his reflections in the course of writing letters addressed to his correspondents, so that we find ourselves faced with very many terms by means of which he tried to visualize the mystery being explored, without however ever fully grasping it: redemption, justification, liberation, reconciliation, and so on. To guide us through this maze, it seemed good to take as our base the symbols that control Paul's terminological language.[19]

To express the relationship obtaining between God and humankind, there is the symbolic pattern of social relationships carried out in various orders: the judicial, the political, the interpersonal. To account for the effect on men and women of the renewal of the covenant in this way, one can call on the symbolism of biological transformation within an individual, one that happens in various ways: entry into life, transformation, assimilation.

These two types of symbolic terms are complementary: the symbolism of the individual happens to illustrate each time the result of what had been begun by the symbolism of social relationships. So, justification bursts forth into life that springs from death, liberation produces a veritable transformation of being and reconciliation tends with all its power to the most intimate kind of identification.

Recognition of this rootedness within human language must not conceal the role of faith experience: this latter invites one to move beyond the symbolic language being used toward the infinite. On the other hand, contact with ordinary language prevents religious language from disappearing into the world of the imaginary.

JUSTIFICATION AND LIFE

The Pauline proclamation of salvation by "justification" calls attention to judicial terminology. From the beginning of the covenant he had established with Israel, God tried his people, the one that continually transgressed his covenant and by this fact found itself under verdict of condemnation. This had to be pronounced at God's tribunal,[20] at Christ's tribunal,[21] before which every human person was bound to appear, not only to undergo judgment but, most of all, to receive pardon. This is how Paul summed up a long indictment in which he convinced the Romans that all were "sinners," deprived of God's grace; that is to say, were cut off from the covenant relationship:

No one can justify himself before God. All who have sinned without the law will also perish without the law, and all who have sinned under the law will be judged by the law.

(Rom 2:12)

And this was so that he could finally exclaim:

But now the righteousness of God has been manifested.

(Rom 3:21)

Within the starting point of Paul's thought, then, a twofold experience holds sway: one involving sin and the other "God's righteousness." In judicial terminology, sin has to be "condemned" so that the guilty party can be "justified."[22] At Damascus, Paul all of a sudden realized that he was no longer under the Law's condemnation but that by faith he had been restored into the covenanted relationship.

What had happened, then, to lead to the declaration of both this condemnation and this justification?

God sent his own Son in the likeness of sinful flesh, and because of sin he condemned sin in the flesh.

(Rom 8:3)

For our sake [*God*] made him to be sin[23] who knew no sin, so that *through* him we might *obtain* the righteousness of God.

(2 Cor 5:21)

The "curse" held out by the Law was concentrated on Jesus, and it found itself to be transformed into a "blessing."[24]

How was it thus juridically possible that an individual's death procured rehabilitation for all? It is not appropriate to reply by basing ourselves on the conception of a "sacrifice for sin," which would have been of benefit to the multitude, for this would depend on cultic terminology and not on that of the juridical world. Moreover, in the preceding texts, the death undergone by Christ was simply the consequence of his having been sent into the sinful world. The suitable response was given in the treatment of Adam, a type of Jesus Christ:

Then as one man's trespass led to condemnation for all men, so one man's
acquittal leads to acquittal and life for all men.

(Rom 5:18)[25]

Paul takes for granted the universal consequence of one person's
action. No doubt, he speaks of Adam as the father of all human
beings, but he presupposes, as well, an anthropology different
from our own. A person is not simply an individual set next to
other individuals; he or she shares in the totality. To express this
thought, the Semites used a notion that in English is designated
as *corporate personality*.[26] While preserving Jacob's individuality,
the Jew knew that the patriarch was also Israel; that is, that in his
loins the whole people was contained. Within this perspective, the
actions of Adam, the ancestor of the human race, had significance
and meaning for all men and women, in such a way that they did
not belong only to him. However, the fact remains that the communitarian diversion of every personality remains a foundational
principle of this way of looking at things. We can call this an
objective "solidarity," real for every human person.[27] In Jesus'
case, Paul describes it vigorously and succinctly: "One has died
for all; therefore all have died" (2 Cor 5:14). Thereby he revealed
his conception of the human person. In addition also, he declares
his faith in the one who is the source of justification. In effect,
Jesus is not like Jacob or any other person, he is the one who is
"without sin," the "Just One."

In accepting the death of *the* sinless one, God condemned sin
in him; this man became *the* human person in whom and through
whom every believer has been reintegrated within the divine covenant. From the fact that Jesus was fully just, a new humanity
has, henceforward, been begun in him.

The reality is broader still. Paul knows that he is justified. So
this "judicial" terminology can induce a mistaken idea, and it
has. Is this justification a simple declaration of righteousness or
does it touch a person's interior being? A first reply can be formulated by means of the biblical notion of the Word. When God
speaks, things happen; his Word is an action. The presupposition
of juridical terminology is clearly expressed with the help of

the symbolism of individuals. This is how Paul will make matters precise.

Paul is aware of the process that vivifies plants in the organic world. At its base are the vegetable images he uses to make observations about the resurrection:

36 You! . . . What you sow does not come to life unless it dies. **37** And what you sow is not the body which is to be, but a bare kernel, perhaps of wheat or some other grain. **38** But God gives it a body as he has chosen, and to each kind of seed its own body.

(1 Cor 15:36–38)

In Paul's eyes, all vivification takes place beginning with a death, even in the case of the germination of plants. So it is as well for the believer. United with Christ's death, he or she comes to life with him. Here, then, is how the reality of baptism is best expressed, as union with Christ's death and resurrection, a passage from death to life. If Jesus' death is thus recognized as the origin of righteousness, his resurrection becomes the prototype of our new life:

3 Do you not know that all of us who have been baptized into Christ Jesus were baptized into his death?[128] **4** We were buried therefore with him (*synetaphēmen*) by baptism into death, so that as Christ was raised from the dead by the glory of the Father, we too might walk in newness of life.

(Rom 6:3–4)

What is this about? No longer is it a case of communion, which depends on the symbolism of assimilation, shown by the preposition *en*, ("in"), but of companionship, shown by the preposition *syn* ("with"). *Corporate personality* is the foundation of companionship with the death of Christ effected in baptism. In Paul's eyes, it was certain the glorified Christ extended the effects of the saving death of the Jesus of history: through the sacrament of baptism the Lord acts in all those who, by their faith, remain united to him. Every believer is thus bound to the event of Christ's cross. In him and with him we have died to sin; baptism symbolizes the absolute aspect of death, burial with the Crucified One.

A consequence follows: entry to a new life must from now on be modeled on the endless resurrection of the living Christ. It is this idea that Paul will apply to the new state of the baptized, in a development within which we detect a close paralleling of the state of the believer and that of Christ himself.

Paul's reasoning is quite simple. Having died with Christ, from now on we live with him, we "are a single plant," "we grow together."[29] The biological timetable is clearly pointed out: starting with death, we enter into life, and a life that is Christ's very life. This is what the following text, laid out in parallel columns, shows:

5 For if we have been united with him (*sym-phytoi*) in a death like his, we shall certainly be . . . in a resurrection [*like his*]. 6 We know that our old self was crucified with him (*syn-estaurōthē*) so that the sinful body might be destroyed, and we might no longer be enslaved to sin. 7 For he who has died is freed from sin.	→8 But if we have died with Christ, we believe that we shall also live with him (*sy-zēsomen*). 9 For we know that Christ being raised from the dead will never die again; death no longer has dominion over him. 10 The death he died he died to sin, once for all, but the life he lives he lives to God.

11 So you also must consider yourselves dead to sin and alive to God in Christ Jesus.

(Rom 6: 5–11)

Meeting Jesus on the cross, Paul experiences his acquittal, he is "rehabilitated," justified, and thereby lives a new life. Henceforth, the believer's state is described with the help of the preposition *syn*: to be "with," to be Jesus Christ's companion. The juridical symbolism finds its crowning point with the help of biological symbolism. In both cases, there is the reality of the transfer from a state of sin–death to the state of righteousness–life; the first tells of the changed condition, the second of the newness of life effected through death.

LIBERATION AND TRANSFORMATION

In addition to juridical terminology, the register of the world of "politics" ("power," domination, oppression) offered Paul another realm of possible expressions to articulate Jesus' death. In fact, the sinner's experience is not only that of being under merited condemnation, but it is also one of oppression from sin, the Law, from death, and finally, from Satan.

Moreover, we can easily grasp that it is by means of another preposition, *hypo*, that Paul's teaching is expressed. Here are several texts:

All are UNDER sin's power.

(Rom 3:9)

You are *no longer* UNDER the Law.

(Rom 6:15)

I am . . . sold UNDER sin.

(Rom 7:14)

Those who observe the Law are UNDER a curse.

(Gal 3:10)

The power of this image is such that Paul is not afraid of defining Jews as "those who are *under* the Law" and believers as those who are "*under* grace."[30] In keeping with this symbolism, we encounter verbs such as "to rule," "to dominate" (*kyrieuō*) and their opposites, "to set free," "to ransom." Death, sin, and the Law, then, come to "dominate,"[31] as if they were mocking the lordship of God and of Christ. The result is a state of slavery, of bondage to the powers; the strength of Paul's terminology is such that Paul comes to say that one is a "slave of righteousness"; sensing, however, that he may be straining the imagery too far, he quickly adds that he uses these all too human words "adapted to your weakness."[32]

Two experiences, doubtless, wrestled in Paul's mind as he sought to give meaning to a metaphor that belonged to the political order. The experience of slavery that was lived out around him, along with the horrors that led to such a condition, but, as well, the Bible's history and religious language. Slaves, then, were set free; but, also and above all, the Hebrew people had been freed from Egypt's bondage and from the Babylonian captivity. This political terminology made possible the means to speak of a transfer from one condition to another: liberation.

There was another set of terms, this one also deriving from the symbolic world of social relationships, but this time in a commercial sense that spoke of the same liberation: that of "ransom." According to family law, the *go'el* (from the Hebrew *ga'al*: "to deliver") was the closest kin on whom devolved the task of buying back goods and persons who had become an alien's property. The Bible applied this designation, *go'el*, to YHWH, Israel's redeemer, thus stressing his familial bond with the people. According to commercial law, one bought back (in Hebrew *pâdâ*: "to deliver against an equivalent") the life of the firstborn or of slaves by means of a ransom. When applied to YHWH buying back Israel,[33] the metaphor drops any reference to a sum of money paid out; the focus is entirely on God who frees from a hopeless condition. Such is the origin of the word *redemption*, whose meaning evidently derives from the fact that God sets his people free from slavery; that is, from sin.

Through his death on the cross, Christ has thus set us free,[34] bought us back,[35] snatched us from,[36] drawn us out of[37] the state of sin, by an act whose effect is not imaginary (as it would be in the Hellenistic mystery cults) but is brought about in the ordinary life of the believer through a constant and progressive "liberation." Paul illustrates this by drawing out the obligation resulting from the new state effected by baptism. The demand of the "new life" (already manifest in the preceding symbolism) is expressed by the slave-free antithesis. This is what Paul says in the follow-up to the text quoted above:

12 Let not sin therefore reign in your mortal bodies, to make you obey their passions. 13 Do not yield your members to sin as instruments of wickedness, but yield yourselves to God as men who have been brought from death to life, and your members to God as instruments of righteousness. 14 For sin will have no dominion over you, since you are not under law but under grace.

(Rom 6:12–14)

A new state follows then; that of freed slaves.

16 Do you not know that if you yield yourselves to any one as obedient slaves, you are slaves of the one whom you obey, either of sin, which leads to death, or of obedience, which leads to righteousness? 17 But thanks be to God, that you who were once slaves of sin have become obedient from the heart to the standard of teaching to which you were committed, 18 and, having been set free from sin, have become slaves of righteousness. 19 I am speaking in human terms, because of your natural limitations. For just as you once yielded your members to impurity and to greater and greater iniquity, so now yield your members to righteousness for sanctification.

20 When you were slaves of sin, you were free in regard to righteousness. 21 But then what return did you get from the things of which you are now ashamed? The end of those things is death. 22 But now that you have been set free from sin and have become slaves of God, the return you get is sanctification and its end, eternal life. 23 For the wages of sin is death, but the free gift of God is eternal life in Christ Jesus our Lord.

(Rom 6:16–23)

Indeed, in all truth, Paul's mind was captivated by the slave/free antithesis. Jesus' death set a condition into motion, an "indicative": liberation, by means of baptism, caused me to die to sin. An "imperative" follows from this: the task of always and everywhere setting myself free. I have to live. Unlike Jesus, who died once for all and accordingly is fully free, my baptismal death is a death only in Jesus, and, not yet, in myself; that death of his has to become actualized in the concrete fabric of my ordinary life. The "following of Jesus" that was typical of the earthly life of Jesus of Nazareth has become, for Paul, following the preceding symbolism, a companionship with the Christ who is alive. According to this symbolism, it becomes an entering into the liberty of God's children.[38]

The same new state is described at another time with the help of the metaphor of a child who is *under* a pedagogue's tutelage and who, having once become an adult, is set free. The advantage of this last metaphor is that it clearly shows the definitive accession to a new condition, that of sonship[39] or daughtership.

The political symbolism of liberation attempts to describe the arrival at a new condition, one that inaugurates the radical transformation of one's being. This transformation does not consist merely in a simple reversal of states, as if the preposition *above* succeeded the preposition *under*; it gets expressed with the aid of another symbol, from the biological order. This latter is difficult to disentangle, for if we are to believe G. Theissen, it originates in what is evidently a mythological realm: saved beings exist in the likeness of their savior. They are assimilated to their redeemer, whose relatives they become even to the extent of a configuration to them. Thus, it is by the use of the metaphors of "image" and "form" (or structure) that the change in one's being is described as that of being freed from slavery or tutelage; the glory itself is mentioned as the agent bringing about the transformation, for it is the attribute of the Savior Jesus.

At the core of his reflection, Paul locates phenomena drawn from nature, which he describes as "differences" in brightness, appearance and form: heavenly bodies and earthly bodies. He believes he is justified in reckoning as possible the radical transformation of a person's being; that is to say, his or her "image":

Just as we have borne the image of the man of dust, we shall also bear the image of the man of heaven.

(1 Cor 15:49)

For we have been

predestined to be conformed to the image of his Son.

(Rom 8:29)

This transformation happens progressively by means of the glory that floods our being and transfigures our face, provided that this transforming power is truly set free in us:

And we all, with unveiled face, beholding the glory of the Lord, are being changed from one degree of glory to another; for this comes from the Lord who is the Spirit.

(2 Cor 3:18)

This activity of the Lord's glory is at work through the glory of Christ, who is God's image:

For it is the God who said, "Let light shine out of darkness," who has shone in our hearts to give the light of the knowledge of the glory of God in the face of Christ.

(2 Cor 4:6)

These verses would require lengthy explanations; we must restrict ourselves to establishing that the believer still lives on earth and that, nonetheless, he is being worked on by a secret power:

20 But our commonwealth is in heaven, and from it we await a Savior, the Lord Jesus Christ, **21** who will change our lowly body to be like his glorious body, by the power which enables him even to subject all things to himself.

(Phil 3:20–21)

The Lord is not limited, then, to setting people free from slavery and freeing people from bondage; he continues to work, not like a master who makes use of many slaves, but from within; progressively flooding into the hearts of those who have been set free in this way so that they can enter the world of love. This is what is being described quite strikingly by the third kind of symbolism, that of reconciliation and assimilation.

RECONCILIATION AND ASSIMILATION

The ways in which are depicted the relationship between God and human persons are varied; so, too, are the symbols used. While the two earlier symbols stressed at the outset the dominant state of the judge or the master, in this third set of symbols interpersonal relationships come to the fore. These presume that neither party is above or below the other, but that they are both on the same level. So, the Bible tells of the covenant set up by God with Israel as one between two partners who, even if originally they were not on an equal footing (the initiative was solely God's), dealt with one another as equals: a kind of contract joined them, mediating terms that were to be observed reciprocally.

As in relationships between human persons, although in this case only one was such, there came about a breach of the understanding, hatred, division, but there was also, between both, reconciliation, love, union. The dominant images are those of separation and assimilation.

In such a symbolism, sin is separation from God, a breaking of the covenant. Paul sees all humanity in this state of rupture when he alludes to the golden calf, with which the Hebrews, by preferring a graven image to the living God, broke the covenant with the Lord.[40] Men and women were, in this way, separated from God and in a state of hostility. But through Christ's cross, reconciliation was brought about. From the enemy that it had been, humankind recovered God's friendship and nearness.

This is what Paul proclaims with joy and triumphantly:

1 Therefore, since we are justified by faith we have peace with God through our Lord Jesus Christ. **2** Through him we have obtained access to this grace in which we stand . . . . **10** For, if while we were enemies we were reconciled to God by the death of his Son, now that we are reconciled, shall we be saved by faith.

(Rom 5:1–2,10)

Paul exults and reckons that his ministry consists precisely in the proclamation of this decisive event:

18 All this is from God, who through Christ reconciled us to himself and gave us the ministry of reconciliation; **19** that is, God was in Christ reconciling the world to himself, not counting their trespasses against them, and entrusting to us the message of reconciliation.

(2 Cor 5:18–19)

In his later letters, Paul extends to the cosmic universe the effect of the reconciliation of humanity with God:

19 For in him all the fullness of God was pleased to dwell, **20** and through him to reconcile to himself all things, whether on earth or in heaven, making peace by the blood of his cross.

(Col 1:19–20)

Underlying this idea of reconciliation is the idea of coming near to, or that of nonseparation. Paul can also dream of an ideal era:

35 Who will separate us from the love of Christ? . . . . **38** For I am sure that neither death, nor life, nor angels, nor principalities, nor things present, nor things to come, nor powers, **39** nor height, nor depth, nor anything else in all creation, will be able to separate us from (*chorizein apo*) the love of God in Christ Jesus our Lord.

(Rom 8:35,38–39)

So, reconciliation is obtained by the superabundant love of God himself and of Christ. This is what is being said, now no longer negatively by the specter of separation (*apo*), but rather positively through the reality of love that unites and is at work on behalf of, in favor of (*hyper*) sinners.[41] It is remarkable to note that, though absent from the two earlier symbols, the formula "to die for" is not found except in association with an allusion to "love." Any idea of substitution seems, then, to be missing from the expression. Here are some examples:

6 *Yes*, while we were yet helpless, at the right time, Christ died for the ungodly. . . . **8** But God shows his love for us in that while we were yet sinners Christ died for us.

(Rom 5:6,8)

Jesus takes the initiative, he is active, though earlier his death had been considered as an object whose worth people speculated about. This is because we remain in the symbolic realm of interpersonal relationships, which possesses an affective connotation. To the "objective" description corresponds Paul's subjective experience, one worthwhile for every believer, and one within which a real, grateful tenderness can be perceived:

I live by faith in the Son of God, who loved me and gave himself for me.

(Gal 2:20)

Jesus in this way manifested his love for me when, without resisting, he "gave himself up" to the iniquity of men and women, perfectly abandoning himself to God's will in utter confidence in the one who could free him from death. In the "for me" in which Paul trusts, we find an echo of the texts of the Last Supper, without, however, their eventual cultic connotation. By his deed, Jesus began a dialogue with every human person: his love expressed in total fidelity bound him indissolubly with every believer. Is this not the meaning that Jesus foretold at his last meal, when he desired to sustain an abiding relationship with his disciples after his death? This was his love, going so far as to give himself in death, which founded the definitive relationship with believers.

In fact, Paul extended to everyone his conviction of being loved in this way as a unique individual. Thus, in order to get his Corinthians to set love above every kind of exalted knowledge (that kind which let them eat meat sacrificed to idols), Paul thrashed his correspondents in the following terms:

And so by your knowledge this weak man is destroyed, the brother for whom Christ died.

(1 Cor 8:11; cf. Rom 4:5)

Having entered the core of love that explained the ultimate disposition of Jesus of Nazareth, Paul can insert into this primordial mystery every relationship that human persons have with one another. For example,

Husbands, love your wives, as Christ loved the Church and gave himself up for her.

(Eph 5:25)

The language of a love that surrenders self for others is not put on to offend the sensibilities of his contemporaries, as long as we do not so interpret the "for me" or the "for us" so that Jesus becomes a substitute for sinners.[42] This would mean departing from the symbolic terminology of interpersonal relationships to enter upon the sacrificial outlook of the old Law.

Jesus' love, thus, was revealed in that he gave his life out of faithfulness to God and to humans. Fair enough! But Paul goes further and, as a believing Jew, goes back to the original source of love, God himself. Basing himself on the biblical principle according to which every good deed must be attributed to God personally, Paul so interprets the unique instance of Jesus Christ surrendering his life out of love:

God *proved* his love for us in that while we were yet sinners Christ died for us.

(Rom 5:8)

Paul even allows a note of tenderness to surface when he probably alludes to Abraham, who led his son Isaac to the place of sacrifice:

[God] who did not spare his own Son but gave him up for us all, will he not also give us all things with him?

(Rom 8:32)

Even today, and without difficulty, we can say in faith that God reconciled us with himself through the death of his Son, as long as we understand that this death is not an isolated happening that possesses some magical power to obtain the salvation of humanity but that, rather, in keeping with the authentic tradition about Jesus of Nazareth, it is the primary expression of a state of faithfulness, as is pointed out in the hymn preserved in the Epistle to the Philippians:

Though [Jesus] was in the form of God, he did not count equality with God a thing to be grasped, **7** but emptied himself taking the form of a servant, being born in the likeness of men. **8** And being found in human form he humbled himself and became obedient unto death, even death on a cross. **9** Therefore God has highly exalted him and bestowed on him the name which is above every name, **10** that at the name of Jesus every knee should bow, in heaven and on earth and under the earth, **11** and every tongue confess that Jesus Christ is Lord, to the glory of God the Father.

(Phil 2:6–11)

If love is the ground of all reconciliation, it tends as well to communion, even to the impossible fusion of beings. This is not merely a case of companionship (*syn*) or of transformation of a being, but one of assimilation, of union, of in-dwelling. This individual symbolism is seen here in two states, that of sexual union and that of nourishment.

Paul compares union with Christ to that of a man with a prostitute, and he declares that he who joins himself to a prostitute becomes but "a single body" with her.[43] And, he goes on, so it is with the believer and Christ Jesus, but with this difference, however: they become together "a single spirit." Undoubtedly, the term "body" signifies a single "person," but Paul wants to emphasize by the word "spirit" that in this way the believer and Christ reach the utter depths of a being, at that very point where nothing enters in, the very secret of existing life.[44]

In the same sense, it is fitting to interpret the breaking down and abolition of barriers between the sexes and between races: you are all *one* in Christ Jesus, he says; not one thing, but one being, so profound is this communion with Christ.

The other symbolism is that of food. Apropos of the Eucharist, Paul states,

16 The bread which we break, is it not a *communion* [*koinōnia*] in the body of Christ? **17** Because there is one bread, we who are many are one body, for we all partake of the one bread.

(1 Cor 10:16–17)

To eat means, in fact, to totally assimilate the other; it means to transform the other into oneself, but with the difference, in this instance, that it is the believer who is transformed into Christ. Though the quality of persons may appear to be absorbed, in fact it continues because it is really a case of persons who remain in a loving dialogue. One could say that the banquet of the Lord who gives himself as nourishment expresses the most perfect of all unions between beings. Now at last, perhaps we can better understand why to celebrate the Eucharist is "to proclaim the Lord's death until he comes," for love and death are bound together.

Finally, the preposition that is used to denominate this new state of being is no longer *syn* ("with") but *en* ("in"), with the depth of meaning that "in Christ Jesus" signifies. There is no need to elaborate on this in a work devoted to Jesus and Paul facing death.[45]

To conclude our investigation into the symbolism of Pauline terminology, it is appropriate to show how the three spheres of the judicial, the political and the interpersonal, complemented by the three realms of the vivifying, the transforming, and the assimilating, cannot be adequate separately, to describe the complexity of "redemption." It is in their mutual interrelationships that the mystery itself can be attended to.

This fact has already been made evident in the prevailing relationships in each of the two kinds of symbolism, the social and the individual. Let us make this more precise in the further case of those relationships obtaining within the three kinds of social symbols. Justification juridically sanctions the cessation of the political conflicts of domination, and reconciliation deepens the relationship between parties who had been opposed. However, only in love is a personal relationship brought about, and this is so not merely by the very statement of grace that constitutes "justification." Lastly, we observe that a single relationship ties the three symbols together. Vivification is expressed by a radical structural transformation, but this can have no meaning except when a profound communion is thereby established between beings.

The considerations mentioned above describe victory over sin, the victory that Paul contemplated when he faced Jesus on the cross. These can be fleshed out by an examination of the manner in which Paul understands the role of Jesus' death when he considered it in the light of two institutions, the Law and sacrifices.

CHRIST'S DEATH AND GOD'S PLAN

Paul was not satisfied with detailing the effects of Christ's death in the lives of believers: justification, liberation, and reconciliation. He was equally at pains to locate this event within God's plan. In fact, his new faith did not lead him to renounce Israel's heritage; for it was the same God who established and then reconstituted the covenant. Far from it. Considering himself to be the authentic heir of his forebears, Paul had to take account of God's interventions in Israel's history. In doing this, Paul did as Jesus had done when, we noted earlier,[46] he gave the death that threatened him a context by referring to events that had marked Israel's pilgrimage under God's ruling hand, namely he saw this death as a share in the tragic destiny of the prophets and of the persecuted Just One. In this way, Jesus gave an impulse to the outlook that typified the primitive Church: those events experienced by him and afterward by the first Christians were seen to have unfolded "according to the Scriptures." Contrary to what we ordinarily think, with this maxim the Church did not try to prove the truth of her facts; rather, the Church attempted to clarify them by situating them within a bigger framework, that is, within God's customary ways as the Bible would have us conceive them. This striking return to the past shows us that the life and death of Jesus were perceived as an eschatological happening, that is, as an event that had "entered upon the end of the ages,"[47] one that gave meaning to every person's life: the Jesus Christ event possessed definitive and universal value.

In his own case, Paul spontaneously clung to the formula "according to the Scriptures," for example, by reworking it and the tradition he had received:

3 Christ died for our sins in accordance with the scriptures . . . . 4 he was raised on the third day in accordance with the scriptures.

(1 Cor 15:3–4)

Paul not only had recourse to a sacred text to justify his propositions[48] or to discover in them the promise, which had been foretold;[49] rather, by doing original work on the tradition concerning Jesus of Nazareth, he also concentrated his focus on those two modes of presence God had institutionalized in the course of past history: the Law and sacrificial worship.

Now, the convenant proposed by God to Israel had been grounded in two ways. First, God's will had been expressed in the Law that Israel undertook to keep; secondly, since this covenant meant liberation from slavery, it demanded of Israel certain cultic practices by means of which the nation manifested to God her repentance and petition for forgiveness. Thus the divine blessing came to be bestowed on the people; then they, having obtained reconciliation by means of their sacrifices, put the Law's commandments into practice.

CHRIST'S DEATH AND GOD'S LAW

The first problem Paul faced after his turnabout on the Damascus Road was the worth of the Law, which quite definitively had condemned Jesus to death on the cross.

By the "Law," Paul understood not the first five books of the Bible, "the Pentateuch," but the Jewish religious system according to whose observance practicing God's commandments had been required for maintaining the covenant and the gift of the blessing. Paul's thought about the Law is highly nuanced and there is no need to hold on onesidedly to the vigorous critique of it which he enunciated. Unable in a few lines to offer anything but a glimpse of the Pauline conception of the Law,[50] I will follow the argumentation of Paul in his letter to the Galatians, which has three phases.[51]

In the first stage of his thinking, Paul juxtaposes Law and Promise. In his eyes, the Law is holy and good because it was given by God to indicate his will. Independent of the minutiae into which the legalistic interpreters had fallen, the Law demanded of the believer flawless observance. However, St. Paul declares, this is an impossible thing. The other side of the coin is that for any person who does not practice it integrally, the Law is the source of a curse instead of a blessing. But how can one extricate oneself from such a fatal trap?

With a bold freedom Jesus had situated observance of the Law within a context of faith and interiority, the very kind of position that the prophets had taken against stiff-necked Israel.[52] Paul scarcely spoke with this kind of authority. But neither in his genius had he suppressed the Law; instead, he situated it within God's plan vis-à-vis something much greater than the Law, namely the blessing it was meant to assure. Four hundred years earlier than the gift of the Law to Moses, the blessing had been promised to Abraham. From this fact it followed that the blessing itself depended not on observance of the Law but on the totally free promise. And this promise was made to all who trusted in God. Accordingly, it is not religious observance, but faith, which makes someone just and obtains for him or her the blessing of the divine covenant.

In the second part of his reasoning, Paul maintained that the inheritor of the blessing was not Isaac but rather Jesus Christ. He was Abraham's true descendant. When Jesus, faithful to the end, expired on the cross, all the curses entailed by the Law died with him. The Law itself died with Christ, not insofar as it was the expression of God's will, but in its function as a means of salvation. In order to express this fact, Paul made use of the terminology of ransom that earlier he had employed with reference to sin:

Christ redeemed us from the curse of the Law, having become a curse for us—for it is written, "Cursed be everyone who hangs on a tree."

(Gal 3:13)

Jesus' death on the cross effected an irreversible rupture within the course of history. Before this death, for centuries, God had sanctioned his covenant with Israel through the mediation of the Law. Henceforth, this covenant is fulfilled directly in Christ.

Through a comparison that seems strange today, Paul in another place shows how he has made the transition from the Law to another master. He observes that just as a woman "subject to a man" is only bound to her husband for the duration of the latter's life, so the believer is bound to the Law (*nomos*) only as long as this latter[53] is still alive. Paul did not delay long enough on this question to make all the points of comparison (as if it were the Law that had died and the believer who had survived); what interested him was to show that the bond between a believer and the Law has been definitively severed by death. So Paul could conclude: since, through the mediation of the crucified body of Christ, the *nomos* has died, henceforth we belong to someone else, to the risen Jesus, the Christ.

You have died to the Law through the body of Christ, so that you may belong to another, to him who has been raised from the dead in order that we may bear fruit for God.

(Rom 7:4)

Therefore, his conclusion follows:

For freedom Christ has set us free.

(Gal 5:1)

Paul spoke of the Law in two different ways. On the one hand, he categorically rejected it: henceforth, it no longer serves as a source of life—it has been supplanted by faith; from this vantage, it is considered as a practice that wrongly claims to be a source of justification. On the other hand, Paul praises it: it is spiritual for it is the very work of God; above all it is summed up in the commandment of love, which alone constitutes the "law of Christ."[54] This twofold aspect of the Law had been made clear to Paul when he was turned around to face the visage of the Risen Lord. The Law's ambiguity had been exploded. Paul understood that in the spirit of the Jews it had usurped a role it ought never to have claimed to play, that of conferring righteousness. Indeed the Law continues to point to righteousness, but it cannot confer it. By pointing out sin, however, the Law had played a salutary role in that, like a pedagogue or, ever better, a warden, it kept the human person conscious of his or her sinful condition and full of hope of the definitive salvation that, along with the promised blessing, would not come except by means of the Spirit given by Christ on the cross.[55]

With this mention of the Holy Spirit, we come to the third stage of Paul's reasoning. In keeping with the Old Testament, which dreamed of a new covenant according to which the divine Law would be inscribed not on tablets of stone but on hearts, Paul showed that in Jesus Christ, the Spirit given to men and women is the very blessing promised to Abraham.

> . . . That in Christ Jesus the blessing of Abraham might come upon the Gentiles, that we might receive the promise of the Spirit through faith.
>
> (Gal 3:14)

The Spirit poured forth into hearts has taken the place of the letter of the Law.[56] In this way Christ has put an end to the reign of the Law by inaugurating the new and definitive reign of the Spirit.

Let us try to make Paul's thought relevant for today. In criticizing the Law of the Old Testament, Paul denounces the ambiguousness of every law, and of every practice of religious observances. Paul does not reject a "code" as one might reject a secondary element over against some kind of "essence" because every concrete will necessarily finds expression in an external code. More precisely, according to biblical terminology, law, insofar as it remains an exterior code, finds fulfillment in the "Law of Christ." This is to say that only Christ gives meaning to whatever law exists. Thanks to the illumination that comes, not by human intelligence solely but from the Holy Spirit, the law of Christ preserves the positive element of the ancient Law. However, just as the Law served only as a pedagogue until the coming of the Christ, who would fulfill it, so from now on every law possesses no worth except as a pointer. From this we draw a weighty conclusion: the "law of Christ" itself, even though it is the fruit of the Spirit and, when put into practice, leads anew to the Spirit, runs the risk of becoming codified.

If by his death Christ put an end to the Jewish law, this was so only to the extent that the Law represented a rule of salvation that in fact was insufficient; with Christ the Law passes over into the realm of the Spirit. And, in turn, the Spirit, makes possible knowledge and observance of the law. We reiterate this in another way. The law bursts in two: on the one hand its purpose passes over into the sphere of the Spirit; on the other hand, its imperfect residue finds expression in the "flesh."[57] As long as the spirit has not absorbed the flesh, there remains between the two a radical antagonism. The Law passes into the domain of the Spirit insofar as it alone can make possible the observance of exterior prescriptions; it passes over also into the domain of Christ insofar as he expresses the Law in its fulness, which is love. It would equally be an illusion to state that every law has lapsed, as it would be to pretend that one would observe the law without acknowledging that only the word of Christ, understood in the Spirit, gives it meaning.[58]

CHRIST'S DEATH AND SACRIFICIAL EXPIATION

In addition to the problem presented by the gift of the Law, Paul was faced with another question that was no less delicate: what had become of the sacrifices his people had offered, the very ones through which, until his return from Damascus, he had hoped for reconciliation with God? At the core of his being Paul thought that, if Christ had put an end to the Law's yoke, he had also set Jewish worship free. Here is how he would henceforth characterize Christian worship:

> Therefore, I exhort you, brothers, in the name of God's mercy, to offer yourselves as a living sacrifice, holy and pleasing to God: this is to be your spiritual worship.
>
> (Rom 12:11)

This is the life of authentic charity that worshipfully expresses one's relationship with God: the sacrifice of Christians is to be found in their lives, in their service to others, in their almsgiving.[59]

Nevertheless, in keeping with that early tradition that regarded Jesus' last meal as a covenant sacrifice,[60] Paul also interpreted Jesus' death as a sacrificial expiation. Does this imply that, in his eyes, Christ's cross ought to be reckoned within the class of ritual sacrifices? Numerous authors think so; but others, on the

contrary, would go so far as to eliminate such sacrificial terminology entirely. In reality, is it not evident that such language is
secondary in Paul's writing since, outside of the traditional narrative of the Last Supper, it only occurs in three other places?
Besides, the symbols that prevail are those of justification, of liberation from sin and of reconciliation, ones we described earlier
without there being need for us to mention any ritual aspect of
sacrifice.

While all this holds true, it remains indispensable for us today
to be precise about the exact meaning of the sacrificial interpretation, especially since this interpretation still belongs to current
terminology. Accordingly, we will attempt to situate the affirmations of the primitive tradition and of Paul within the history
of sacrifices.[61]

Whether it be social or individual in type, sacrificial terminology
is symbolic language analogous to that which was described in the
first section of this chapter. In this case, the issue is that of a human
relationship to the deity; to foster this, human beings spontaneously devised a system of prohibitions that had to be kept (indicating the sacredness of the deity) and a system of reparation
for transgressions committed. Such reparation had to be carried
out (in order to restore communication with God). Thus there
was begun a relationship between God and human persons, one
that was maintained by means of taboos and sacrifices. So, human
persons were placed within a system wherein God, like a lord,
imposed on them certain rules, certain rites as means of communication. This relationship with God was conceived in the manner of an exchange of goods or gifts, the human agents being
bound to prescriptions that, in fact, they had themselves imposed
in God's name. As R. Girard so well put it, human beings thus
projected onto God their very own violence and they caused it to
turn back against themselves.[62]

It would be erroneous to so understand the rites of the Old
Testament in the preceding way, as if Israel had not entirely transformed the meaning of sacrifices by way of her own experience

of the God of history. Without doubt it often preserved rites akin to those of the ancient religions, but their meaning of them had been deeply modified.

We will take up again an effort at defining sacrifice in the Old Testament.[63] By sacrifice, we mean an animal or vegetable offering to God, presented to God on an altar and withdrawn by means of its partial or entire destruction from any profane use. The symbolism appears more clearly in animal sacrifice because of the significance given in the Bible to blood: the blood represented life itself, something that belongs to God alone and that could not be consumed along with the animal's flesh.[64] The immolation (the putting to death of an animal) had no particular meaning; the flesh was roasted and shared among the faithful as a meal, while the blood was poured out on the altar, which symbolized God himself.[65] What precisely was going on? A believer or a people sought intimacy with God through the sharing of an irrevocable gift. The offerers sought to bridge the gap created between themselves and God by sin or by the violation of a prohibition. They symbolized this desire by an offering, and they approached God through the mediation of the blood poured out on the altar. Thanks to this "expiation,"[66] God himself re-established contact with them and rendered them pleasing anew to his eyes. The covenant was symbolically renewed; communion was rediscovered.

The ritual sacrifice of the Jews was principally represented by the Feast of the Great Pardon or Atonement (*kippourim*, from *kipper*: "to cover, to pardon," "to expiate"): God pardoned the sins of the whole people, who were somehow gathered together in the people present before him; he proclaimed his pardon by accepting the rite of the sprinkling of blood on an enormous golden table adorned with two golden cherubim, set up underneath the ark (which corresponded to the altar of Sinai), YHWH's throne, where of old he had communicated his commands.[67] This "propitiatory" (*kapporet*) was the place where God, who was present, remitted the sins of the entire people. The High Priest, on this occasion only, entered into the Holy of Holies[68] in order to carry out the rite of the sprinkling of the blood on the golden table and, afterward, on the people; yet it was God alone who "erased, covered" the sins.

Another sacrifice, also fundamental to Jewish worship, was the paschal sacrifice that commemorated, by means of the paschal lamb, their liberation from bondage in Egypt, the prototype of liberation from sin[69] and the date of birth of the Jewish people as such. It was *the* sacrifice above all others observed in Jesus' time and that of Paul.

Essential differences, accordingly, distinguished Jewish sacrifices from the violent sacrifices of the other Mediterranean religions. We single out one in particular. The Jewish notion of sacrifice did not include the destruction of a victim that would have been offered in exchange (substitution) for a human person or as a reparation for sin or as a blood debt to be paid to a wrathful deity. When the Old Testament spoke of blood, it thought not of suffering but of life.

To these differences, we add this observation, that paralleling sacrificial practice ran a current of thought that spiritualized worship; it was an idea very strongly felt in Judaism. Faced with the kind of formalism that had already been denounced by the prophets,[70] some believers questioned the ritual aspect of bloody sacrifices and joined the adherents of the covenant in their hearts,[71] as, for example, the Baptist sect did.

Furthermore, in the same era, a sapiential current of thought extended a relationship with God to every person and, bypassing the rites of Jewish worship, situated sacrifice in the interior offering;[72] the writing *Pseudo-Philo* preserved only the practice of bread offerings.[73] Similarly, the current of thought represented at Qumran or among the Therapeutists limited themselves to offering sacred meals.[74]

Finally, it is fitting to recall how the first Christians put great emphasis on the fourth of the Servant of YHWH songs, a poem that had been practically ignored in the Jewish tradition,[75] for in it Christians found so many similarities to Christ's death. For, when the Servant "gives his life," we find in this the transformation of a ritual sacrifice into a personal sacrifice; that is, the esteeming of the love that was the basis of the sacrifice (which thereby essentially points to the "gift of self"), even if there was detected in the offering of self a "sacrifice of expiation." To the definition of sacrifice given above we may thus fittingly adduce the possibility of a "personal" interpretation of Christ's sacrifice.

It is now time for us to run through the three passages in which Paul made use of the tradition to state that Christ had fulfilled the Jewish sacrifices by his death.

The first passage evidently makes allusion to the paschal ritual since it allegorizes the believer's need "to purify (oneself) from the old leaven so as to become a batch of unleavened dough," a clear transposition of Jewish terms dealing with the radical cleansing of the house in which the Passover meal was to be celebrated. This was done to root out every trace of fermentation before the paschal lamb was consumed. In this context, Paul could add, "Christ, our Passover, has been immolated" (1 Cor 5:7), not in the sense that Christ then would be the ritual sacrifice above all others, but in the sense that he had himself in his very being replaced the Jewish rituals, and this by means of the obedience he had manifested right up to his death on the cross.[76]

In the second passage (1 Cor 10:16–22), Paul has inherited the eucharistic formula according to which the covenant is established in the blood of Christ, his body having been handed over "for you."[77] The context in which Paul spoke of the Eucharist, namely his defense of Christians eating meat that had been sacrificed to idols, shows that he saw in the eucharistic liturgy a practice analogous to pagan sacrifices.[78] What does this mean? From the context, we conclude that the eucharistic practice was thus properly depicted as a sacrificial rite; but this does not signify thereby that Jesus' death itself was equivalent, in Paul's eyes, to a ritual sacrifice: on the contrary, the tradition to which Paul adhered was oriented to the personal sacrifice of Jesus who obediently gave his life and so re-established the covenant.

Finally, we come to the third passage, the one in which Paul most explicitly refers to the sacrificial tradition of the Old Testament:

23 All have sinned and have been deprived of God's glory; **24** but they have been freely justified by his grace by means of the deliverance fulfilled in Christ Jesus, **25** the one whom God destined to be the instrument of propitiation through his blood, which is received by faith.

(Rom 3:23–25)

Let us enumerate the characteristics of Jesus' "sacrifice."[79] "Deliverance" (Gk. *apolytrōsis,* "redemption") comes about not by Jewish rites but through Jesus Christ. How? By Jesus' becoming himself the essence of what happened on the occasion of the Jewish Feast of the Great Pardon, that is to say, becoming our reconciliation with God. Henceforth, reconciliation is effected not by animals being sacrificed but by Jesus' personal mediation, and this mediation is accomplished through his blood. We must carefully refrain from regarding this "blood" from the perspective of the bloody sacrifices in other religions, or even within the framework of Jewish sacrifices, as if Jesus had shed his blood in the way sacrificed animals do. Jesus' blood corresponds to that of YHWH's Servant who "gave his life" for the many. As we see, Paul thus found himself at the confluence of the various currents that animated Jewish spirituality. Certainly he evoked thoughts of the feast of Yom Kippur, just as he also alluded to the paschal festival, and as he took a position on pagan sacrifices. But this terminology is simply a support for a reality that infinitely exceeds ancient practices.

If the preceding description stands established, do we have to conclude from it that we must forego use of even the word "sacrifice"? Such a solution, it appears to me, would be too drastic. The tradition has preserved the term and, since in the past it underwent a constant evolution tending toward an ever greater degree of spitualization, so it should help us today in prolonging the transformation of the communication now existing between God and humankind. This communication no longer goes on by means of taboos and rituals but is sustained in the dialogue between God and human persons. Or, rather, it is God who takes up the human's role. Let me explain. No longer is it the case that men and women offer sacrifice to God, rather now God hands his Son over to them. From that symbolic order of communication exercised by means of sacrificial victims, we pass over to the order of interpersonal communication in the gratuity of love. So now it remains possible to speak of "sacrifice," but on condition that in so doing we pick up echoes of the firmly rooted disposition of ecstatic dialogue Jesus expects in his disciples: "The one who loses his life keeps it safe; the one who wants to hold on to his life, loses it . . . . Anyone who does not deny self cannot be my disciple."

As St. Paul says, we are no longer children bound by the guardianship of law and sacrifices, but we are sons and daughters who, through the Spirit, can enter into dialogue with God himself. To give expression to Christ's death there is no need now to refer to the sacrifices of the Old Testament, except to note their end, their disappearance: in Christ Jesus the cultic order is dead and has ceded its place to the Spirit. This is what Jesus said so magnificently to the Samaritan woman: "The hour is coming when true worshippers will adore the Father in spirit and in truth."[80]

CONCLUSION

It is not our intention to take up again the main points of a treatise on the "redemption"; however, it is appropriate to pull together some points gleaned from our investigation into Pauline thought, particularly from the perspective of the terms Paul held onto.

1. Our first observation concerns the plurality of terms Paul used to declare what Christ's death on the cross meant. Among the wide variety of expressions that were possible, one in particular among them seems to have been relegated to secondary status: the cultic interpretation found in only three texts in all the Pauline writings. And yet, doubtless because of an unfortunate interpretation given to the Epistle to the Hebrews,[81] this one interpretation has for so long dominated Christian teaching. We have had to insist then, that in Paul the cultic terminology of the Old Testament has been transformed into existential language. Moreover,

in this transformation it linked up with the usage found in the New Testament as a whole. Whenever cultic terminology continues to be employed, this is so only in regard to Old Testament realities,[82] to describe how Jesus fulfilled these by his personal "sacrifice,"[83] or, lastly, to describe the worship that henceforth characterizes Christian existence as "spiritual worship."[84]

2. In the second place, we take note of presuppositions one ought to have in mind when hearing Paul's terminology. A first presupposition is that of the existence of God, the God who made a covenant with humanity through Israel and who intends to persevere right to the end in his commitment. A second presupposition is that humankind is sinful; men and women broke the covenant established by God and henceforth they abide in a state of bondage, in a ruptured relationship. Out of this arises the problem of how to conciliate, how to reconcile the two parties to the agreement forming the covenant. Finally, a third presupposition is that Jesus, the Just One, has become by virtue of his resurrection the Lord of all humanity, and so all that he was and all that he did possesses universal significance.

3. Armed with these three principles, what, then, does the death of Jesus mean in Paul's eyes? It is that we share in a renewal process and that we are living a "rendering explicit" of the words of Jesus himself.

Essentially, Jesus' death was the crowning of a life of faithfulness, of love for God and for the human race. His death possesses no worth in itself, as if it could magically suffice to bring about special effects, as if it had been desired by Jesus or by God as a definite means to salvation. Jesus was "delivered over" to death; God "delivered" his own Son up to death. This means that their love was such that nothing asked was repugnant to Jesus; it means that Jesus went to the end in meeting the requirements of faithfulness.

4. Such terminology was satisfactory to express the fact that Christ's death delivers from the slavery of sin; other terms declared that sinners had been justified or had been reconciled with God. Other terms deepened the reality so described by using sym-

bols associated with individual personal experiences: birth into life, gradual transformation, assimilation to another. Finally, the human symbolism describing the relationship between God and humankind was recast from top to bottom. No longer were there to be instances of communicating with God by means of animal or vegetable sacrifices (supposed to represent man's disposition) or by observances that put men and women under the yoke of a crushing law. Rather, each person was invited to commune with God through the loving Spirit poured into our hearts, which builds up the body of Christ.

5. Appreciating the symbolism underlying the various terms regarding "redemption"allows us to take them seriously without at the same time letting ourselves be snared by these words. However, this is precisely what happened when people applied literally to God human realities while at the same time they lost sight of their metaphorical nature. Thus, people spoke of sin's "offense" against God and of God's intention to punish and to chastize. Also, from the human viewpoint they spoke of "reparation," of "satisfaction," and of "merit" by which the human Jesus "satisfied" divine justice. All these words could effectively conceal an aspect of truth that classical theology pointed to; but currents of thought and the tendencies made possible by these terms led to a distressing attribution to both God and human persons of inadmissible dispositions; for example, when reading that God "handed over" his Son people understood by this that God had delivered him up to punishment or reprobation.

6. A healthy understanding of Jesus' death (namely Paul's) immediately helps to reveal how *theory* became *praxis*. Paul articulated his understanding of Christ's death by showing how baptism makes it real in our day-to-day living: this death is not only intellectually comprehended by the believer, it is active in him or her. The Eucharist actualizes this active nature of Christ's death (what Paul calls his "dying,")[85] so that it exercises its influence in ordinary life and produces its effects in those who draw near to us. Through this same reality, the believer is protected from the danger of sacramental practice being transformed into

acts of magic. Finally, when Paul stresses that "worship" is "spiritual" and that it manifests itself in ordinary life, this does not mean that there is generally no worth in worship. If worship continues to have a role to play in Christian life, this is no longer because it exists in continuity with Jewish worship, which has been abolished in definitive fashion; rather, taking its cue from the human condition itself, worship ceaselessly recreates the symbolic nature of people as believers. As one philosopher put it to me, "the human person is an animal who makes symbols." If Jewish worship is dead, Christian worship must ceaselessly be reborn and through the word, and the bread, re-express the Lord's active presence in the assembled community.

NOTES

1. Gal 3:13; cf. Dt 27:26.
2. Phil 3:5.
3. Dt 21:23; Gal 3:13.
4. Cf. Acts 22:3–5; 26:9–12; Gal 1:13f.
5. Gal 1:15f; Phil 3:12; cf. X. Léon-Dufour, *Resurrection* (p. 75, n. 65), 101–119.
6. 1 Cor 2:2–5.
7. Gal 3:1.
8. 1 Cor 11:26.
9. Mk 15:21p,30,32: cf. Acts 2:36; 4:10.
10. Mk 8:34p; Mt 10:38p; pp. 36–37.
11. 1 Cor 1:23; 2:2; 2 Cor 3:4; Gal 3:1; 6:14; Phil 2:1.
12. 1 Cor 1:17f; Gal 5:11; 6:12,14: Eph 2:16; Phil 3:18; Col 1:10.
13. Cf. Eph 9:1; 18:1; Trall 11:2; Rom 5:3; Phd 8:2; Sm 1:1.
14. Gal 6:12.
15. Phil 3:18f.
16. 1 Cor 6:12; 10:23.
17. 2 Cor 4:10; cf. 6:4–10; 12:9; Phil 3:4–11.
18. So, K. Kertelge, "Das Verständnis des Todes Jesu bei Paulus," in *Der Tod Jesu. Deutungen im Neuen Testament* (Freiburg-in-B.: Herder, 1976), pp. 114–136.
19. G. Theissen, "Soziologische Symbolik in den paulinischen Schriften," *KuD* 20 (1974), 282–304.
20. Rom 14:10.
21. 2 Cor 5:10.
22. J. Mateos (*Nueva Biblia Española* [Madrid: Cristiandad, 1975] p. 1975) proposes to translate it by *rehabilitación*, which we cannot render by "rehabilitation" because in English the word can equally well refer to an innocent party restored to his legitimate rights as to a guilty person reintegrated to a normal life.

23. Paul, a faithful reflector of the common faith, holds back from saying "to sin": Jesus was without sin.
24. Gal 2:13f.
25. Cf. p. 209.
26. J. de Fraine, *Adam et son lignage. Études sur la notion de "personnalité corporative" dans la Bible* (Bruges: DDB, 1959), especially pp. 202–217.
27. Not to be confused with an activity of "sympathy."
28. "Baptized into." In Greek, the preposition *eis*, and not *en*, shows that Paul does not mean to suggest some kind of insertion into a mystical Christ, as if baptism plunged the individual into a new element, namely Christ. So, in 1 Cor 10:2, the Hebrews were "baptized into Moses in the cloud and in the sea": henceforth they belonged to Moses, the leader of the people. Cf. Gal 3:27.
29. Such is the first meaning of *sym-phytoi*.
30. Rom 6:14; 1 Cor 9:20 (three times); Gal 3:23; 4:4, 21; 5:18.
31. Rom 6:9,14; 7:1.
32. Rom 6:18f.
33. Dt 7:8; 13:6; cf. Dt 9:26; 15:15; 21:8; 24:8; Neh 1:10; Ps 78:42; Mi 6:4.
34. *Eleutheroō*: Rom 6:18,20,22; 8:2,21; 2 Cor 3:17; Gal 2:4; 5:1,13.
35. *Apolytrōsis* Rom 3:24; 8:23; 1 Cor 1:30; Eph 1:7,14; 4:30; Col 1:14.
   Agorazō: 1 Cor 6:20; 7:23. *Lytrousthai*: Ti 2:14.
36. *Ex-aireō* Gal 1:4.
37. *Apeleutheros*: 1 Cor 7:22. *Exagorazō*: Gal 3:13; 4:5.
38. Rom 8:2; Gal 5:1,13.
39. Gal 3:23,25; 4:2,4.
40. The terms in Rom 1 recall the sin of the Hebrews in the desert, although they, properly speaking, have in view the sins of the pagans.
41. *Hyper* said of God: Rom 8:31f; 2 Cor 5:21; of Christ: Rom 5:6–8; 14:15; 1 Cor 15:3; 2 Cor 5:14f; Gal 1:4; 2:20; 3:13; Eph 5:2,25; 1 Thess 5:10; 1 Tim 2:6; Ti 2:14; 1 Pt 2:21; 3:18; 1 Jn 3:16. Cf. K. Romaniuk, *L'Amour du Père et du Fils dans la sotériologie de Saint Paul* (Rome: La Représentation, 1961), especially pp. 54–95.
42. This, moreover, is why, from the sixteenth to the twentieth century, it was thought that Jesus had taken upon himself our sins and undergone the wrath of God. Cf. P. Grelot, *Péché originel et Rédemption* (Paris: Desclée, 1973), pp. 205–218, which reproduces the texts of theologians such as Luther, Calvin, Estius, Cornelius a Lapide, of orators like Bossuet, Monsabré, or Msgr. Gay, of poets like Milton or of popular songs like "Minuit Chrétien." Cf. Dorothee Sölle, *Christ the Representative: An Essay in Theology after the "Death of God"* (Trans. David Lewis; London: SCM, 1967).
43. 1 Cor 6:15–17.
44. 1 Cor 2:11.
45. Cf. L. Cerfaux, *Christ in the Theology of St. Paul* (New York: Herder and Herder, 1959), and *The Christian in the Theology of St. Paul* (New York: Herder and Herder, 1967).
46. Cf. pp. 56–63.
47. 1 Cor 10:11. Ordinarily it is translated, perhaps out of weariness, "We who touch the end of time" something that modifies, without good reason, the structure of the Greek sentence.

48. Rom 4:3; 9:17; 10:11; 11:2; Gal 4:30; cf. 1 Tim 5:18.
49. Rom 1:2; 16:26; Gal 3:8.
50. See the developments of L. Cerfaux (above, n. 45) from *Christ* (pp. 147–151) to *The Christian* (pp. 431–443).
51. Gal 3:6–29. Cf. X. Léon-Dufour, "Une lecture chrétienne de l'Ancien Testament. Ga 3.6 à 4.20," in *L'Évangile hier et aujourd'hui*, Festschrift F. J. Leenhardt (Geneva, 1968), pp. 109–115.
52. In his discussions with the religious authorities, Jesus spontaneously linked his interventions to the prophetic invectives of Hosea (Mt 9:13; 12:7), of Isaiah (Mt 11:23; 13:14f; 15:8f) or to the injunctions of Moses (Mt 15:4; 19:7; 22:32,37,39).
53. Rom 7:1–6. In Greek, the word for law is *nomos* and belongs to the masculine gender.
54. Gal 6:2.
55. Cf. Jn 19:34.
56. Rom 8:2, where the expression "law of the Spirit" designates not a law that would be animated by the Holy Spirit, but a new regime that supplants that of the Law.
57. Here "faith" consists in the pretension of proving one's righteousness by one's own works. Cf. *DBT*, pp. 185–188.
58. Cf. X. Léon-Dufour, *Évangiles* (p. 74, n. 32) 415–420.
59. Cf. Phil 2:17; 4:18; see also, in the same line of thought, Heb 13:5; 1 Pt 2:5. S. Lyonnet, "La nature du culte dans le Nouveau Testament," in J. P. Jossua and Y. Congar, eds., *La Liturgie après Vatican II* (Paris: Cerf, 1969) pp. 357–384.
60. 1 Cor 11:23–25. Cf. above, pp. 86–87.
61. It is clear that here we can do no more than trace in a working sketch the evolution of this idea, basing ourselves on the work of specialists, especially J. de Vaux (cf. below, n. 63); J. Cazeneuve, *Les Rites et la Condition humaine* (PUF, 1958); M. Eliade, *Patterns in Comparative Religion* (New York: Sheed & Ward, 1958).
62. R. Girard, *La Violence et le Sacré* (Grasset, 1974).
63. J. de Vaux, *Les Sacrifices de L'Ancien Testament* (Paris: Gabalda, 1964) and *Les Institutions de L'Ancien Testament*, vol. 2, 2nd ed. (Paris: Cerf, 1967), pp. 340–347. Cf. A. Vergote, "La mort rédemptrice du Christ à la lumière de l'anthropologie," in *Mort pour nos péchés* (Brussels, 1976), pp. 45–83.
64. Lv 17:11,14; Dt 12:16.
65. Lv 1:1,5,11; cf. Ex 24:6,8.
66. Cf. S. Lyonnet, *DBT*, 155–156, as well as *De peccato et redemptione*, II, *De vocabulario redemptionis* (Rome: 1960). Cf. also p. xxiii.
67. Lv 16; cf. Ex 25:17f,22; 1 Sm 4:4.
68. Cf. Heb 8–10 (especially 9:7,11–14, 24–28; 10:3).
69. Ex 12:5,13, and so on; 1 Pt 1:19.
70. Hos 6:6; Am 4:4f; 5:21; Is 1:11–18; Mi 6:6f; Jer 7:21–23.
71. Jer 31:31–34; Ez 36:26f.
72. Ps 40:7; 50:8–14; Prv 15:8; 21:3; Sir 34:18–20; 35:1–3.
73. *LAB* 21:7; 26:7; 49:8.
74. *1 QS* 10:14f; Philo, *Quaest. Ex.* II, 69: *Vit. Cont.* No. 64–82; cf. C. Perrot, "Le repas du Seigneur," *MD* 123 (1975), pp. 34–40.

75. Cf. J. Jeremias, "Pais theou," *TDNT* 5 (1967), 677–717.
76. Cf. Ps 40:7 quoted in Heb 10:4–10; cf. p. 115.
77. On *hyper*, cf. above, n. 41.
78. 1 Cor 10:16–22.
79. Cf. S. Lyonnet, *De vocabulario redemptionis* (above, n. 66), pp. 97–134.
80. Jn 4:23.
81. For example, the interpretation found in R. Girard, *Des choses cachées* (p. 47, n. 129), pp. 251–254.
82. Cf. S. Lyonnet (above, n. 59), pp. 368–379. As well as Lk 2:37; Acts 26:7; Rom 9:4; Heb 9:1,6; Rv 7:15; 22:3.
83. Eph 5:2; Heb 9:23,26; 10:12,26.
84. Rom 12:1; Phil 2:17; 1 Pt 2:5; Rv 1:6; 10:5; 20:6.
85. Cf. below, p. 266, n. 16.

6. Death, Where Is Your Victory?

Paul attempted to translate and to communicate his experience of the living Christ. In every way he proclaimed that, through his death and resurrection, Christ re-established the covenant between human beings and God: they have been justified, liberated, reconciled, brought to life, transfigured and brought into communion with God and one another. All good and true. And we can rejoice without restraint. Yet, if the death of Jesus who was obedient unto the cross in this way obtained salvation and life for us, how did Paul understand our own personal deaths, the ones awaiting us at the close of our lives?

Theodore of Cyr spoke a word to Paul saying, "You define your terms by beginning with the end."[1] In truth it is the end indeed that causes one to grasp the facts about the world to come; for out of that world comes a sense of eternity that gives meaning to time, to life, to death. This, then, is the reason why Paul could speak of death: his own experience of the Risen One had placed him at the end of time. He could define death and from there tackle the thorny problem of the connection between death and sin: in what way can we say death is "natural" and to what extent is death the fruit of sin? Finally, in his correspondence with the Thessalonians, he graphically showed the way in which death had been conquered and how it remains our hope. As we have seen,[2] to the Jews who observed it, death had a twofold visage: it is at one and the same time a natural phenomenon and an occurrence bound up with sin. The following two probes will reveal the depth of understanding Paul confers on death.

THE ESSENCE OF DEATH

What happens at the moment of death? According to the Bible, the soul strictly speaking does not leave the body as it would if it had been enveloped within it; rather, the whole human person descends into the grubby existence found in Sheol. Today we might say that because of this the soul finds it impossible to communicate normally with other people, a state that lasts until the end of time, when the resurrection will restore to each being its proper integrity. A believer would not be content, however, to affirm his or her belief in the resurrection, but rather tries to grasp how this will take place, with a hope of casting new light thereby on what death is in itself. Such were the problems that Paul addressed in the fifteenth chapter of 1 Corinthians.

Since we will treat this text more fully in our next chapter, we will mention only the main points now. Paul wanted to justify belief in the resurrection of the dead. After showing where its foundation lay, in the Resurrection of Jesus (15:1–11), Paul drew out conclusions that flow from this faith at least insofar as these touched on the problem that had been troubling the Corinthians. Paul did so in three units laid out in chiastic fashion (A B A'). In two instances Paul reasoned *per absurdum*: if Christ has not been raised, then our faith, our hope has no content, and we, people who have been deceived, are the most unfortunate of people (vv. 12–19); or, put in a new way, if Christ has not been raised, let's eat and drink! (vv. 29–34). Between these two lines of thought we find the positive argumentation (vv. 20–28), whose purpose is that of pointing out our solidarity with the risen Christ, who has already won the victory both in principle and in fact. If, then, Christ is the "first fruits," we, too, may be certain of being raised up.

Beginning with Verse 35, Paul set about showing how our resurrection comes about. God, he said, can create spiritual bodies (vv. 35–44) along the lines set forth in the Heavenly Person (vv. 45–49). How? By means of a universal transformation of human beings at the end of time: all will witness the triumph over death

(vv. 50–53); then, to wrap up his treatment, Paul gives expression to a final hymn of praise (vv. 54–58).

The long passage found in Verses 35–36 addresses the question posed by the Corinthians: "How are the dead raised up? With what kind of bodies will they come (back)?" (v. 35). This difficulty of theirs manifests doubt concerning the resurrection, treating it as impossible. Here again Paul is vigorous in his reaction: by doubting in this manner, the Corinthians show themselves ignorant of the truth that death conditions all of life (v. 36). However, if death is necessary for life to progress, what ought one to think when the whole body has just disappeared? Then, apparently, it is no longer an instance of growth but of a return to nonexistence.

To come to grips with the weighty anxiety pressing on the spirits of their contemporaries, authors of the Jewish tradition oscillated between two types of images—sometimes material ones, at other times spiritual ones. In the first view, for example, it was believed in certain Jewish quarters that a bone from the spinal column, shaped like an almond, was incorruptible; since it was different in each person, it could allow for each person to be recognized at the end of time.[3] In opposition to such a theory, admittedly an extreme one, we find the answer Jesus gave to the doubting Sadducees, one that takes up an Enoch tradition: "At the resurrection there is neither wife nor husband; but people will be like the angels in heaven."[4] That is to say, we cannot imagine heaven, which is to come, on any earthly model. How, then, can one talk about a state that no one has ever laid eyes on? Still, according to Jewish thinking, life cannot be conceptualized without bodies. Ultimately, then, the how of the resurrection depends on one's notion of the body: "With what kind of body will they come back?"

The answer given is simple: they will return with a transformed body. A mysterious declaration brings this out:

51 We shall not all sleep, but we shall all be changed, **52** in a moment, in the twinkling of an eye, at the last trumpet (for the trumpet will sound), and the dead will be raised imperishable, and we shall all be changed [*transformed*].

(1 Cor 15:51–52)

The reference to a trumpet is a typical instance of the apocalyptic language found in this passage; on the last day those who will be at rest in the cemetery,[5] having by their burials been handed over to corruption, will pass from corruptible to incorruptible life. The rest, those still alive on this last day, will, themselves also, have to be transformed. What is essential, then, in each of these alternatives, is entry into the other world. A consequence of this fact is as follows: what is required for passage from one state to another is not corruption but rather change. To put it another way, properly speaking, there is not continuity between earth and heaven. Paul had already said so when addressing the Thessalonians:

We who are alive, who are left, shall be caught up together with them in the clouds to meet the Lord in the air.

(1 Thess 4:17)

In this equally apocalyptic scenario, Paul is at pains to underline for his correspondents the fact that at the moment of the Parousia the "survivors" will not take precedence over those who are already dead and must therefore first of all be raised, but they will be simply "snatched up" from the earth. Paul is dealing with a limited case here because at the Parousia time will in fact no longer exist, nor will there be any possibility of corruption. This is the reason why the "survivors" best exemplify what the transition from earth to heaven consists in—not the destruction of the body but its transformation.

Can one still, then, maintain as the characteristic feature of death the dissolution of the body? From the fact that dissolution is its most apparent characteristic we run the risk of concluding that therein lies what is essential to death; yet death's meaning is found not there but in its opposite, the transfiguration of the body. This can take place after the body's dissolution or directly, with the living body as the starting point. Death, then, is either a stage on the way to transformation or the transformation itself. Paul does not specify what exactly this transformation consists in; and this is a good thing, for if he had he would have pretended to master the other side of death. Nevertheless, he considers himself able to imagine this mysterious change by contrasting it with what is left behind on earth: flesh and blood, corruptibility, mortality, dust. This is what is suggested by the three antitheses we will now examine.

THE FIRST ANTITHESIS: ONE KIND–ANOTHER KIND

Paul recalls first of all a general principle that we have already met, one that every person ought to admit, that in the vegetable world there is a diversity of bodies; nevertheless, within this diversity, we can speak of continuity.

37 What you sow is not the body which is to be, but a bare kernel, perhaps of wheat or of some other grain. **38** But God gives it a body as he has chosen, and to each kind of seed its own body. . . . **42** So it is with the resurrection of the dead. What is sown is perishable, what is raised is imperishable. **43** It is sown in dishonor, it is raised in glory. It is sown in weakness, it is raised in power.

(1 Cor 15:37–38, 42–43)

In the eyes of an intelligent person there is diversity in the vegetative world; so, why not in the world of human beings? Let us, then, accept in principle that there could be a human body other than that of our experience.

Moreover, we note that there is a continuity between these various instances of "one kind" and "another kind." No doubt in keeping with the thought patterns of his time, Paul attributed this continuity to God's intervention; but when he did so it was not to offer some sort of biological teaching that we would consider outmoded today. Rather, he taught as he did to affirm that God the Creator was the guarantor and even the author of every deep-seated instance of continuity. It would not serve any purpose to seek proof for his assertion; it was only an analogy. Paul did not teach that germination was the result of a miraculous intervention by God, only that the resurrection was the outcome of a divine intervention. So, then, it would be vain to try to find continuity in the material order between corpse and a risen body. The disproportionate relation that Paul noted between the seed and the plant cannot be grounded except in God who gives it a body.[6] At one and the same time we can say that it is God who recreates the body, and that it is sowing that is manifested in divers ways. However, I have to admit that the resurrected body is of "another" kind than the "one" that I had known; also that, despite this, there is a real continuity between the two, a continuity maintained by God.

THE SECOND ANTITHESIS: PHYSICAL–SPIRITUAL; EARTHLY–HEAVENLY

44 It is sown a physical body, it is raised a spiritual body. If there is a physical body, there is also a spiritual body. **45** Thus it is written, "The first *man*, Adam, *became a* living being"; the last Adam became a life-giving spirit. **46** But it is not the spiritual which is first but the physical, and then the spiritual. **47** The first *man* [was] *from the dust, [coming] from the earth*, the second man [comes] from heaven. **48** As was the man of dust, so are those who are of the dust; and as is the man of heaven, so are those who are of heaven. **49** Just as we have borne the image of the man of dust, we shall also bear the image of the man of heaven.

(1 Cor 15:44–49)

As the starting point of Pauline reflection, we find this text of Genesis: "The Lord God molded the man out of dust taken from the ground. He breathed into his nostrils the breath of life and the man became a living being."[7] Continuity in the midst of diversity, expressed in the analogy of the development in plants, in this case manifests itself through Paul's theology of the two Adams.[8] In it, we move from the "physical body" to the "spiritual body." The physical body is an organism endowed with life and composed of two elements: the "dust"[9] (which is earthly) and the (heavenly) breath of life, which is loaned to humankind. We note that Paul does not depict the human person as a "soul" incarnated in matter, but rather as dust that has become a living soul. Contrasted with this first human person, we find the second human person described as "a life-giving spirit." In order to grasp the specific nuance here, we need to go back to the original text of Genesis where the "breath of life" (*pnoēn zōes*) is distinguished from the "spirit" (*pneuma*). In effect, the latter is properly designated as heavenly and does not reside in the human person, a conviction we discover in a developed rabbinic text, which uses as its starting point the prophet Ezekiel and describes the kind of relationship that is required to unite the vivifying spirit with the creature.[10]

An application to our condition is easy to make. We have been fashioned in the likeness of dust; one day we will bear the likeness of heaven. Since we are one with the first Adam, we shall also be one with the second. In this way Paul tells of a life that participates in two worlds, the earthly and the heavenly, a fact that allows us to specify difference in nature and the divers origins of the human person when these are considered before and after death.[11]

So, an answer has already been provided for the Corinthians, namely that we shall rise with a "heavenly body" in the likeness of the second Adam, the risen Christ. What, then, becomes of the continuity between the two bodies; isn't there still a radical difference? This is the subject of Paul's third antithesis.

THE THIRD ANTITHESIS: CORRUPTIBLE-INCORRUPTIBLE

50 I tell you this, brethren: flesh and blood cannot inherit the kingdom of God, nor does the perishable inherit the imperishable. . . . **53** For this perishable nature must put on the imperishable, and this mortal nature must put on immortality. **54** When the perishable puts on the imperishable, and the mortal puts on immortality, then shall come to pass the saying that is written: "Death is swallowed up in victory."

(1 Cor 50–54)

To the contrast in origins there is added here a contrast between the natures of the "bodies," something that allows for the articulation of the absolute necessity of a transformation. The notions inherent in the words "impossibility" (*ou dynatai*) and "must" (*dei*) confirm what was stated above concerning the essence of death, namely, that it involves a radical transformation.

The physical, what is made of dust—what is understood by the words "flesh" and "blood" of our life—all this is destined to disappear, while the spiritual person, the one whose origin is in heaven, is incorruptible. Everything, therefore, is transitory because the actual organism, being physical, must be clothed with something else that is incorruptible, immortal. This is the only specification brought to bear on the second term in the ongoing process. Afterward, Paul, returning to the mystery in which the process originates, appeals to the author of the incorruptibilty, who is both heavenly and spiritual: the second Adam has become the source of incorruptibility. Paul can then draw the conclusion that at the resurrection an incorruptible and immortal "organism" will be created for the believer.

Since we are unable to be any more specific about the final state of the change, we can, instead, focus our attention on the change itself. The transition to glory does not necessarily require either sleep or decay, but only a transformation that can take place either after sleep or in an instant. For the rest, as we noted earlier, there is what Paul told the Thessalonians ("We will be snatched up") or what he told the Philippians:

20 Our commonwealth is in heaven, and from it we await a Savior, the Lord Jesus Christ, **21** who will change our lowly body to be like his glorious body, by the power which enables him even to subject all things to himself.

(Phil 3:20–21)[12]

To visualize the risen body, one only has to think of the glorified body of Jesus. What is made of "dust" is referred to here as "lowliness" or "wretchedness" (*tapeinōsis*). Again, the conforming, the transforming, the transfiguring of our bodies is paralleled with Christ's.

At the end of this short inquiry, we can draw several conclusions. Death possesses two aspects: decay and change. To give thoughtful expression to death, one needs to consider the transition from what is sown to the plant that grows, a process that depicts in an excellent way continuity in the midst of diversity.

Better still one ought to keep one's eyes set on Jesus in glory, the one who already enjoys our very own anticipated spiritual body.[13] We are driven by this back to our personal knowledge of Jesus Christ. However, one question still remains, rooted as it is in our understanding of Christ's death: Why is this transformation still necessary? Is it bound up with the human condition, as certain texts we studied earlier (physical-spiritual) seemed to suggest? Or rather, is it due to our sins as the corruptible-incorruptible antithesis seems to suggest (even if it is not mentioned even once in this context)? This is what we now have to explore.

SIN, THE STING OF DEATH

In the texts examined thus far, Paul attempted to describe the transition involved in death by means of several antitheses that were analogous but not identical to each other. In our movement through one pair to another there was discernible a slight slip, one that led to the discovery of sin's presence at work within death itself.

The contrast in the pair "of the dust"—"heavenly" (or "physical"—"spiritual") pointed to the creature's state in its constitutive weakness, apart from any moral value judgment: the earth cannot be at heaven's origin. Earth cannot produce heaven; the physical organism cannot furnish the Spirit.[14] In one sense, the human being is mortal by nature.

In translating "physical" by "animal," the *Traduction oecuménique de la Bible* suggests that from this point of view, the human person is on the same level as a beast; even if this is not a felicitous translation, it does remain true that this interpretation picks up the passionate questioning attitude found in Ecclesiastes:

19 For the fate of the sons of men and the fate of beasts is the same; as one dies, so dies the other. They all have the same breath, and man has no advantage over the beasts; for all is vanity. 20 All go to one place; all are from the dust, and all turn to dust again. 21 Who knows whether the spirit of the *sons of Adam* goes upwards and the spirit of the beasts goes down to the earth?

(Eccl 3:19–21)[15]

In order to produce a living organism God loaned his breath, the one that returns upward; when God takes it back, this organism dies. Put in other words, the human person's condition is mortal, just like the animal's. But, despite this, the breath loaned by God is not in every regard identical to the breath that animates beasts, for the latter ultimately remains on earth. What difference, then, is there precisely? The second antithesis will elaborate on this.

The "corruptible"—"incorruptible" antithesis, in itself, does not say any more than the previous one, for it is equivalent to "perishable"—"imperishable." However, its immediate context suggests that we can conceive of a further dimension, that of sin. In fact, Paul concludes his treatment by declaring that death is bound up with sin:

55 O Death, where is thy victory?
   O Death, where is thy sting?

56 The sting of Death is Sin [*It is Sin*], and the power of Sin is the Law. 57 But thanks be to God, who gives us the victory through our Lord Jesus Christ!

(1 Cor 15:55–57)

With this the actors in the drama come onto the stage: death, sin, and the Law, against whom are ranged grace and Jesus Christ; these characters will come into full view in the great passage from the Epistle to the Romans that will now engage our attention.

To start with, we should unravel several consequences that follow from the earlier texts. Naturally, a human being cannot on his own bring about the transition that leads to the Kingdom of God; it is not by means of his or her own power that a person crosses from earth to heaven. There is more still that needs to be said. The human person has allowed himself or herself to be captured by sin, which causes one to do not only perishable but also corrupt deeds, ones from which at the moment of death he or she will have to be completely cut off. Certainly a man or woman does not perform only these kinds of deeds since those done in God are good deeds. But what we call "sin" is the outcome of activity done "apart from God." Hence death manifests another countenance, one that demands a complete break with what is corruptible, whatever has been effected in human persons by what is merely human and in which God has no place. How could this corruption enter the Kingdom of God?

This double dimension of death must remain as the backdrop for our reading of a fundamental text from the Epistle to the Romans: Verses 12 to 21 of Chapter 5.

In order to read correctly this famous passage, it has to be located within the totality of the epistle.[16] It serves as the conclusion of the epistle's first part (Rom 1:19–5:21), in the course of which Paul first of all demonstrated that every person, Jew as well as Greek, is a sinner and merits the condemnation of death (1:19–3:20) and then that, in Jesus Christ, justification is henceforth granted to whoever believes (3:21–5:11). This reconciliation, he now points out, is universal (5:12–21). To show how this is so, Paul recaps the history of salvation with the aid of personifications. In this way he universalizes all sins in "sin," synthesizes every condemnation to death in "death," and finally evokes the person of "Adam," the "epitome of sinners," so that, by pointing to its opposite, he can show the universal significance of the activity of Jesus Christ.

The logic of this first part of the epistle can be traced as follows: (1) All humans are sinners. (2) Jesus alone is true righteousness. (3) Through him this righteousness becomes universal. (4) How can the individual man or woman obtain a share in this new state? By recourse to the One—all[17] relationship.

Unable to undertake a detailed analysis of this difficult passage here, I will consider only what relates to the understanding of death it contains. When reading this text one must avoid historicizing the person of Adam; his only function is to provide a "type" whose "antitype" is Christ.[18] In this way, Paul shows that through this relationship of type to antitype Christ's action, like Adam's, in fact possesses universal significance. In order to show that the act of one person has significance for all, Paul argues as follows:

Verses 12–14   A rough sketch of his reasoning, which at first fails but then is taken up and is successful in Verse 18.

Verses 15–17   A caution that one not be deluded by the affinities between their works but rather note their difference.

Verses 19–20   A confrontation with the dramatic characters, their similarities and differences; at this point the comparison picks up the ideas of Verses 12–14, based on the fact that Verse 18 had correctly formulated the situation.

Let us read the complete text of Romans 5:12–21 as it has been graphed:

12 Therefore as sin came into the world through one man
and death through sin,
and so death spread to all men
because all men sinned . . .

13 sin indeed was in the world before the Law was given, but sin is not counted where there is no law.

14 Yet death reigned from Adam to Moses,
even over those whose sins were not like the transgression
of Adam, who was a type of the one who was to come. . . .

15 But the free gift is not like the trespass.
For if by the offense   →how much more, *by the grace*
of one   of one man Jesus Christ have
many   *many*
died *abounded in God's grace and the free gift of God.*

16 And the free gift is not like the effect of that one man's sin:
for the judgment   →but the free gift
following one trespass   following many trespasses
brought condemnation   brings justification.

17 If because of the trespass → much more will those who receive the abundance

of one man — of grace and the free gift

Death — righteousness in life

reigned through that one man — reign through one man Jesus Christ.

18 As one man's → so one man's

trespass — act of righteousness

led to condemnation — [*means*] *righteousness of life*

for all men — for all men.

19 For as by one man's → so by one man's

disobedience — obedience

many were made sinners — many will be made righteous.

20 Law came in, → but where sin increased,

to increase the trespass; — grace abounded all the more,

21 so that, as Sin reigned → Grace also might reign

in — through righteousness to eternal life

Death, — [through Jesus Christ our Lord].

This passage is proverbially difficult to understand: for, in fact, Paul begins with a comparison ("just as . . .") to which he does not give a parallel ("so . . ."). After this comparison is begun and not completed, he continues with his work of sketching comparisons (vv. 12–17) by looking at the works produced by Adam and by Jesus Christ: deeds, consequences, effects. It is only in Verse 18 that he feels he can resume the points of comparison and there the comparison becomes perfectly balanced. So, it is appropriate to give expression to our treatment by beginning with Verse 18:

> Then, as one man's trespass
> [led to] condemnation for all men,
> so one man's act of righteousness
> [leads to] acquittal and life for all men.

Wishing in this way to show that Jesus' work has universal significance, Paul emphasizes what he considers to be evident, namely that Adam's fault has brought about a condemnation that touches everyone. Now, it is precisely this condemnation that is the condemnation to death, exactly the opposite of the "justification of life" obtained by Christ. Already we see that in Paul's eyes death is the result of condemnation and not a simply natural phenomenon. How can he demonstrate this? The earlier verses lead to this conclusion.

Verse 12 is introduced by a *dia touto* ("therefore") that picks up what had been said in Chapters 1–5 of the epistle, namely that the reconciliation won by Christ (Rom 5:11) is a universal reconciliation:

12 Therefore, as sin came into the world through one man and death through Sin, and so death spread to all men because all men sinned. . . .

According to this teaching, it is on account of sin and not on Adam's account that death made its appearance in the world. Death appears here as a power, itself, at work by means of sin, which is its "sting," as Paul told the Corinthians. The term "death" is ambiguous: is it merely death that we experience, or spiritual death, or Death as a power? It seems that in this passage we cannot reduce death to a biological phenomenon. If death has a relationship with sin, this is because death is not simply natural and because it expresses a power at work in the world, one that Paul designates with the name of sin.

Paul in fact added "and so death spread to all men because all men sinned." For him, death experienced as a universal phenomenon signifies the state of sin. This interpretation evidently depends on our translation: death is not *caused by* sins (to any extent whatever), but at the biological level is the *indicator* that all human persons have sinned.[19] Since we all die, it is the sign that we all sin.

This Pauline reasoning seems to be based on evidence. Everyone admits the phenomenon of death. "Observe carefully with the eyes of faith," Paul says; "You will see then that death has a dimension that is out of the ordinary. It is not merely biological but also and essentially something else. It repudiates any relationship with sin, showing that we are all in some way sinners." One ought not, then, speak of "death" for animals but rather of "decomposition," particularly since, in the phenomenon of "death," we see in addition to the awareness of decomposition an experience of being torn away. This awareness reveals that there is something besides the biological phenomenon and lays one open to interpreting it as the condition of sin. Quite rightly people have discovered in this text a teaching about "original sin," at least the fact that this does not imply the original sin of an individaul Adam but the universal sin of all human persons.

To sum up, death for each person is not the penalty for his or her individual sin. As a universal phenomenon, sin sends one back to a universal and mysterious fact: all humans have sinned. This, then, is what faith has laid hold of by induction. Temporal death is the first level but, because of its relationship with sin, it signifies eschatological death, which is separation from God.

With Verses 13–14 Paul begins to reason as he had done once before in the Epistle to the Galatians,[20] namely by taking into account God's plan: Israel's election and the Law intervene. In effect, the universalism indicated in Verse 12 would be more immediately intelligible if there had not been the issues of Israel's particularity or the Law. Whence the Jewish reader's objection: "How could death hold sway over everyone since there is no account taken of sin when there is no Law? Before Moses, death could not have been universal." Prior to formulating this objection Paul held firmly to his line of thought: "Even prior to the Law there was already sin in the world." After raising the difficulty we have just mentioned, Paul affirmed the fact of universal death: this is because "sin" is not necessarily bound up with the Law. In the preceding chapter of this work, we saw that Paul went back beyond Moses to Abraham in order to locate the Law in relation to the promise.[21] Now, he goes even further back, to Adam. In the time of the first man the Law did not yet exist to keep track of sins but, nonetheless, death existed—and so also sin—given that death signifies universal sin.

13 Sin indeed was in the world before the Law was given. But sin is not counted where there is no Law; **14** yet death reigned from Adam to Moses, even over those whose sins were not like the transgression of Adam, who was a type of the one who was to come. . . .

(Rom 5:13–14)

Paul spoke of the Law because he was a Jew. Since he has to describe God's plan, he must always mention the Law, a key period in the divine economy. So, in Romans 2:7–16 he had spoken of the privileges of the Jews in order to show that the Law does not lead to justification. Likewise Paul located himself in relation to Abraham (3:27–4:25). Judeo-Christianity was not a philosophy but a history woven out of events: Abraham, the Law, and so very many encounters with God of which Paul had to give an accounting. All humans, including among them members of the chosen people, are locked within an "economy" leading to death,[22] one inaugurated by Adam who represents and includes all of sinful humanity, which was subject to the power of death until Christ's definitive victory.

These two verses merely repeat the statement of Verse 12, that there is an intrinsic link between death and sin. Death symbolizes sin, the sinful condition of humankind.[23] Death both *is* and *is not* sin at work. Awareness of corruptibility shows the aspect of death under which sin is at work. In Paul's view, there is no longer a "natural" death for humans.

Verses 15–17 develop the parallelism indicated at the end of the previous verse: Adam as "a type of the one who was to come." We must not in fact be deluded by Adam's work: for over against transgression there is ranged grace; condemnation is countered by justification; and against death we find life lined up as if life and death were two radically different consequences.

With regard to Verses 19–21, these merely pick up Verses 12– 14 in order to specify the comparison between Adam and Christ. For our purposes, there is scarcely anything to be gleaned from these verses beyond what has already been noted, except that we observe that here the term "sin" replaces "death" to indicate the power holding sway (v. 17). In this way the issues are uncovered:

physical death, visible to all, dominates, but the true reign is that of sin, which perpetrates the work of death. Death thus expresses sin at work. Disintegration and decay are unmasked: they are sin in its virulent form. Thus is faith afforded a vision perceptive enough to detect the symbolic dimension of reality.

The closing part of 1 Corinthians reveals its full meaning: sin is the sting of death. In the vision of faith, we repeat, death is thus not simply a biological phenomenon; it is not, as in an animal's death, simply decomposition. Rather, it "symbolizes" the condition of being separated from God, which we call sin; it symbolizes eschatological death. Moreover, anyone who knows with the Bible that the human person is a being dependent on God for breath (because God alone is the Living One and so God alone is the life giver) knows clearly, too, that to separate oneself from God is to be separated from the source of life, to destroy oneself and to go to definitive death.

THE DEFEAT OF DEATH

But the human person does not go fatally to definitive death. In Jesus Christ, the life-giving Second Adam each person can be reborn into the life he or she lost in the First Adam. Fully human, Jesus was in solidarity with the world of sin,[24] but he was also in perfect harmony with God, and this to such an extent that his radical faithfulness kept him in the world of divine life. This is what is said in the letter to the Philippians: by virtue of his obedience unto death, which was sin's condemnation, he has been made Lord.[25] Victorious over sin, Jesus triumphed over death.

Let us be more specific about this revelation by Paul. In Adam all were sinners; in Jesus Christ all are sharers in grace. Humanity is likened unto a sphere that Adam smashed by separating it from God; within this broken sphere, all are born into death. Jesus entered into this sphere; being without sin, he himself became the principle for a new sphere. Jesus is the head of a new humanity.

This is only intelligible in all its depth if one grasps the notion of *corporate personality*, which we took up earlier.[26] Neither

Adam nor Jesus are simply heads of a race; they actually constitute a single body with those who are their descendants either through the flesh or through faith. This depiction is founded not on the concepts of cause and effect but rather on the concepts of one's condition and one's solidarity. Adam is neither the cause nor the source of my sin, he is merely the one who introduced sin into the world. Through Adam's deed, I am born into a relationship with the power of sin; this is what is called "original sin." In passing into the new sphere, bound up through Jesus Christ to God, the human person rediscovers life, that is to say, grace.

Since Christ is the New Adam, he exhausts the significance of the first Adam, "the type of the one who is to come." He is the antitype, the very reality awaited. Also I must understand my relationship to Adam, my state as a human being and sinner, not by beginning with my relationship to Adam but by laying hold of my state in Jesus Christ. Paul did not speak of Adam and then of Christ; if he could speak of Adam it was because he had known Jesus Christ. So he could write to the Corinthians:

21 For as by a man came death, by a man has come also the resurrection of the dead. **22** For as in Adam all die, so also in Christ shall all be made alive.

(1 Cor 15:21–22)

From Adam I inherit not only my humanity but also my mortal condition, which is a consequence of sin's entry into the world. In this sense, I am congenitally bound to Adam's sin, but, it must be carefully noted, Adam only opened the door to sin; it was sin that conferred on death its aspect of a violent tearing away. But now, by faith, I am bound to the new Adam, who has triumphed over sin.

Paul did not only elaborate a theory concerning Jesus' victory over death, he had to console some young converts who found themselves tormented by the loss of their loved ones. This is the way in which Paul endeavored to reply to his correspondents' question:

We would not have you ignorant, brethern, concerning those who are asleep, that you may not grieve as others do who have no hope.

(1 Thess 4:13)

After a lengthy treatment of the new condition of the children of light, he concluded,

Therefore, encourage one another and build one another up, just as you are doing.

(1 Thess 5:11)

There he took up again an earlier exhortation:

Therefore, comfort one another with these words.

(1 Thess 4:18)

To the normal sadness every experience of death causes, Paul opposes the hope on which one can base one's conviction that one will not be abandoned. Why this is so is what we must now make clear.

THE SITUATION

The young community of Thessalonica was preoccupied about the fate of fellow Christian believers who had "fallen asleep."[27] As John Chrysostom would say later, "the place of burial is called a 'cemetery' so that you may know that those who have ended their lives and rest there are not dead but rather are stretched out and are sleeping."[28] The dead are thus said to be reclining and dozing in expectation of the awakening foretold by Scripture. In this way, death could be denominated "sleep" (Gk. *koimēsis*)[29] and believers reflected this thought, as an inscription from the second and third centuries found in Thessalonica witnesses:

Calocerus to (the memory of) his beloved parents
Macedonius and Sosigenia
their place of rest until the resurrection.[30]

In addition to this conviction common during that period, the conviction concerning the imminent Parousia had made a deep impression on Paul and the Thessalonians. The Parousia—that is, the glorious coming of the Lord Jesus—should not have been late in coming and found some asleep and others alive. Thus, Paul spoke of "us who are alive, who are left"[31] and of the eventuality foreseen for the day of the Parousia: "whether we wake or sleep."[32]

But between Paul and his correspondents a difference of view leads to Paul's reproach:

You *ought* not grieve as others do who have no hope.

(1 Thess 4:13)

What does this mean? The pagans (the "others," according to Paul) do not possess certitude concerning the afterlife, because they do not know God.[33] In fact, according to popular beliefs, people were fatalistic as is shown in the letter of a certain Irenus to Taonnomphris and Philo found in a papyrus of the second or third centuries:

Courage (*Eupsychein*)! I, also, weep in sadness with the . . . as I wept over Didymus. And everything that is appropriate I perform, as do all of mine. . . . But, in fact, we can do nothing against this. So, mutually console yourselves. Be well![34]

The Old Testament seems to share Irenus' philosophy:

17 . . . Observe the mourning according to *the dead person's* merit, for one day, or two, to avoid criticism; then, be comforted for your sorrow.
20 . . . Drive (*sorrow*) away, remembering the end of life.
21 . . . There is no coming back; you do the dead no good, and you injure yourself.

(Sir 38:17, 20–21)

These two texts are surprising because of their "common sense"; they are also unsettling by their absence of hope. Are we not right then in associating the faithful of Thessalonica with the authors of these sentiments, with these "others" about whom Paul speaks, since they themselves live in expectation of the Parousia. However, their expectation is not identical with hope, which presupposes faith in the resurrection and allows one to overcome sadness in the face of death. We cannot compare Irenus's conclusion with Paul's exhortation: "Comfort one another!" A hypothesis may allow us to account for the circumstances described: the glare of the Parousia may have concealed from the Thessalonians Paul's thought about the resurrection of the dead. So much were they dazzled by it that they pratically overlooked the fact that their dead would share with them the joy of the Lord's coming.

PAUL'S REPLY

In listening to this apparently detached answer, we must not imagine that Paul is an unfeeling man; for example, he confided to his friends in Philippi the sadness that weighed on him with the thought of the possible loss of Epaphroditus, his travel and battle companion:

Indeed he was ill, near to death. But God had mercy on him, not only on him but on me also, lest I should have sorrow on sorrow.

(Phil 2:27)

We listen to Paul. He does not reason, as we might spontaneously do, by referring to a long delay that would separate his correspondents from the Parousia and that might see themselves also stretched out in a cemetery. In any case, he did not seize on the opportunity to declare that the Parousia is not imminent; moreover, perhaps he did not think this or dare to say such a thing and elsewhere he even freely places himself among those who seemingly will still be alive on the day of the end.

Paul does not cast a doubt on the faith of the Thessalonians in the resurrection of the dead; he simply wishes to relocate it in relation to the Parousia. This is his reasoning process:

Since we believe that Jesus died and rose again, even *those who have fallen asleep, God will bring them (back) through Jesus and with him [axei syn autōi]*.

(1 Thess 4:14)

This sentence is wobbly. The reasoning ought to have been "since we believe . . . , let us also believe that God will raise up those who are asleep." But Paul did not ask that people believe this, he presupposed it. His concern pushed him even further ahead: Jesus will not abandon to the cemetery our beloved dead, they will also be, even they, "with him."

How can this be possible? What, then, will be the scenario at the Parousia? Paul uses an apocalyptic arsenal whose "incidental reality" we ought not to try and make too specific (the word of command, the archangel, the trumpet, the descent, the snatching up into the air), except for one thing only: the living will not have any advantage over the dead.

15 For this we declare to you by the word of the Lord, that we who are alive, who are left until the coming of the Lord, shall not precede those who *are dead*.

(1 Thess 4:15)

And his description of the meeting with the Lord is as follows:

16 For the Lord himself will descend from heaven with a cry of command, with the archangel's call and with the sound of the trumpet of God. And the dead in Christ will rise first; **17** then we who are alive, who are left, shall be caught up [*harpagēsometha*] together with them [*hama syn autois*] in the clouds to meet the Lord [*eis apantēsin*] in the air; and so we shall always be with the Lord.

(1 Thess 4:16–17)

If the dead rise first of all, this is because they have to be made alive again, like those who will be still alive at the Parousia; thus it is those who are alive who will come to meet the Lord, or, more precisely, who will be "snatched up" from this earth. To be able to do this—that is, to go into the air—they will have to have been transformed, a necessity that we established earlier on.[35] This scenario, which depends on apocalyptic imagery, provides the equivalent of this necessity ("to be snatched up"). In addition it refers to the practice of "joyous entrances" made by a sovereign. Just as long ago Moses made the Hebrew people go to meet God outside the camp, as Jerusalem did before Jesus' entry into the Holy City, and as young maidens went out to meet the Bride-groom,[36] so will it be at the eachatological meeting. Then Jesus will go down from heaven to earth, and we will all descend with him. Then there will be the final judgment: all will reign on earth.[37]

As interesting as this dramaturgy might appear to be in helping us visualize the snatching up of people from the earth, it does not, for all that, point out the goal of Paul's instruction. His point is that "all together" we will receive the Lord's blessing. The theme of the Thessalonians' sadness from this perspective is essentially that of separation at the key moment of the Parousia. There was among them neither an error (as if the resurrection would not take place[38]) nor a concern about priority status in the final procession. Their sorrow was in not being together at the meeting with the Lord, something that implied a mistake about the moment of the resurrection but not about its facticity.

What then is the joy of the Parousia? Paul seems not to have thought about some kind of mystical union or about some sort of enjoyment of the "beatific vision" that might typify an individual's experience of heavenly joy. Paul does not deny this, clearly, but he has a regard for something else: he insists on the communitarian dimension of a life of companionship with the Lord, and he avers his agreement with the ancient prophecy of Ezekiel: "I will gather them together again and bring them back into the land of Israel."[39]

Thanks to the Thessalonians who, out of their sense of community, came into error regarding the moment and manner of the resurrection, Paul revealed the communitarian dimension of heavenly happiness. Does he not in this way[40] answer ahead of time the anguished question of those afflicted by their bereavement: will I find again those whom I have loved so much?

CONCLUSION

Has Paul enabled us to make strides in our understanding of the mystery of the death of human beings? The preceding pages certainly will not have answered all the questions we ask today, particularly about death and sin. Nothing has been said about sin's origin or about its nature; this would require lengthy treatments that are out of place here. Moreover, we can ask ourselves the nature of Paul's specific contribution to the understanding of our topic.

Unlike a contemporary mind, which is encumbered by a certain degraded Hellenistic philosophy, someone familiar with Scripture would not fail to affirm that Paul's thought is profoundly biblical. When we inquired about the presupposition of Jesus of Nazareth's thought,[41] we noted death's twofold aspect: the fulfillment of a life full of days or a premature experience of being torn away from this world. This twofold aspect is found again in Paul but more neatly bound up with sin. Not according to the classical formulation: if Adam had not sinned, we would not have been given up to death. Let us not charge Adam with all our woes, but let us admit that since death touches all of us we are all in solidarity with the world of sin into which he introduced us. So, for Paul, because death essentially consists in the radical transformation of our human condition, it also appears as a being torn away from this earth, something that is, let us say it, both sad and practically unjust. Paul states clearly that this is the consequence of sin.

What is radically new Paul owes to his experience of the Risen Jesus. Certainly the Old Testament hoped for the triumph of life over death but for Paul that hope has already been realized: because one man has been snatched away from death, all will themselves be snatched away from death. The condition is that one cling tightly to this man in whom everyone is totally renewed. What is new, on the last line of the ledger, is Jesus Christ who comes to give sense to the nonesense of death. Paul contemplated God's victory in his Son. Hope without doubt continues to animate the Christian but it rests henceforth on the certitude that death has been overcome: "O Death, where is your victory?"

NOTES

1. Theodore of Cyr on 1 Cor 1:18 (PG 82:236): *Apo tou telous tas prosēgorias titheis* (a text poorly reproduced by ICC as *tas katēgorias*).
2. Cf. above, pp. 4–11.
3. The Apocalypse of Baruch (first century after Jesus Christ) poses the same question as the Corinthians, and there the answer given is that the dead, after

making themselves recognized by their close acquaintances, will afterward have an appearance similar to the one they had on earth. Then the transformation takes place (*Ap. Bar.* 49:2–50:4). The gospel Resurrection narratives follow the same evidently Semitic pattern (cf. X. Léon-Dufour, *Resurrection* [above, p. 75, n. 65], pp. 42 and 320, n. 40].

4. Mt. 22:32 p; En 51:4.

5. Cf. below, pp. 215–216.

6. Already in 2 Mc 7:20–23.

7. Gn 2:7, in Greek *kai eplasen ho Theos ton anthrōpon choun apo tēs gēs, kai enephysen eis to prosōpon autou pnoēn zōēs, kai egeneto ho anthrōpos eis psychēn zōsan.* In addition, see Jb 12:10; 34:14f; Ps 78:38; 104:29f.

8. There can be no question of a "primordial man" nor of a pre-existent Christ, but only of the Christ of Easter; cf. E. Schweizer, "Choikos", *TDNT* 9 (1974), 472–479.

9. Unlike the word *pēlos,* "clay," the term *chous:* "dust" tells of a reality that has no consistency in itself, but receives this from God alone.

10. Ez 37:14. Cf. R. Martin-Achard, *De la mort à la résurrection* (Neuchatel: Delachaux, 1956), p. 83, taken up and developed by B. Schneider, "The Corporate Meaning and Background of 1 Cor 15:45*b*," *CBQ* 29 (1967), 463.

11. Virgil Gheorgiu, *Après la vingt-cinquième heure* (Plon, 1966) in a passage that, to my embarrassment, I could not find again, tells how he answered police officers who asked him about his civil status: "I am from above."

12. Cf. 1 Cor 15:27; 2 Cor 3:18.

13. On 2 Cor 5, cf. pp. 253–257.

14. Cf. Jn 3:6: "That which is born of the flesh is flesh . . . *unless one is born from above, no one can enter the Kingdom of God.*"

15. "*Before* the dust returns to the earth as it was, and the spirit returns to the God who gave it" (Eccl 12:7; cf. Gn 2:7; 3:19; Jb 34:14; Ps 104:29; 146:4; Sir 40:11).

16. On the different outlines proposed for the Epistle to the Romans, cf. A. Robert and A. Feuillet, *Introduction to the New Testament,* trans. P. Skehan *et al.*; (New York: Desclée Company, 1965), pp. 454–456. See my own outline in *RSR* 51 (1963), 94–95.

17. Cf. pp. 164–166.

18. Refer to the commentaries; for example, that of J. Huby *L' Épitre aux Romains* (Paris: Beauchesne, 1957) or that of F. J. Leenhardt *The Epistle to the Romans* (Cleveland: World Publishing Co., 1961) or, more simply, *TOB,* p. 463, n. *m.*

19. The phrase *eph'hōi* allows for two possible interpretations that are defensible grammatically: (1) It expresses a type of causality, either direct (equivalent to *hoti,* as in 2 Cor 5:4) or dependent on another causality (as, perhaps, in Phil 3:12 and 4:10). According to this interpretation, personal sins are the cause of death (so, the *TOB*) or the condition to be fulfilled so that sin produces its effect of death (so, S. Lyonnet in the *Jerusalem Bible*; cf. *Bib* 36 [1955], 436–456). The first of these is not convincing as Pauline, for it is only really used by Paul a single time; the second meaning is only attested in general literature as a condition to be fulfilled in the future, while in this case the condition is past (the aorist tense). (2) The phrase *eph'hōi* is composed of the preposition *epi,* followed by a pronoun that refers back to a noun or to the preceding

clause. The preposition *epi* often indicates "that on account of which" or "that on which"; in other words, the basis for the preceding statement (cf. Rom 8:20) 1 Cor 9:10; Phil 3:9; 1 Tim 6:17). Thus, Lyonnet admits that the expression can be understood as: "by reason of the state of death (brought about by Adam's sin) all have sinned"; the relative pronoun *hos* has in view the whole proposition rather than the noun *thanatos*. According to T. Zahn, *Der Brief des Paulus an die Römer* (Leipzig: A. Deichert, 1910), p. 267, the phrase signifies the historical consequence: "by reason of which all have sinned" ("*auf grund hiervon sündigten alle*"), and it is through such a contingency that all have sinned. According to our interpretation, the expression rather has in view the "logical" consequence that one must deduce from the actual situation. Death has come to all men and women; from this (as a logical consequence of which, as a result of which) one can conclude that all have sinned, or that is an indication that all have sinned.

20. Cf. pp. 180–184.
21. Cf. pp. 180–181.
22. This expression comes from the *TOB*, p. 463, n. *k*; cf. Rom 11:32; Gal 3:22.
23. Here, as elsewhere, the word "to symbolize" is used in its contemporary meaning as expressed by thinkers. Unlike the signifying "sign," which is always distinct from what is signified, the symbol both is and is not the reality that it symbolizes. Symbolic operation consists in the revelation of the relationship that unites two analogous realities, even though they belong to two different worlds (cf. p. 30). There is merely one death, the physical kind verifiable by all; but this occurrence can symbolize to faith the spiritual death that sin is.
24. Rom 8:3.
25. Phil 2:6–11; cited pp. 176–177.
26. Cf. pp. 164–166.
27. Gk. *koimēthentes*, ordinarily translated "the dead" (4:13).
28. Chrysostom: *hoi teteleutēkotes kai enthauta keimenoi ou tethnēkasin, alla koimōntai kai kathendousi* (*PG* 49:393).
29. Hermas, *Vision*, III: 11.
30. *To koimētērion eōs anastaseos.*
31. 1 Thess 4:17.
32. 1 Thess 5:10.
33. 1 Thess 4:5; Eph 2:12.
34. A letter cited by A. Festugière, *L'Idéal religieux des Grecs et l'Évangile* (Paris: Gabalda, 1932), p. 158. What, in fact, is the value of "fusion in ether"? (p. 145).
35. Cf. above, pp. 199–201.
36. Ex 19:17; Jn 12:18; Mt 25:1,6. Cf. J. Dupont, *SYN CHRISTOI. L'union avec le Christ suivant saint Paul* (Paris: Desclée de Brouwer, 1952), pp. 64–73.
37. Rv 5:10; cf. 1 Cor 4:8.
38. 1 Cor 15:36.
39. Ez 37:21: "*synaxō kai eisaxō autous eis tēn gēn Israēl.*"
40. "*Axei syn autōi*" (1 Thess 4:13), "*hama pantote syn Kyriōi esometha*" (4:17), "*hama syn autōi zēsomen*" (5:10), "*episynagogē ep'auton*" (2 Thess 2:1). Cf. the Appendix to this book: "Beyond Death."
41. Cf. above, pp. 5–6.

7. Suffering and the Hope of the World

"O Death, where is your victory?" One could just as easily juxtapose another cry over against Paul's victory shout: "O Christ, where is your victory?" How is it that human history is as much an interweaving of indescribable suffering after Christ's resurrection as it was before? There is no need to paint these sufferings in all their hues, for they are quite vividly present in everyone's consciousness. And yet Paul's triumphant shout still echoes today.

In reality, through his contact with the living Christ, Paul became convinced that God's life is stronger than death and Christ's cross has meaning. Through this entry into the secret of the end of time, he could affirm and maintain that even if entry to the Kingdom of Heaven demands a radical transformation, death has nonetheless been vanquished not only in fact in Jesus Christ but also in principle for every human person. Given these facts, what is to be thought of suffering, which is the true prelude to death?

The Bible never tried to explain suffering, even though it searched out its worth as a learning and even a purifying trial. Job bowed down before the incomprehensible mystery of God, while the Servant of YHWH took upon himself the sin of the people. But this was no more than discourse or prophecy so that as a result even today a Jew can be satisfied with putting off the cessation of suffering and death until the end of time. For his part, Jesus experienced human suffering to the full, leaving it up to God to reply to the scandal involved in suffering:

In the days [*of the life*] of his flesh, he offered up prayers and supplications, with loud cries and tears, to *the One* who was able to save him from death, and he was heard for his godly fear.

(Heb 5:7)

Paul, for his part, when confronted with someone who had crossed over through death, felt he had to go further: if death has been conquered, does not suffering have to be on the point of disappearing from the world? Is it not an untenable paradox to hold at one and the same time to victory over death and to the continued existence of suffering?

The alternative is to localize this within a paradox that is even more comprehensive. The Christian by faith lives out a radical tension between the "already" and the "not yet"; this means that the ideal is guaranteed but the real continues to hold sway. At this point we make the observation that the more an ideal is elevated, the greater scope there is for deception when one notices that facts are so far from confirming that ideal. Is this not the case with what we call suffering? When one cannot reduce it merely to sorrow, suffering consists essentially in an awareness that there is a gulf between what one knows has, in principle, been accomplished and what one holds in fact? To believe that Jesus is risen and death overcome does not mean suppressing suffering; on the contrary, it means making suffering more painful. Let us add that it also means encouragement to struggle more vigorously to eliminate it or, at least, to diminish it.

Paul was a realist. Moreover, he was compelled to come to understand the ideal in which he firmly believed by facing up to the suffering he underwent. Right from the start he situated the tension in relation to the mystery of the Risen One; then, he pointed out the role of the Holy Spirit. The operations of Christ and the Spirit respectively were brought to bear on suffering and hope. But to read Paul is to see hope well up more clearly from the person of Christ while the animating presence of the Spirit shared a closer relationship with sufferings that people underwent. These observations, then, suggest the two themes we will develop in this chapter.

CHRIST AND HUMAN HOPE

According to a classic formulation, Jesus is exalted in glory with the Father, whence he shall come at the end of time to judge the living and the dead. In this view Christ would have handed matters over to the Holy Spirit while he awaited the glorious day of his Parousia. This way of looking at things, so well articulated by Luke, highlights the significance of the work of Jesus Christ. However, it entails with it a very real risk, that of portraying the Savior as immobile and in expectation in heaven, while in the world men and women continue to work, to struggle and to suffer. How could one accept with joyous hearts this disinterestedness of Christ? Would Christ in the end merely be the model just person who, after his sojourn on earth, has gone to rest in heaven? But is he not present as well in the midst of men and women who suffer?

Now Paul had a second way of depicting Christ's glorious life, one that saw him always laboring until the end of time. Little by little this perspective was replaced with the one mentioned earlier, but it still possesses incontestable merit, something I would like to expound before pointing to Paul's other, more abstract but no less significant, terminology on this topic.

CHRIST STRUGGLING TO THE END

In the fifteenth chapter of 1 Corinthians, whose structure we have already outlined,[1] Paul tried to persuade his correspondents about the resurrection of the dead, which they doubted. He describes the way in which the resurrection will take place. There are three stages in its accomplishment: first of all, Christ's resurrection, then the bringing to full life of both the survivors and the dead until, finally, there comes the victory. Let us read over the text:

20 In fact Christ has been raised, the first fruits of those who *are dead.* 21 For as by a man came death, by a man has come also the resurrection of the dead. 22 For as in Adam all die, so also in Chrsit shall all be made alive. 23 But each in his own order: Christ the first fruits, then at his coming those who belong to Christ. 24 Then comes the end, when he delivers the Kingdom to God the Father after destroying every rule and every authority and power. 25 (For he must reign *until he has put all his enemies under his feet.*) 26 The last enemy to be destroyed is Death. 27 "For *he has put all things in subjection under his feet.*" But when it says

"All things are put in subjection under him" it is plain that he is excepted who put all things under him. **28** When all things are subjected to him, then the Son himself will also be subjected to Him who put all things under him, that God may be all in all.

(1 Cor 15:20–28)

The scenario may appear to depend on mythological constructions; however, by comparison with other descriptions, it is somewhat stark: no question here of a trumpet or an archangel's voice, still less of apostasy, a man of lawlessness, a son of perdition, an Antichrist, or a restraining power.[2] All this apocalyptic paraphernalia has been left aside. The only features remaining are the enemies who are at work in history: the heavenly powers, and death. In addition, the assignation of the final actions has been preserved. But this is not the essential point; what matters is Christ's role, not at the "Parousia" but at the "end."

Before this "end," at the moment when he will hand over the rule to God, there will be a space of time during which Christ will have been continuing the battle against the enemies, against these very heavenly powers who wreak harm on men and women.[3] Paul takes up the warring style of Psalm 110 to describe Christ's activity as he aims to establish God's rule.[4] During all this remaining time, then, Christ is laboring to bring about the destruction in this world here below of the last enemy, death.[5]

It is in just such a context that suffering takes on meaning. It is an integral aspect of our life prior to the end of time. If from a purely natural viewpoint this struggle can be inserted within a conception of humanity moving sorrowfully toward a communion of persons, in our view it appears as a reflection of the struggle that is being waged without respite against the power of death. And Christ is with us to direct the battle.

FAITH TRIUMPHS OVER DEATH

Paul did not merely show how Christ cooperates with us in the struggle against death and suffering. He carefully scrutinized personal experiences of suffering that seemed to counterbalance God's promise and to upset a believer's equilibrium. Of such a kind was the crisis that threatened Abraham, our father in faith. Paul saw in Abraham a type of the believer caught up in the trials of life:

He is the father of us all **17** . . . in the presence of the *One* in whom he believed, who gives life to the dead and calls into existence the things that do not exist. **18** In hope he believed against hope, that he should become the father of many nations; as he had been told, "So shall your descendants be." **19** He did not weaken in faith when he considered his own body, which was as good as dead [*nenekrōmenon*]—because he was about a hundred years old—or when he considered the womb of Sarah *which had been touched by* death [*nekrōsis*] **20** No distrust made him waver concerning the promise of God, but he grew strong in his faith as he gave glory to God, **21** fully convinced that God was able to do what he had promised.

(Rom 4:17–21)

Abraham, the trustee of the divine promise of a posterity without number, saw himself threatened by death, incapable of raising up life. But he abided in the presence of the God who gives life to the dead and calls into being that which is not. On the one hand, he stared death in the face; on the other, he understood that life was to be found in God. His faith consisted in "hoping against all hope" that God could transform all things and "fill up with power" his servant.

Christian faith, according to Paul, does not consist in admitting certain truths; rather, it means being in dialogue with God. Further, given that the human condition is replete with trials and miseries, faith is grounded in God, who can deliver from the evil which threatens to be crushing. Quite clearly, this does not explain away suffering, but only indicates the outlook one can have toward it. Leaping toward God in the face of death, faith in this way becomes "hope."

IN THE FACE OF SUFFERING, HOPE

Shortly after his treatment of the patriarch Abraham, Paul concluded the first part of his epistle by generalizing the objective situation in which we find ourselves, a condition effected by faith in Christ, which has justified us. Without any doubt he proclaims that the victory has been definitively won, but he then goes on to locate victory immediately within a context of the "tribulations" of which we are necessarily victims; tribulations and victory—neither exists without the other.

Yes, Paul writes, death has been vanquished and we do possess life; the covenant has been reestablished and we are hoping for glory:

> 1 Therefore, since we are justified by faith we have peace with God through our Lord Jesus Christ. 2 Through him we have obtained access to this grace in which we stand, and we rejoice in our hope of sharing the glory of God.
>
> (Rom 5:1–2)

But alongside this evidence there appears other, conflicting evidence. Brusquely, Paul evokes the distresses that overwhelm us, but he does so only to declare that, since there is a confidence[6] based on hope of glory, so likewise there is confidence "in tribulations":

> 3 More than that, we rejoice in our sufferings, knowing that suffering produces endurance, 4 and endurance produces character, and character produces hope, 5 and hope does not disappoint us, because God's love has been poured into our hearts through the Holy Spirit who has been given us.
>
> (Rom 5:3–5)

This is a foundational text. Our mortal condidtion, similar to Abraham's, is the trace felt here below of our condition as sinners. This is why believers remain persons in a permanent state of conflict. On the one hand, they are certain that the victory has been won; on the other, they grant that the clashes of this present world have not, for all that, come to a halt.

This paradox is seized around the waist. Two words run head on into one another and yet mutually enrich each other. On one side, *suffering* is undergone, sickness, barrenness, a whole collection of experiences that fall under the heading of "tribulations." Encountering this group head on is *hope*, which proclaims, despite appearances to the contrary, its very own certitude, one that belongs to another order. Tribulation appears as the sequel in this world to a struggle engaged in to the "end" with the power of death. Hope keeps us with our heads high, with the result that Paul cannot speak correctly of suffering without also immediately evoking hope.

Paul had inherited from the primitive community an existential definition of the Christian as a person animated by faith, hope, and charity: this triad constituted the Christian's being.[7] It is difficult to account for hope's origins, for the noun "hope" is never found in the gospels and the verb "to hope" is entirely absent from Mark and is found but once in each of the other three gospels. Always it is Paul who makes of it a "category;" that is to say, the mainspring of his theological thought. In the text quoted above, hope comes in as a recapitulation of two other attributes, "perseverance" or "constancy" (Gk. *hypomonē*) and of "tested fidelity" (Gk. *dokimē*), the attribute of someone who has endured a trial. These three expressions strive to take within their scope an extent of time during which the Christian has remained steadfast in faith. Ultimately, it is thanks to love, the third term in the triad, that hope does not "deceive." In effect, in contrast to hope, which tends entirely to what is not yet possessed, love already is the object of one's experience, thanks to the Spirit who has been given.

The virtue of hope (Fr. *esperance*) looks to what it does not have a hold on, and, in this sense, it is identical with "a hope" (Fr. *espoir*) extended toward what is to come (the future). But while "a hope" (*espoir*) is never certain of gaining possession of its object, hope (*esperance*) possesses certitude, because faith is firm and because love has been experienced. As with hope in the Old Testament, so Christian hope is still oriented toward the abundance of the goods of the covenant, but its foundation is the unshakeable rock of Christ's resurrection. Henceforth, even if the sorrowful tension between the "not yet" and the "already now" continues with even greater intensity, the Spirit who has been given acts as surety for hope in its efforts to hold on despite everything. This, then, is what Paul now magnificently demonstrates in facing head on the very fact of suffering.

THE HOLY SPIRIT AND SUFFERING

Just as he concluded the first part of the development of the Epistle to the Romans with a consideration of hope in the midst of tribulations, so Paul concludes the second part of his treatment by describing the new life of the believer who undergoes suffering. This, then, is the account of the believer's objective condition in Christ, along with the moral imperatives that flow from it.[8] From Romans 7:7 to 8:30, he describes how, thanks to life in the Spirit, the new life is lived out. The two phases of his treatment are presented successively, not in their objectivity as regimes (as had been done in the treatment of Romans 1:18–5:11), but in their subjective actualization, which answers how an individual can live in the Spirit.

Now, it is by means of a diptych that the two views of the Christian "I" have been represented. Existing at the outset under the Law and without the Spirit and then delivered over to sin and death, the "I" commits suicide.[9] Though the first panel in the diptych shows the fruit of sin (7:7–25), the other, more positive one, details how God's Spirit comes to set "Me" free and gives "Me" life (8:1–17). Paul considers himself authorized to declare that we are truly "set free." Following this double presentation of the new life, Paul concludes in double time, just as he did in the first part: first, with considerations on the life that is exposed to suffering (8:18–30, which parallels 5:1–11), and then with a triumphal hymn to God's love, giving thanks for all that has been given (8:31–39).

According to the state of the text, which we shall consider in detail, that is Romans 8:18–30, the "spiritual life" is not only a struggle against the spirit and the flesh, but is already the Spirit's victory, which, faith knows, has in principle been won over sin and the flesh. The Christian's present existence immediately runs up against suffering, and, by virtue of this very fact, requires the exercise of hope.

18 I consider that the sufferings of this present time are not worth comparing with the glory that is to be revealed to us (*eis hēmas*). **19** For the creation waits with eager longing for the revealing of the sons of God; **20** for the creation was subjected to futility, not of its own will but by the will of him who subjected it in hope; **21** because the creation itself will be set free from its bondage to decay and obtain the glorious liberty of the children of God. **22** We know that the whole creation has been groaning in travail together until now. **23** And not only the creation! But we ourselves, who have the first fruits of the Spirit, groan inwardly as we wait for adoption as sons, the redemption of our bodies. **24** For in this hope we were saved. Now hope that is seen is not hope. For who hopes for what he sees? **25** But if we hope for what we do not see, we *spy it out* with patience.
26 Likewise the Spirit helps us in our weakness; for we do not know how to pray as we ought, but the Spirit himself intercedes for us with sighs too deep for words. **27** And he who searches the hearts of men knows what is the mind of the Spirit, because the Spirit intercedes for the saints according to the will of God.
28 We know that in everything God works for good with those who love him, who are called according to his purpose. **29** For those whom he fore-knew he also predestined to be conformed to the image of his Son, in order that he might be the first-born among many brethren. **30** And those whom he predestined he also called; and those whom he called he also justified; and those whom he justified he also glorified.

(Rom 8:18–30)

When we display the text's movement with a chart, we notice immediately that Paul's thought finds its expression in opposed pairs, as much in Chapter 8 as it had in Romans 5:1–5, the only two places in the epistle where there is reference to hope.

In these two passages glory and suffering are never enumerated in succession: we always come across them in contrasts, in "opposed pairs." Further, it is useful never to come to grips with one of the terms without doing the same with the other. For Paul, to speak of suffering is intolerable unless one speaks also of hope; moreover, tribulations that are undergone become mediators of

	Rom 5	Rom 8
Contrast 1: victory/ suffering	peace (1), glory (2) tribulations (3)	glory (18) sufferings (17, 18)
Contrast 2: suffering/ hope	perseverance (3, 4) hope (2, 4, 5)	waiting (19, 23, 25) hope (20, 24, 25)
Foundation guaranteeing the tension	God's love (5) the Holy Spirit (5)	God's love (35) the Spirit (13–16, 26, 27)

hope. He adds, as well, that love dwells in one's heart to allow the tension between suffering and hope to be endured.

STATING THE PROBLEM: THE FACT OF SUFFERING

I consider that the sufferings of this present time are not worth comparing with the glory that is to be revealed to us.

(Rom 8:18)

From the start, Paul confronts the painful fact of sufferings: but does he not thereby call into question the reality of the victory won by Christ over death's power and minions? In order to get inside Paul's thought, one has to recall that, as a good Jew, he sets the "now" of the "present time" in opposition to the "time to come."[10] The end of time brings clarity to the present.[11] Here Paul balances out sufferings and glory.

Paul, in classical fashion, understood by sufferings the pains of work, the trials of one's body and heart; the term also refers to the eschatological tribulations,[12] those trials that were to act as preludes to the Parousia. Of just such a kind was Israel's long-standing complaint, which found its culmination in the new situation created by Christ's coming.

In regard to the glory that balances off suffering, this means the "eschatological" glory, already mysteriously active in the present age but a glory that, in the end, will reveal "in our favor"[13] the splendor of the mystery of Jesus Christ. Elsewhere Paul stated this truth more precisely:

This slight momentary affliction is preparing us for an eternal weight of glory beyond all comparison.

(2 Cor 4:17)

According to the context, this glory consists in divine sonship, in total freedom, in the "redemption of our bodies."

Two movements punctuate the following development. First, creation itself, then believers—the two together—give utterance to their expectation of glory. These two movements are tied together by the vocabulary of hope. The family of *elpis* words, which belongs to the earliest catechism,[14] resounds on seven different occasions in this passage, especially in the digression found in Verses 24–25. The word is accompanied by all kinds of terms that signify expectant waiting: *apekdechomai*, is a violent waiting, which here is translated quite expressively as "to spy out attentively," sometimes referring to creation (v. 19) as well as to believers (vv. 23 and 25); the rare word *apokaradokia*,[15] is the attitude of craning one's neck or head to observe what is going on, with a note of tension in waiting for something or someone, translated here as "stalking"; *hypomonē*, is another aspect of hope, that which stands firm, perseveres, is constant. All the situations are ones of expectant waiting: the yearning and deep desire that rise up from the secret regions of one's being, the groanings in the travail of giving birth, whether that of the creation or that of believers or of the Spirit himself. All of these experiences suggest an atmosphere of victorious hope, which reinforces the weakness, suffering, and slavery of the present moment, with which they stand in stark contrast; the future expressions are judiciously used to point out the marvels of glory: the freedom of the children of God, the redemption of our bodies.

BIRTH PANGS AND CREATION'S HOPE

19 For the creation waits with eager longing for the revealing of the sons of God; **20** for the creation was subjected to futility, not of its own will but by the will of him who subjected it in hope; **21** because the creation itself will be set free from its bondage to decay and obtain the glorious liberty of the children of God. **22** We know that the whole creation has been groaning in travail together until now.

(Rom 8:19–22)

This magnificent text sets one dreaming as one gazes on a depiction of a nature that yearns with all its powers for final liberation. What exactly does this mean? We need to be more precise about the exact meaning of some words: *creation, futility, subjection.*

Creation designates the created world, considered first of all in itself, independently of the life of believers of which there will be mention in the development that follows (v. 23); it means the world in general—men and nature—which the Bible continually shows to be in solidarity both in joy and in pain.[16] To illustrate this, it is helpful to recall that the covenant of Sinai had been transposed in the Noachic covenant.[17] The bow in the clouds (or rainbow) signified the covenant made between God and the earth. Unlike the Greeks who admired the harmony of the cosmos, the Jews were first of all sensitive to the world of humans and, thus, to the fidelity of the God of love, for they did not conceive of man without God, even less of the universe without man: the universe did not exist in some autonomous fashion but was tied to the historical act of God's creating man. The universe, accordingly was also in solidarity with man's sin and so came under the influence of its consequences; on the other hand, since man must one day bring creation to perfection, creation attentively "spies out" the manifestation of the sons of God that will one day restore its stability and its brilliance.

Now, for Paul, this creation "has been made subject to *futility*." By this term Paul did not strictly understand the state of simple creation, for in Romans 1:21 men are said to have "become" futile because they did not render glory to God; instead they worshipped creation rather than the Creator.[18] Sin, which consists in taking creation for one's god or in taking one's self for God, entails as its consequence not the fragility inherent in the human condition, but according to Hebrew etymology a "lightness."[19] The meaning

of this word is clearly manifest to one who can admit, along with
the Bible, that only God brings to life, sustains and "gives weight"
to creation. When this bond with God is severed, man no longer
is anything but an appearance, something superficial; he becomes
unstable and is no longer rooted, since his root is the living God.
So, he becomes a liar, inconsistent and, to the degree that he pre-
tends to be solid, deceitful.

The consequence of this state of "futility" is *corruption*,[20] that
is, a state of division and continual disintegration. Creation finds
itself in bondage to corruption by the fact that it has been subjected to "futility." Having lost its point of attachment, which had
assured it of stability and firmness, creation kept floating at the
whim of human caprice and ended up disintegrating into the dust
from which it sprang.

Creation had not wanted this *subjection* to futility; the subject
state had been imposed on it. In fact, creation in God's plan—
namely, solidarity with the destiny of humans—was to have
shared in the promised glory. But it had become subject to futility.
By whom, Paul did not specify. On this point, likewise, exegetes
have been divided. Some consider creation was made subject by
Satan, but, we might ask, why should he have gotten involved
in such a way? Others ascribe responsibility for this subjection to
Adam (and sinful man) or to God himself.[21] The use of the passive
voice without an agent being designated ("had been subjected")
suggests that God is the author of this action, through an inter-
mediary, Adam. Clearly this was not an instance of a god exer-
cising "vengeful authority."[22] Rather, was it the normal outcome
of God's plan as this had been so clearly revealed in the first chapter of the Epistle to the Romans: "God handed them over, " that
is, he abandoned them to the consequences of their sin—to futility—to *non*glory, to perversion.

Since he is involved in the beginning of this subjection, God
has not let its course develop according to some sort of fateful
determinism, but rather has introduced into the process a horizon
of *hope*.[23] Our translation is at pains to stress the following in-

terpretation: it is not, properly speaking, creation that "keeps hope," but rather God who does so by situating creation on a foundation of hope.[24]

Paul attributes to hope what is proper to man: a hope for liberation from bondage and for a passing over from corruption to glory. He chose to speak in generalities about hope's object, concentrating his attention instead on man who is hope's *raison d'etre* and who still has yet to recover his nature as a "son of God"; only when that happens will creation be united in the "glorious freedom of the children of God." Just as a human person's body is mortal and so is destined for corruption, so creation, which was made subject to futility, appears as the extension of our body's condition. But, just as our body also has to be ransomed and transfigured, so, too, creation, through our consciousness, itself also has to hope to be set free from its corruption. This hope is tied to a glory that must be recovered, the glory man has lost and causes to be lost as the result of his sin.

In awaiting the revelation of glory, creation is like a woman who brings forth a child to the light of day. This comparison is typically biblical: the theme of the woman who is about to give birth sometimes indicates the inevitable aspect of the eschatological judgment, at other times it indicates the prelude to a new world about to be born.[25] The value of the comparison lies in the fact that it associates the joyous certainty of a coming birth with the passing away of sorrow: through and beyond suffering, life is already being revealed. This, then, is what the groanings of creation in the travail of giving birth mean.[26]

Two conclusions are called for from this reading of these verses. In the first place, the awareness that Paul did not think about a human person's destiny apart from that of the whole of creation. According to an image often alluded to, "the universe is not a simple pedestal with man as its statue; one can much more aptly compare it to a gigantic stem of which humanity is the flower."[27] Creation in this way shares in human existence and human destiny. Another conclusion follows: in creation's "labor" there is a dimension that is not "natural"; creation does not behave exactly as it would have if man did not find himself in the state of sin.

Because of this, therefore, just as actual physical death symbolizes to the eyes of the believer the state of sin in which he finds himself, so creation's sorrowful travail, the bondage of corruption wherein it groans, and all this suffering must symbolize for it something that goes beyond the simple difficulties that creation undergoes to reach fulfillment. But, at the same time, the believer knows that salvation also reaches into this other dimension of himself that the universe constitutes: this travail is the bringing to birth of a new world that will reveal the liberty of the sons of God.

BELIEVERS WAIT EXPECTANTLY

And not only the creation! But we ourselves, who have the first fruits of the Spirit, groan inwardly as we wait for adoption as sons, the redemption of our bodies.

(Rom 8:23)

Human waiting is analogous to, but not identical with, that of creation. In effect, we already possess a foretaste and a guarantee of eschatological freedom in that we have the "pledge of the Spirit."[28] And this is the reason we are conscious of our waiting and why we see that creation, itself, also is engaged in waiting. In our turn from now on we are attentively spying out the liberation of our bodies that will bring our filial adoption to fulfillment. Like creation, the body is in servitude to sin and, thus, is destined for death; it has to be "bought back," be set free itself from the bondage to which it finds itself reduced. This affirmation will be clarified in our reading of the passage from the second epistle to the Corinthians, to be done in the next chapter; for the moment, it is enough for us to refer to our reading in the preceding chapter of the movement by which we pass from the "physical body" to the "spiritual body." This passing is not an escape from the body but rather is the body's being brought to fulfillment; this movement does not come about except by way of suffering, and this is why we groan as we wait for the day of our liberation.

BELIEVERS HOPE

24 For in this hope we were saved. Now hope that is seen is not hope. For who hopes for what he sees? **25** But if we hope for what we do not see, we wait for it with patience.

(Rom 8:24–25)

The believer does not live only in expectation, however intense that waiting might be: rather, the believer is propelled by hope, for hope adds to expectation the certainty of obtaining what we are awaiting. Salvation, even though already given, is still to come: one must, for this reason, live in an atmosphere of hope.[29] The follow-up to Verse 24 is a development, somewhat rabbinical in style, over the seeing—not seeing contrast, which, in fact, typifies hope's attitude. Concretely, this signifies that, if we were not to be aware at each moment of the mortal condition of our bodies, we would end up by imaging that we already fully possess our salvation. Needs, quarrels, even wars are so many stimuli to keep us on the lookout for the moment when we will be able to meet one another as brothers and sisters. However negative and odious it might be, in this light suffering takes on meaning: it keeps us in a state of waiting for glory. Hope, which is one of the necessary dimensions of our faith life, is continually being nourished by the paradox of our life as believers: already possessing salvation by means of the pledge of the Spirit and still waiting for salvation to be brought to its fulfillment in our bodies. Suffering prevents me from getting bogged down on this earth, in this still incomplete creation. Like creation I am in a state of waiting; more than creation I am full of hope.[30]

OUR HOPE TAKEN UP INTO THE HEART OF GOD

26 Likewise the Spirit helps us in our weakness; for we do not know how to pray as we ought, but the Spirit himself intercedes for us with

sighs too deep for words. **27** And he who searches the hearts of men knows what is the mind of the Spirit, because the Spirit intercedes for the saints according to the will of God.
28 We know that in everything God works for good with those who love him, who are called according to his purpose. **29** For those whom he fore-knew he also predestined to be conformed to the image of his Son, in order that he might be the first-born among many brethren. **30** And those whom he predestined he also called; and those whom he called he also justified; and those whom he justified he also glorified.

(Rom 8:26–30)

What then does it mean to hope? Because it does not possess its goal, hope gets transformed into a constant demand; but the faith animating this prayer is "weak," unlike that found in Abraham when he considered his body "already as good as dead"— for he "did not weaken in his faith."[31] Would that the example of Abraham, a model for believers, might keep us from despairing in the face our "powerlessness" to "raise up life from a barren womb," or to transform our own bodies and the whole world!

In any case, we are not alone in this hope. Paul reiterates what he had said earlier, that we do possess the "pledge" of the Spirit. This pledge is active in each of us. Just as man transforms creation's expectation into a veritable hope, so the Spirit is able to transform human groanings into authentic prayer. Groanings and yearnings had existed before, but they had not reached the point of being uttered.

The Spirit has been presented by Paul in a fashion analogous to what Christ had said when he spoke of the "Paraclete" in the Johannine tradition. In the Synoptics, by contrast, there had been no mention of the Spirit in what we would call a strictly theological sense. Only John and Paul had given to the Spirit an active role in the believer's life; and they did this in diverse ways. In John, the Spirit is Christ's advocate within the conscience of believers. In Paul, the Spirit (who testifies with us to our sonship[32]), helps the Christian in weakness; and in temptation to despair the Spirit brings the Christian to give utterance to his or her yearning.

Before all else, the believer recognizes that he does not pray "as he ought." Probably Paul is here echoing the confession of a man who, in the magical papyri of his period spoke as follows: "O you, whoever you are, give me what you know!" In antiquity the human person did not dare articulate his prayer for fear of drawing down on himself a thunderbolt from the gods because of some error or disrespect on his part. Still, there is some advantage for us in such a view, because the Spirit causes us to proclaim God as Father without, for all that, our having been able to plumb God's mysterious designs. Here, then, is the role of the Spirit who gives meaning to our groanings, which are "too deep for words"[33]—as much to those who take up creation's groaning once more like a child's pain, as in the case of the groaning of believers by means of which our experience of tension is expressed. All this is beyond our Spirit but not beyond God who searches our hearts. Unlike ourselves, who do not know, God does know what is the drive and the "yearning" of the Spirit, namely the Spirit's intercession on behalf of the saints. Man himself cannot express the true language of God, but the Spirit who formulates this yearning that is "according to God" can give expression to our desire for life and peace.[34]

Hence, it appears from these verses that genuine prayer must begin with an avowal of ignorance about its own object or, even more so, about ourselves, the ones formulating the prayer. One may say about prayer what was said about justification: it is begotten in the very moments when it becomes forgetful of self.[35] Prayer is expressed, first of all, by groanings too deep for words, thereby signifying that the Spirit who moves our spirits goes beyond our understanding. All things considered, prayer consists in recognition of the plan for our glorification that is guaranteed by God from this very moment. This, then, is the point that still needs explanation.

Even though we do not know how to pray as we ought, we do know this much at least:[36] through the Spirit's intervention, we have access to God's secret designs. A trinitarian movement exists in every prayer; it begins with the Spirit, moves by way of the Son (in whose image we have to be conformed), and issues in the Father's glory.

In principle, "God makes everything work together for the good of those who love him, for those who have been called according to his primordial and eternal purpose." Paul has in mind all believers when he names them "those who love God."[37] This designation, which is quite rare in Paul, is immediately corrected. For example, in 1 Corinthians 8:3 Paul said, "If anyone loves God, he is known by Him." In this text, likewise, the subsequent verse (Rom 8:29) invites us to acknowledge that we are "fore-known" by God. Those who "love God" are only responding to a prevenient love; and, thus, God's action in favor of those who love Him seals the recognition that has been accepted and proclaimed by man.[38]

In this principle of prayer, we understand that the unfolding of history, which is so disconcerting because of the sufferings that have been let loose, is being guided by God who follows a plan determined ahead of time (*prothesis*). This plan, anterior to (*pro*) human history, is effected in the course of time, assuming the consequences of man's sin but also looking toward his liberation, and in this way issuing in God's glory.

When God makes everything work together for the good of those who love him, this is because he loves the Son, it is because God has decided to enable believers to be conformed to the Son's image: for there is a kinship structure between the believer and the Son. Now, the Son himself is God's likeness,[39] and we are, bit by bit, being transformed into his likeness[40] through the work of the Spirit. In the end, God wants us, with his first-born, to form one immense family of which he is the eldest.

After this return to origins,[41] Paul plunges into the course of the ages,[42] ending up at the end of time.[43] Between protology and eschatology is situated the unfolding of history. And here Paul enumerates the principal divine actions: call, justification, glorification. He expresses these in the aorist tense (one of the Greek ways of expressing past time) so as to declare better that we are already in possession of these goods, including glory.

CONCLUSION

And so, no more than the Old Testament did, Paul did not claim to have found an explanation for the universal phenomenon of suffering. He could not do so, just as he could not "explain" death. These are the givens of human experience that are inexplicable. Jesus, himself, did not explain suffering but he took a stand on it by performing many healing miracles[44] and by accepting the cross.[45]

For his part, Paul accepted death and suffering. He also assigned it meaning. He showed that he was heir to the biblical tradition endorsed by Jesus, one that told of the "necessity" that the prophet suffer and also spoke of the persecution of the Just One.[46] In his own way Paul took up the great notion of the design of God in which suffering had a place; he did so by referring either to its eventual meaning or to the outlook one should take toward it. Having recognized the secret dimension of suffering (a function of one's ability to discern the work of sin, the true root of evil in the world), the Christian can locate suffering in relation to the glory prepared for us, thereby appropriating the virtue of hope. Finally, the Christian has eyes set on Christ who, with him or her, wages the battle to the end.

To find in this way a meaning for suffering that begins with sin (which subjected the whole of creation to corruption), does not thereby hand creation over to the fatalism of suffering in stoic fashion or out of some mystique of hope in the evolution of the human species.[47] Paul holds nothing in contempt; he does not even claim that Jesus "blessed" human suffering. But Paul does invite the Christian to cooperate with Christ in the struggle against sin and, so, against suffering. Suffering, like death and like sin, must be hated, and the believer must ceaselessly struggle with Christ against sin, death, and suffering up to the day when, having been overcome, the Christian humbly hands himself or herself over to the one who can provide deliverance forever.

In this battle, the Christian is not alone. He or she lives in communion with the entire creation, which groans in travail to give birth and, so, also in communion with all men and women who, in their way, stand up to suffering and struggle that it be done away with here below. He or she struggles with other believers and ultimately with Christ. And, through the Spirit, the Christian comes to know the meaning of God's plan, a plan for glory. Suffering makes a yearning spring up; and the Spirit bestows a plenitude of meaning on this desire. Prayer "transforms" the Christian's groaning before the absurd, thanks to the Spirit that inspires him or her. Far from paralyzing him or her in an illusory kind of resignation, hope stimulates the Christian to action in this world, knowing, as that hope does, that heaven is not so much beyond this world as "within" it. For love anticipates even here in this world the glory that there will be at the end.

Sometimes people say, "If Jesus had truly won the victory, there would be no more conflicts or wars." Might this be an imaginary triumph? Not according to the word a poet attributed to Jesus, "It was not war that I came to suppress, so much as peace that I came to add in abundance."[48] The Spirit makes this peace radiate in the believer's heart, a peace enabling him or her to give meaning to the groaning of creation, which is unaware.

NOTES

1. Cf. p. 198.
2. 2 Thess 2:1–4.
3. H. Schlier, *Principalities and Powers in the New Testament* (*Quaestiones Disputatae 3*; New York: Herder and Herder, 1961).
4. Cf. M. Gorgues, *À la droite de Dieu. Résurrecton de Jésus et actualisation du Ps 110,1 dans le Nouveau Testament* (Paris: Gabalda, 1978). The subject of the verb in Verses 25 and 27 seems to be Christ himself.
5. Cf. 1 Cor 15:26; Rv 20:14; 21:4. Death, like sin, has to be hated; and the believer, like Christ, has to fight against sin and death without a let-up.
6. The Greek *kauchēsis*, which sometimes refers to boasting, cannot be uniformly translated as "pride" (against the *TOB*): it means self-assurance, confidence, basing onself on God (and not oneself). Cf. entry "Pride," *DBT*, 2nd ed. (1973), p. 359, and entry "Confidence," *Dictionary of the New Testament* (San Francisco; Harper & Row, 1980), p. 145.
7. From the very first New Testament writings, the triad of "virtues" (faith, hope, love) is mentioned: 1 Thess 1:3; 5:8; 2 Cor 13:13; Col 1:4f; Heb 10:22–24; 1 Pt 1:21f.
8. Rom 6:1–7:6; cf. pp. 170–171.

9. Thus, according to Graham Greene, in *The Heart of the Matter* (Middlesex: Penguin, 1978), Scobie, aware of his interior division and personal disarray, moves fatally toward suicide.
10. Rom 3:21,26; 5:9,11; 7:6; 11:30f; 13:11.
11. 1 Cor 10:11; cf. p. 194, n. 47.
12. Cf. Rom 5:3; 8:35; 1 Cor 7:26–28; 2 Cor 1:5–7; 4:11,17; 11:23–28; Phil 1:29; Col 1:24; 4*EZ* 13:16–19; *Ap. Bar.* 25:1.
13. The preposition *eis* is followed by a personal pronoun in the accusative case; so, it is appropriate to translate it not as "in us" but "in our regard."
14. Cf. R. Bultmann, *"Elpis,"* *TDNT* 2 (1964), 530–532.
15. Only here and in Phil 1:20.
16. Cf. A. M. Dubarle, "Foi en la création et sentiment de créature dans l'Ancien Testament," *LV* 48 (1960), 21–42.
17. Gn 8:21f; 9:9–13; Jer 33:20,25; Acts 14:16f; 4*EZ* 7:11f; *Ap. Bar.* 51:12f; 32:6. S. Lyonnet has remarkably pointed out the difference of conception on this point between the Bible and Hellenism: "La rédemption de l'univers," *LV* 48 (1960), 43–62, especially pp. 47–48. Cf. also A. Viard, "Expectatio Creaturae," *RB* 69 (1952), 337–354.
18. Rom 1:21,25.
19. This key word of Ecclesiastes (in Hebrew *hèbèl*, in Greek *mataiotēs*) symbolizes, in the first place, a "breath," "nothingness." It serves as a designation of idols (Acts 14:15; 1 Cor 3:20 = Ps 94:11) or the consequences of moral or religious disorder (Rom 1:21; Eph 4:17).
20. In Greek *phthora*: "the act of corrupting, corruption." H. Schlier, *Der Römerbrief* (Freiburg-im-B.: Herder, 1977), pp. 260–261, has clearly shown, through engagement with numerous commentators, that vanity designates something "more fundamental" than the corruption that is its consequence; it characterizes the creature as such.
21. I gravitate toward J. Huby's interpretation, over against what S. Lyonnet or H. Schlier say, for they insist on the role of Adam and of the human person as sinner. Undoubtedly, Adam was the one who let sin enter the world, but it is God who in the end is responsible for the situation, above all for the fact that hope has been given.
22. S. Lyonnet justly reacts against this interpretation.
23. Paul could allude to the divine promise made in Paradise: *"The woman* shall bruise your head," (Gn 3:15), the "protogospel" of Christians, which heralds the triumph of the Messiah, born of a woman. Cf. S. Lyonnet, in J. Huby, *L'Épitre aux Romains*, 2nd ed. (Paris: Beauchesne, 1957), p. 613.
24. *Eph'elpidi*, wherein the preposition *epi* indicates the foundation, the base, the support.
25. A classical theme in the Bible: Is 26:17; 66:8; Jer 22:23f; Hos 13:13; Mi 4:9f; Mt 24:8; Mk 13:8; Jn 16:21; Acts 2:24; 1 Thess 5:3; Rv 12:2; *En* 62:4; 4 *Ez* 4:40; *1 QH* III:7ff.
26. P. Claudel, "All suffering which there is in the world is not the sorrow of an agony, but that of giving birth" (*Conversations dans le Loir-et-Cher* (Gallimard, 1935), p. 255; quoted in J. Huby, *L'Épitre aux Romains*, p. 297.
27. J. Huby, *L'Épitre aux Romains*, p. 297.
28. The word "first fruits" (Gk. *aparchē*) indicates that which announces a coming good (Rom 11:16; 1 Cor 15:20,23; 16:15), but it can be the equivalent of the

"pledge" or "down payment" (Gk. *arrabōn*), which indicates an anticipated sharing in the coming good in its totality (Rom 8:9; 1 Cor 7:40). "The pledge which the Spirit is": an epexegetical genitive.

29. Saved not by the fact that we hope for the coming Spirit nor by hope—M. F. Lacan, "*Nous sommes sauvés par l'espérance*" (Rom VIII, 24) in *À la rencontre de Dieu*, Mémorial A. Gelin (Le Puy: Editions Xavier Mappus, 1961), pp. 331–339. Put in another way, our salvation, acquired in principle, does not, however, suppress hope; we live in an atmosphere of hope.

30. "I suffer and so I am. This is more exact and more profound than Descartes' *Cogito*. Suffering belongs to one's very personal existence and personal consciousness. . . . Dostoyevski saw in suffering the sole cause of the birth of consciousness. . . . It is not the wickedest men who suffer the most, but the best. . . . The spiritual problem consists in the transforming of obscure suffering, which has as its end a human person's loss, into a transfigured suffering that is the way to salvation," N. Berdiaff, *Dialectique existentielle du divin et de l'humain*" (J. B. Janin, 1947), pp. 89, 96, 100.

31. Rom 4:19.

32. Rom 8:15.

33. The Greek *alalētos* designates not glossolalia but, for example, "what one may not say" (2 Cor 12:4) or that which cannot find speech, what God alone can comprehend (cf. 1 Cor 2:6–16).

34. Rom 8:6f.

35. Jb 40:5f.

36. This translation ties Verse 28 to Verse 26; in fact, the *to gar ouk oidamen* addresses the *oidamen de*: "for, undoubtedly, we do not know . . . but we know." For Greek expression *gar* with a different significance, see X. Léon-Dufour, *Études d'Évangile* (Paris: Seuil, 1965), pp. 73–75.

37. "Those who love God," a typically Jewish expression, from Ex 20:6 or Dt 6:5, passing by way of Mt 22:37; Mk 12:30; Lk 10:27; 1 Cor 2:9.

38. The fundamental sin of men and women is the nonrecognition of their state as creatures: Rom 1:21; it destroys the very tie that constitutes creation.

39. 2 Cor 4:4; Col 1:15.

40. 2 Cor 3:18; Phil 3:21.

41. *Proegnō*, cf. Rom 11:12; 1 Pt 1:2,20, and *pro-orisen*, both aorists corrected by the prefix *pro*.

42. Historical aorists: *ekalesen, edikaiōsen*.

43. *Edoxasen*: an aorist of anticipation.

44. According to the interpretation of Matthew, who, in the course of a collection of miracle narratives, quotes Isaiah: "*It was he* who took our infirmities and bore our diseases" (Mt 8:17, adapting Is 53:4).

45. Cf. pp. 89–117.

46. Cf. pp. 56–63.

47. Is this not what R. Garaudy lets us understand in his confession *Parole d'homme* (R. Laffont, 1975)?

48. The poet was Paul Claudel.

8. Paul Faces Death

As we tried to show in the three preceding chapters, it was in relation to Christ's death that Paul had elaborated his understanding of death and suffering. These corresponded to our presentation of Jesus' thought when he was faced with the death of others. Now it remains for us to specify, to the degree possible, what Paul's reaction had been to the possibility of his own death. This is not an impossible task whatever the truth of the only tradition we have (from Clement of Rome at the end of the first century), which reports that Paul died as a martyr, probably around the Year 67. If the New Testament is silent on this point, this is because its interest lies not with the death of disciples but with the death of Jesus Christ. This is why Jesus' attitude was treated in three chapters while, in Paul's case, several pages will now be enough.

Let us note immediately that there is a difficulty that renders our treatment somewhat risky. When Paul spoke of death, he spontaneously used the pronoun "we." Since it seems that this cannot be an instance of the royal we, it is highly probable that Paul linked his companions in the apostolate to the same experience. Is it, then, possible for us to extend to all believers what Paul says? No doubt, the state of affairs is in the first instance a case of the "apostolic" sufferings, that is, those sufferings endured as part of the mission of evangelization; in addition, however shocking this might be, we note that Paul never demanded of his converts direct collaboration in his apostolate. However, since the properly apostolic dimension of all Christian existence later became part of the Church's consciousness, we are justified in considering that the Pauline assertions are relevant for all believers.

There would appear to be two major aspects to Paul's viewpoint. First, Paul noted that death was at work in him within his setbacks and sufferings, and he tried to find out the meaning behind this truth. Secondly, Paul saw his death coming, which leads to our question: Did he welcome it stoically or with fear and trembling, and, if the latter, could he do so without remembering Jesus in Gethsemane? In any case, Paul's outlook does not seem to be as relaxed as it was when he addressed the Thessalonians in the passage we probed in Chapter 7.

Paul spoke to the Thessalonians about their deceased brothers and sisters, but not about their own deaths. The perspective of a communitarian existence in heaven is relatively easy to grasp when it touches others and when one thinks that one will be among the living at the Parousia. But when one must die oneself and die this death without having fulfilled one's human career or without having seen the rule of love established on earth, then the problem becomes tragic because it is the problem of *my* death.

Paul doubtless knew, as he told the Corinthians, that Christians will have to be "changed"; the prospect of surviving right up to the Parousia allowed him to soften the stark reality of decomposition, which normally sets in at death. But were the specter of death to draw near, how would Paul react then? On two separate occasions he confided his sentiments in this regard, first in a serene way to the Philippians and afterward in sorrowful fashion to the Corinthians, with the result that we can assert that Paul depicted death both with a beloved face and also with a horrifying visage.

THE BELOVED FACE OF DEATH (PHIL 1:23)

In a lengthy outpouring of himself,[1] Paul confided his sentiments to the Philippians while a prisoner confronted with the possibility of his own death. Not that he had actually experienced this in a real way, but he did envisage it as a positive eventuality. Paul no longer was living in the somewhat naive state of exultation, as he did earlier when he wrote to the Thessalonians: at that time, the issue concerned other people and, to boot, Christians who had no essential role to play in the spreading of the Good News. Now he who is the one responsible for the apostolate finds himself in prison while others, as he puts it, preach Christ "out of rivalry. . . thinking that they will add even more to my suffering in prison."[2] Paul, however, effects a sublime rectification of this thinking: far from dallying over niggardly considerations about prestige or of personal jealousy, he sets his eyes on Christ alone:

What is the difference? The fact is that in every way, whether in pretense or in truth Christ is proclaimed.

(Phil 1:18)

And later, having stated that he rejoices in everything, he continues,

20 . . . with full courage now as always Christ will be honored in my body whether by life or by death. **21** For to me to live is Christ, and to die is gain.

(Phil 1:20–21)

Apparently, Paul is insane enough to bring to a single level death and life in this way; he thereby restores meaning to life beyond death. Within Paul's biblical perspective, such "gain" could not refer to deliverance of the soul, which until then had been held captive within the body; rather, in dying he wins out by becoming fully one "with Christ." This somewhat abrupt assertion demonstrates the freedom that the believer should have in looking at life and at death, and this because it is Christ alone who justifies each and grounds both one and the other. Still, since this "freedom" runs the risk of being misinterpreted, Paul adds,

22 If it is to be life in the flesh, that means fruitful labor for me. Yet which I shall choose I cannot tell. **23** I am hard pressed between the two. My desire is to depart and be with Christ, for that is far better. **24** But to remain in the flesh is more necessary on your account.

(Phil 1:22–24)

The affirmation is a clear one: to depart is "to be with Christ," a condition that Paul earlier, in his correspondence with the Thessalonians, seemed to reserve to the time of the Parousia. But there is a difference. Now it is no longer Christ who comes on the clouds; instead it is Paul who goes to him. In this sense, *his* death is his sharing in the death of the world. And, in fact, death here is a "change," as he depicted it within a Parousia context further on in the same letter:

20 But our commonwealth is in heaven, and from it we await a Savior, the Lord Jesus Christ, **21** who will change our lowly body to be like his glorious body, by the power which enables him even to subject all things to himself.

(Phil 3:20–21)

By deepening his focus on being "with Christ" in the early text and in this text anticipating from the very moment of death what formerly he had reserved for the end of time, Paul's thought shows development *vis-à-vis* the content of 1 Thessalonians. Does this development consist simply in making explicit his thought or does it rather depend on a discovery brought about by contact with Hellenistic aspirations for happiness in the beyond?[3] This is difficult to answer. Without wanting to eliminate all influences from the milieu in which Paul found himself, we can direct our thoughts along the following lines: Paul was conscious that one's relationship to Christ entailed important consequences. The "sleep" people habitually alluded to cannot be conceived as a diminishment in comparison with our life here below (= in the flesh). From now on, just as the final Day had become anticipated in the lives of the "children of the Day,"[4] so now the *syn Christoi* ("with Christ") of the Parousia can be seen as anticipated in the moment of one's death: this would then be a clear revelation of the meaning of the *en Christoi* ("in Christ") experience lived in faith here on earth.

Whatever the literary origin of *syn Christoi* may be, it is clear that Paul did proclaim a new truth: at death the believer will find himself or herself immediately with Christ.

In agreement with Jesus, we stated above that heaven is God himself;[5] with Paul we can now say that heaven is "being with Christ" or even heaven is "being together with Christ." What more needs to be added? Just that one point still remains obscure:

what happens between death and the Parousia? This question has raised a great deal of further speculation concerning the "intervening time" or the "interim." We will return to this issue in the Appendix to this work,[6] for the question presupposes that one has dealt with the problem of the language we use to speak of the "time that follows" death. Here we must be content to give consideration to another of Paul's confidences, a much more tragic one.

TAKING ON DEATH

Shortly after writing to the Philippians, Paul alluded once again to his own death in the course of the second letter that remains to us of his correspondence with the Corinthians.[7] Paul's predicament was a setback, one even more radical than the imprisonment he underwent at Philippi: it had been a setback to his health, a setback at the hands of Jews and, finally, a setback in relation to the faithful of Corinth, who charged him with fickleness and a tendency to dominate. We can easily comprehend why the thought of death haunted his spirit; nevertheless, the perspective of life being triumphant was never forgotten. In fact, life through death comes to constitute Paul's horizon. Two texts reveal his thought in this regard.

IN COMBAT WITH DEATH (2 COR 1:8–10)

Earlier on, in the synthesis he sketched out in Romans 6, Paul had elaborated his presentation of the paschal mystery: baptized into the death and resurrection of Christ, the believer lives simultaneously a condition (he or she is dead-alive) and an obligation (die-live!).[8] So far, so good; there is, however, quite a gap between theory and praxis. Now, Paul deals with a real experience. It is one thing for someone to speak of the need to die in order to live; it is still another for that same person to undergo death without yet knowing the kind of life that is to be its outcome or, rather, it is still another thing to discern within a death that presses upon one the very life that, little by little, is being revealed.

Paul shared his experience:

8 For we do not want you to be ignorant, brethren, of the affliction we experienced in Asia; for we were so utterly, unbearably crushed that we despaired of life itself. **9** Why, we felt that we had received the sentence of death; but that was to make us rely not on ourselves but on God who raises the dead; **10** he delivered us from so deadly a peril, and he will deliver us; on him we must set our hope that he will deliver us again.

(2 Cor 1:8–10)

Paul had just gone through an "abnormal" trial, one of such a kind *(tēlikoutou)* that it was not simply an instance again of the various kinds of dangers he often had encountered before. This trial was recent (in Asia) and it continued still (the future tense of v. 10), though the original occurrence was narrated in the Greek aorist tense *(ebarēthēmen* in v. 8); it even constituted a permanent halt to death, as the Greek perfect tense indicated *(eschēkamen* in v. 9). These are the assured data, against which every hypothesis concerning the tribulation Paul underwent must be measured.[9]

What interests us is not the bare fact of the trial but rather the meaning Paul assigned to it. Brought into the presence of the one who alone can "liberate" him, Paul applies to himself what he had recounted objectively with regard to our father Abraham; like Abraham he has to "believe in the One who raised up from the dead our Lord Jesus."[10] We need to examine the whole letter, for it was in its entirety composed in light of the blow inflicted by the trial; we will see that the death-life antithesis has now been changed into one of tribulation-consolation[11] and that a ministry of glory presupposes the apostle's state of humiliation:[12] indeed, life issues forth from death. But if we were to develop this we would be extending ourselves beyond the proper goal of our chapter, namely Paul's personal reaction to death, which came on the scene to threaten him.

THE TWOFOLD FACE OF DEATH (2 COR 4:16–5:20)

To appreciate in full that tragic text in which Paul revealed his authentic reaction as a man to the reality of death, which had drawn near, we must here, as we did elsewhere, recall Paul's situation. Paul had just eloquently celebrated the ministry entrusted to him: he declared that it was a veritable treasury of glory. What really characterized the apostolic ministry was that the ministers were poor beggars. The grounds for this paradoxical state—one would have to wait a long time before the ambassadors would share here below in the glory of their offices—reside in the need jealously to safeguard the prerogatives of God, who, alone, is the one at work through the agency of his ministers. Paul often repeats this through the length of this epistle: God is the one who strengthens, anoints, and bestows the pledge of Holy Spirit; who brings one into Christ's triumphal victory procession; who causes his glorious light to shine in our hearts even though of ourselves we are merely darkness. Truly, it is God who is present, always and everywhere.[13]

But human persons are predisposed to stop at once at the instrument of this divine power and thus divest God of his glory.[14] Also, to ensure the spiritual dimension of this ministry, it is fitting that the ministers reveal themselves as the dregs of humanity; this is a theme Paul had developed earlier for the Corinthians in his first epistle.[15] Here Paul is not content merely to stress the fact of humiliations; he goes on to reveal that God's glory is operative amid the humiliations. Life is winning the victory over the death of its messenger, and life is even now being communicated to those who are faithful. We read in the text:

7 But we have this treasure in earthen vessels, to show that the transcendent power belongs to God and not to us. **8** We are afflicted in every way, but not crushed; perplexed, but not driven to despair; **9** persecuted, but not forsaken; struck down, but not destroyed; **10** always carrying in the body the death *[nekrōsis*[16]*]* of Jesus, so that the life of Jesus may also be manifested in our bodies. **11** For while we live we are always being given up to death for Jesus' sake, so that the life of Jesus may be manifested in our mortal flesh. **12** So death is at work in us, but life in you.

(2 Cor 4:7–12)

Life's struggle against death takes on a strange coloration, for it is out of the death being endured by the apostles that life issues for the good of believers. One could forthwith be reminded of a love that knows no limits in its self-giving; for example, the love

Paul demonstrated to the benefit of his faithful Corinthians.[17] Love indeed is lifegiving. But the welling forth of love in Paul's case is a much more profound reality, for Christ is the one who "causes him to die" and who communicates to him a "life force." Accordingly, a marvellous dissociation is found to be at work; for while death is at work in Paul, others are being brought to life. From this it does not follow that individuals are sacrificed for their neighbor's good; in fact, Paul is mindful that he himself will also be the beneficiary of the glory being bestowed on others:

13 Since we have the same spirit of faith as he had who wrote, "I believed, and so I spoke," we too believe, and so we speak, **14** knowing that he who raised the Lord Jesus will raise us also with Jesus and bring us with you into his presence. **15** For it is all for your sake, so that as grace extends to more and more people it may increase thanksgiving, to the glory of God.

(2 Cor 4:13–15)

The notion of a pure sacrifice of oneself to benefit a collectivity, widespread though it may be today,[18] offers no *raison d'être* to the Christian: for it is together that we will be happy in the most definitive way. Thus the issue is one of frontally facing death, a power that, although it is able to ravage, is unable to offer any resistance to faith. Paul continues his argument grandly:

16 So we do not lose heart. Though our outer nature is wasting away, our inner nature is being renewed every day. **17** For this slight momentary affliction is preparing for us an eternal weight of glory beyond all comparison, **18** because we look not to the things that are seen but to the things that are unseen; for the things that are seen are transient, but the things that are unseen are eternal.

(2 Cor 4:16–18)

Who can speak this way? Only one who has experienced the *nekrōsis* ("dying") of Jesus in his own body. Faith's claim is indeed a splendid one: the spiritual person who is begotten in baptism can never stop growing, because life is at work. Afterward Paul, when he thinks of what awaits him beyond death, weighs in a balance his trials, which are light, he says, in comparison with the heavy weight of glory that awaits him. What interests Paul, in fact, is a reality that one cannot see but that lasts forever. And yet the reality of death continues to impose itself. Paul's horizon simply gets bigger. Above and beyond this enunciated viewpoint, which properly speaking may be called apostolic, Paul goes on to depict the human condition in general. The subsequent outline describes the path that every man or woman embarks on at death.

As a starting point, Paul alluded to the ideal he yearned for: it was to pass from this life into a glorious dwelling place by means of life's progressive invasion of his personal being, a process that little by little would overcome the reality of death.

1 For we know that if the earthly tent we live in is destroyed, we have a building *[which comes]* from God, a house not made with hands, eternal *[which comes]* in the heavens. 2 Here indeed we groan, and long to put on our dwelling *[which comes] from Heaven,* 3 so that by putting [it] on we may not be found naked. 4 For while we are still in this tent, we sigh with anxiety; not that we would be unclothed, but that we would be further clothed, so that what is mortal may be swallowed up by life. 5 He who has prepared us for this very thing is God, who has given us the Spirit as a guarantee.

(2 Cor 5:1–5)

It is an article of faith that, over and above our earthly dwelling (which is headed for destruction), we have access to a dwelling place that comes from God. What are we to understand by this "dwelling"? All kinds of answers have been suggested, including heavenly beatitude, a spiritual body that is either interim or definitive in nature, and a glorious body to be received at the Parousia. But as André Feuillet has so well explained,[19] these diverse representations do not actually take into account the totality of the text we have. On the contrary, if we take note that this "dwelling" is called "a dwelling not made by human hands" (an allusion to Jesus' saying about the Temple), the task of identification is easy: the dwelling that comes from God is, quite simply, Christ himself.

And, whereas Paul did not say that we shall have a glorious body on high, he does assert that now already "we have" an eter-

nal dwelling place. What more needs to be said except that we
have in heaven Jesus' glorified body?

And so, we maintain that we have two bodies, a claim that may
appear to be paradoxical unless, that is, we recall the Pauline doctrine concerning the two Adams, which he exposed in the first
epistle to the Corinthians:[20] just as there are two Adams (the
earthly one being the issue of the dust while the heavenly one
comes from heaven), so he maintains that there exist two dwelling
places. In this text Paul says nothing regarding the nature of *our*
glorified bodies in relation to Christ's body. The answer to this
question must be found in the letter to the Philippians, where he
observes that the Lord will transform our wretched body in order
to make it like or conformed to Jesus' glorified body. From this
we may conclude that, in principle, there is only one glorious
body, Christ's, and also that Christians will have a glorious body
made like unto his unique body.[21]

In Verses 2–4, Paul revealed the result that flowed from this
newly established fact, namely that this body yearns for glory.
This very desire comes to expression in the form of groanings,[22]
because this deep human longing is that, without any kind of
uprooting, one might pass over directly into heaven. Now, man
knows full well that this desire cannot be satisfied; he would very
much wish not to be found even for a moment naked, that is,
without a body. The dream of one's continuing in existence is
deeply inscribed within human beings, even if a man or woman
knows that reality itself does not correspond with this dream.
Hence, groaning and dejection coexist with a point of view that
sees that what is mortal in us will not simply be absorbed by life
and that a rupture will have to take place.

Following the lines of another image, that of clothing, Paul
taught the need of the same necessary condition. We ardently desire to put on the new clothing of our heavenly dwelling over our
present body, so as to thereby avoid being found naked,[23] that is,
without clothing or without the body that death will have de-
composed. This does not mean wearing two sets of clothing, one
on top of the other, nor of a yearning to change bodies, as one

might change clothes to put on new ones completely different from the first ones. To be clothed again means to be transfigured in the image of the glorified Lord's body.

Several commentators have seen in this a statement regarding the condition of the "separated soul," a provisional condition of waiting for the resurrection at the end of time. But the context does not permit such a reading; in fact, we do not have a reference here to the final resurrection, but rather to a natural desire to see heaven immediately as the prolongation of life on this earth. We recall here what Paul had said about that borderline case concerning those who at that time would not have "fallen asleep" but would be the survivors: death essentially consists in "transformation."[24] Now, Paul repeats that we all wish to be found in this very situation of the privileged and that we want thereby to escape the stripping off, normal though it might be, of our mortal body. This is the odious face of death. But just as God has not made creation subject without also giving it a horizon of hope along with the first fruits of the Spirit, so Paul ends Verse 5 by proclaiming his fundamental conviction: without doubt it is the Lord who has set us in such a state, but he also has given us the pledge of the Spirit. There exists in each of us an anticipation of the heavenly dwelling place, a foretaste and guarantee of what is to come.[25]

This evocation radically modified the course of the development of Pauline thought. It is almost as if, after having descended into the deep pit of death and decomposition, Paul again became aware of the hope rooted in his heart through the Spirit. In a second stage of his thought, which will be read now, Paul showed the beloved face of death, namely his view that we shall "dwell in the Lord's presence." By means of our passage through death, our deepest desires will be fulfilled and we will then be happy to "change dwellings."[26]

6 So we are always of good courage; we know that while we are at home in the body we are away from the Lord, **7** for we walk by faith, not by sight. **8** We are of good courage, and we would rather be away from the body and at home with the Lord. **9** So whether we are at home or away, we make it our aim to please him. **10** For we must all appear before the judgment seat of Christ, so that each one may receive good or evil, according to what he has done in the body.

(2 Cor 5:6–10)

It is the breath of the Spirit that has swept away the fog that obscures man's deepest longing. Doubtless, the desire that one never be found "naked" perdures still, but there remains an even more pressing desire, that of going to dwell in the Lord's presence. In effect, in this earthly body we are outside our truest dwelling place, for to live in faith is not yet to live by sight. We live in tension, and that is normal; without doubt, then, two desires coexist with one another in us, but it is the desire to be with the Lord that carries the day.

The outcome of this situation is that we find ourselves existing in a state of radical freedom *vis-à-vis* life and death. What is essential lies elsewhere for us, in a concern to do our best in this world, knowing that the Lord will reward us according to our deed. Transposing this treatment, we might say that earthly activity (in deed or intention) is the measure for all time of the degree of our sharing in the Lord's glory. I will be forever what I have been on earth; but then the reality will be seen in its full light.

DEATH WITHIN PAUL'S LIFE

Faithful to the spirit of Jesus who called his disciples to lose their lives in order to preserve them,[27] Paul put his theory into practice. In fact, one of the characteristics of Paul's thought is the relationship it establishes with our daily life. In Paul one finds no "theory" that does not also get expressed in "praxis"; and there is no praxis that is not founded on an interpretation of this theory. The theory is the "word of the cross," but it has consequences in practice; this is the first aspect of Paul's treatment. In turn, practice reveals its deep meaning, namely a movement from death to life.

CRUCIFIED WITH CHRIST

The mystery of Christ coming forth alive out of death finds expression in the word of the cross and in the ritual of baptism. The cross of Jesus has obtained reconciliation with God; baptism then assimilates the believer into the paschal mystery, causing him or her to become a "new creature." Dead in Christ and raised to life, the Christian finds himself or herself engaged in the process of living a new life. Here is how Paul expressed this in his weighty formulations:

19 For I through the law died to the law, that I might live to God. **20** I have been crucified with Christ; it is no longer I who live, but Christ who lives in me; and the life I now live in the flesh I live by faith in the Son of God, who loved me and gave himself for me.

(Gal 2:19–20)

24 And those who belong to Christ Jesus have crucified the flesh with its passions and desires. **25** If we live by the Spirit, let us also walk by the Spirit.

(Gal 5:24–25)

The nature of the inexpiable conflict between the "spirit" and the "flesh" Paul treated in this same epistle to the Galatians in a text that we cannot reproduce because of its length.[28] In reading it we come to realize what sad caricatures have been fashioned out of authentically Christian "mortification." This, as we have already pointed out in dealing with the words of Jesus,[29] has nothing to do with self-hatred, nor with despising the body nor, still less, with a disdain of sexuality. In Paul's eyes, the "flesh" is heir to sin, which the Law caused to multiply, while the "Spirit" personifies all that is good in what the Law intended and in what has been fulfilled through the gift of the Spirit. Between these two powers there is an unyielding opposition at work in the Christian's heart: though he or she can live according to the flesh, he or she ought to live according to the spirit. The struggle against the flesh is nothing other than a struggle against the sin to which it is heir, a struggle against death, which was introduced into the world by sin.

This Christian warfare is made possible by the fact that Christ, in taking on this body of flesh,[30] was "made to be sin."[31] Having come in the flesh's sinful condition, he condemned sin in his very flesh.[32] This, then, is the reason why the Christian in Christ, has, crucified the flesh and won the victory in battle. The spirit, which carries on the struggle, is animated by the Holy Spirit that has been given.[33]

If, then, there is death in the Christian's life, this is so with an assurance of victory. The latter is the glory that has been promised at the Lord's manifestation at the end of time. The victory also takes visible form in the person of Christ who is at God's right hand. Here, then, is what Paul developed in the Epistle to the Colossians, centered no longer simply on the paschal mystery but on Christ exalted in Heaven.

1 If then you have been raised with Christ, seek the things that are above, where Christ is, seated at the right hand of God. 2 Set your minds on things that are above, not on things that are on earth. 3 For you have died, and your life is hid with Christ in God. 4 When Christ who is our life appears, then you also will appear with him in glory.

(Col 3:1–4)

An inference is drawn out of this truth: "Put to death therefore what is earthly in you,"[34] an inference that only appears frightening when it is separated from the Christian's baptismal state. This "mortification" is carried out not from some morbid kind of instinct, but out of a desire to live, out of love for Christ and not out of self-hatred; it is practiced with discernment so that one may always be increasingly set free from sin, as one lives with one's eyes fixed on Christ and on those who surround him. These are, in effect, the circumstances and the demands of a fraternal kind of life, the necessities of an apostolic life, which inserts death into daily life. Having said this much, it is appropriate now to describe the atmosphere that typifies Paul's thought. There is nothing of the kill-joy in it. On the contrary, thanksgiving is the soul of Christian life: believers ought to be *eucharistoi*[35] ("full of thanksgiving"), overflowing with avowals of their indebtedness in all things.[36]

FROM DEATH TO LIFE

Paul's conduct gave witness to the mystery of a life that was blossoming forth through death. The following is an especially clear autobiographical assertion of this reality of his:

8 Indeed I count everything as loss because of the surpassing worth of knowing Christ Jesus my Lord. For his sake I have suffered the loss of all things, and count them as refuse, in order that I may gain Christ 9 and be found in him, not having a righteousness of my own, based on law, but that which is through faith in Christ, the righteousness from God that depends on faith; 10 that I may know him and the power of his resurrection, and may share his sufferings, becoming like him in his death, 11 that if possible I may attain the resurrection from the dead.

(Phil 3:8–11)

With just such an assurance Paul reckoned his life to be an apprenticeship into the mystery of death within life; he spoke of a "communion in the sufferings [of Jesus]" when, at the end of his treatment of the Christian battle, he mentioned to the Romans:

. . . we suffer with him in order that we may also be glorified with him.

(Rom 8:17)

Paul's apostolic life had been a continual experience of suffering, as we have noted already at the beginning of this chapter. He who had received extraordinary graces was in fact tested by a "thorn in the flesh given to keep [him] from being proud."[37] This led him to assert paradoxically:

For the sake of Christ, then, I am content with weaknesses, insults, hardships, persecutions and calamities; for when I am weak, then I am strong.

(2 Cor 12:10)

Previously in this same chapter we read a passage in which Paul testified that he was ceaselessly being "given up to death for Jesus' sake."[38] We quote now from another passage, which likewise had been directed to the Corinthians:

9 For I think that God has exhibited us apostles as last of all, like men sentenced to death; because we have become a spectacle to the world, to angels and to men. 10 We are fools for Christ's sake, but you are wise

in Christ. We are weak, but you are strong. You are held in honour, but we in disrepute. **11** To the present hour we hunger and thirst, we are ill-clad and buffeted and homeless, **12** and we labor, working with our own hands. When reviled, we bless; when persecuted, we endure; **13** when slandered, we try to conciliate; we have become, and are now, as the refuse of the world, the offscouring of all things.

(1 Cor 4:9–13)

Beneath the last words employed here by Paul (Gk. *peripsēma* and *perikatharma),* there lies hidden a linguistic usage still current today in the Near East. The word can be used as a term of re-proach: "Get out of here, scum!"—or piece of garbage, refuse of humanity, dregs of society, dirt, filth, trash, slops, dishwater. However, it also had come into use in an expression used when one wanted to honor an important personage: "May I be treated as your expiatory victim!" How can a single phrase like this sig-nify two quite diverse realities, scum and an expiatory victim?

This semantic difficulty is clarified by an historical custom,[39] according to which someone was reckoned to be either scum him-self or to signify an expiatory victim. In fact, it seems well es-tablished that in the Hellenistic world there was an annual rite during which people drove out a man who had been previously charged with the acts of wickedness or the evils of a city. People addressed him saying, "Become our *peripsēma,* and even our sal-vation and redemption!"[40] Then he was taken to the sea as an offering to Poseidon.[41] This *pharmakos* or medicine man became taboo by taking upon himself the "defilements" of the city. People chose a single individual, one not particularly noble or blame-worthy (and more generally from among those condemned to death or no-goods[42]); this starveling then was fed sumptuously during the year that preceded the "sacrifice." In principle, his death was brought about by drowning in the sea, through some instinct directed toward purification; sometimes, also, it was carried out by stoning or by the wretched one's being hurled down from the top of a rocky crag. Often afterward, however, arrangements were made so that the victim could save himself.

The *peripsēma* in this way personified salvation: being put to death signified the taking away of an evil which had oppressed the people.[43] In calling himself a *peripsēma,* Paul regarded himself as the object of contemptuous ridicule on the part of all: his life was wretched according to the sages of this world. Paul set this meaning right and saw in his life of humiliation his cooperation in the salvation of all. In fact, the term *pantōn* ("all") was attached to *peripsēma* to show that he stands alone and unique before the entire collectivity of the people.[44] Paul described himself as one "condemned to death," and as the dregs of humanity. Finally come his references to the antitheses: in place of a curse, there is the blessing; by means of someone condemned, there is salvation. These parallel his role as the victim sent away but who is the bearer of pardon and universal redemption. Paul adds the words "as if," perhaps because he knows that Jesus Christ alone is the redeemer.[45]

The above view is merely an hypothesis, but the totality of Paul's utterances make it highly plausible. Paul would never be satisfied only with declaring that he "bears on his body the marks (Gk. *stigmata)* of Jesus;"[46] in addition, he would see in these sufferings a true coredemption. This is what our study of this last text has made clear.

PAUL'S SUFFERINGS AND THOSE OF JESUS

Paul often recalled "his" sufferings; once indeed, as we noted,[47] he even was unafraid to designate them by means of the expression the *"nekrōsis* of Jesus carried about in our body, so that the life of Jesus also might be manifest in our body." Everything takes place as if still now Jesus is engaged in dying through his disciples. The context of the passage lets us realize that this death is at work in the apostles so that life might be passed on to the faithful. There is no substitution at all here, but rather we find an instance of mutual exchange, an exchange in which life replaces death. Thus, Christ's death is today still at work mysteriously to bring about life.

The interpretation given above finds solid support in a surprising text that has prompted many misgivings in people's minds because it seems to suggest that Paul could be adding something to the redemption effected by Christ. The text is found in the Epistle to the Colossians, which is held to be authentic by the vast majority of exegetes. Paul was a prisoner and confided to his correspondents the meaning he attributed to his sufferings:

> Now I rejoice in my sufferings for your sake, and in my flesh I complete what is lacking in Christ's afflictions for the sake of his body, that is, the Church.
>
> (Col 1:24)

Jacob Kresmer has published a thesis on this controverted text, reporting the various interpretations given to it through the ages and proposing an exegesis around which we will rally.[48] Let us now take up the meaning of the different terms found in the text.

The "tribulations" (Gk. *thlipseis,* a word deriving from *thlibō:* "to rub, to press") were the trials that Israel underwent, especially in Egypt or during the Exile,[49] so that the expression took on the meaning of a category of thought. So, one can speak of the "day (or time) of tribulation." This meaning can even be applied to conjugal life,[50] to poverty,[51] to the pains of childbirth,[52] but above all it was used of the trials undergone by the apostles, their persecutions and mistreatment because of the faith. In Paul they are linked to the era of the end time, which even now has been anticipated. Paul likens his own "sufferings" to the tribulations of Christ.

The genitive "tribulations *of Christ"* is a subjective genitive, that is, it refers to the tribulations that Christ himself experienced. As a matter of fact, Jesus of Nazareth suffered great tribulations during his lifetime; they led him to the cross.

Now there exists a "lack" in these tribulations, and Paul declared that he came to "complete" them. The Greek verb translated in this way is a complex one: *ant-ana-plēroō,* in which *ana* does not mean "anew" but rather indicates an action of "filling, of completing, or of filling to overflowing," while the *anti* part adds the notion of substitution, the idea that something or someone replaces what is lacking in another.

What follows is the interpretation, based on John Chrysostom, proposed by J. Kremer, one which I have modified slightly.[53] Christ's work still continues on today; it keeps on opening out now and will continue to do so until the end of time; this reality is made possible through the apostolic work of his disciples. Christ, now risen and glorified, is the explosion of his personality into the world. This explosion goes on in the course of time, a fact that suggests a lack in Jesus of Nazareth: limited as he was in his being of flesh, he was unable to radiate fully into our world before his death. Paul interpreted his own sufferings, then, as the fulfillment of what had been lacking in Christ's tribulations. He presupposed that the envoy (which he himself was) represented the sender:[54] from now on Jesus of Nazareth expresses himself through the action and apostolic tribulations of his disciples.

Pointing as it does above all to Paul and to the apostles, does this affirmation hold also for apostolic workers in general? The conclusion seems self-evident. Does it hold equally well for all Christians who suffer? This application is an easy one to make, and it fits directly in the line taken by Paul's thought, as St. Augustine has observed. Still one must admit that this extension cannot immediately be read from the text except on one condition, the presupposition that each believer shares in some way or other in Christ's apostolic activity.

These tribulations of Christ are to be undergone and accepted "for the sake of his body, which is the Church." As a matter of fact, Jesus underwent his death and his sufferings so that the Church could be founded and established; for the Church is the Body of Christ.

CONCLUSION

The confidences entrusted to us by Paul raise a question that is difficult to resolve. How could this man full of get-up and go, simultaneously tender and full of temper, a dreamer of conquests ever further afield, how could this man extol as he did the "language of the cross"? How could he have boasted about the suffering he bore in his body and in the thousand apostolic concerns he endured for the sake of his faithful? I do not think that we can make him out to be a man who took pleasure in his setbacks, what today we might call today a person of masochistic disposition. Clearly because of his character Paul was bound to draw down on himself "tribulations" a more "even-tempered" person would have ignored; however, it remains true that a systematization of suffering such as he accomplished cannot simply be accounted for by the defects of his temperament.

Looking at the problem from every angle, I end up thinking that Paul's behavior in proclaiming the Good News, in effecting binding relationships with non-Jews, in demanding conduct by others worthy of their baptism, and so on—all these dynamics provoked a reaction from the people in the various localities. First, there was the synagogue, which was furious at seeing this heretic snatch away adherents; then, there were the Judeo-Christians, displeased to see the Christian faith bursting forth beyond the limits of the Jewish Law; next, there were Christian brothers and sisters, who were annoyed by the demands made of them by their founder. A whole world of people kept rising up against this kind of spoilsport. When Paul suffered persecutions at their hands, it was not because he went looking for them. They came as a corollary to, and as a consequence of, his gospel.

When persecutions flooded in on him, Paul recognized in them a reflection of what Jesus himself had undergone; he likened his own lot to the paschal one experienced by Jesus. "Mortification" was not sought for its own sake, neither by Paul nor by Jesus. It came Paul's way because he was faithful to the message he had been charged with proclaiming. The "cross," "suffering," and persecutions in themselves had no meaning, but only as the consequence of the preaching of the gospel. Hence, they may be considered as the actualization of the *nekrōsis* ("dying") of Jesus, as an expression of absolute fidelity to God and to human beings.

NOTES

1. Phil 1:12–26. Written to Ephesus, the letter seems to date form the year 56 or 57.
2. Phil 1:17.

266 / PAUL FACES DEATH

3. So thinks J. Dupont, *L'Union* (p. 222, n. 36), p. 184.
4. 1 Thess 5:5; Eph 5:8–14.
5. Cf. pp. 20–21.
6. Cf. Appendix, below, "Beyond Death," pp. 282–298.
7. 2 Corinthians was probably written by Paul at Philippi between December 57 and January 58, in order to reestablish harmonious relationships among the Corinthians, in view of his intended visit and to favor the collection. Independently of questions about the unity of the letter (Chapters 8–9 and 10–13 come from somewhere else), our passage belongs to a block that extends from Chapters 1 to 7 (except for 6:14–7:1).
8. Cf. pp. 170–171.
9. The riot of the silversmiths at Ephesus produced few serious consequences (Acts 19:23). The persecution of the Jews, begun in Asia, continued under the form of plots to be avoided (Acts 20:3; 21:27; Rom 15:31), a trial neither characteristic nor new. Spontaneously, one thinks of the onset of some serious sickness that still threatened: epilepsy; intermittent fevers; malaria; eye migraines. These are plausible but undemonstrable suppositions (cf. 2 Cor 12:7; Gal 4:15).
10. Rom 4:24.
11. 2 Cor 1:6f: *"Are we afflicted?* It is for your comfort and salvation. *Are we consoled?* It is for your comfort, which you experience when you patiently endure the same sufferings that we suffer. Our hope *(for you)* is unshakeable; for we know that as you share in our sufferings, you will also share in our comfort."
12. 2 Cor 3:1–5:10.
13. 2 Cor 1:21f; 2:13; 3:18; 4:6.
14. The incident at Lystra, reported by Luke (Acts 14:11–18), was typical. Seeing the activity of Paul and Barnabas, people wanted to offer a sacrifice to the two apostles: "The gods have come down to us in the likeness of men!" They called Barnabas *Zeus* and Paul *Hermes.* Also Barnabas and Paul cried out, "Men, why are you doing this? We also are men, of like nature with you!"
15. 1 Cor 4:9–13. The text is quoted on pp. 260–261. It is clear, as the conclusion of this chapter underscores, that Paul's behavior was not masochistic.
16. The Greek word *nekrōsis,* from *nekros,* "dead" (an adjective), and *nekroō,* "to put to death," can, with some difficulty, be translated by "mortification," a term that has taken on quite precise shades of meaning in contemporary speech. The *TOB,* sadly, translates it by "agony." The word means "death activating," "death in the process of being brought about"; this is *"nekrōsis,"* an action that kills, which continues on even after the individual's death. The only other use of it in the New Testament is in Rom 4:19, à propos of Sarah's sterile womb. Here, Paul does not oppose to "life" the Greek word *thanatos* (which ordinarily he situates in his contrasts: Rom 7:10; 8:6,38; 1 Cor 3:22; Phil 1:20), as he does two verses further on. Why? Probably to signify that Jesus is in the process of *making* his apostles *die.* *Zoē* becomes "the power of life."
17. 2 Cor 11:29; 12:15.
18. Even, so it seems, in the writings of R. Garaudy.
19. "Exégèse de 2 Co 5, 1–10 et contribution à l'étude des fondements de l'eschatologie paulinienne," *RSR* 44 (1956), 161–192, 360–402.

20. 1 Cor 15:44–49; cf. pp. 202–203.
21. There is only one body, Christ's body. It follows that, in heaven, human beings will be distinguished from one another, not by their bodies, but by virtue of the depth of their beings, which will express themselves variously in the body of Christ.
22. Paul uses the same term to describe the (unspeakable) groanings of the whole creation: Rom 8:23,26; cf. p. 240.
23. Verse 5:3 is variously translated; we rejoin that of Osty, but depart from that of the *TOB,* wherein one reads, "provided that we are found dressed and not naked." The deepest desire is to not be found without anything, for nakedness consists in being without a body, without the possibility of self-expression by reason of the bodily decomposition that we know. Paul desires to be found in the condition in which the resurrection coincides with the Parousia; that is, in which death consists in a simple transformation (1 Cor 15:51).
24. Cf. pp. 199–205.
25. Cf. on Rom 8:20,23, pp. 233–238.
26. "Changer de domicile"; cf. J. Dupont, *L'Union* (above, p. 222, n. 36), pp. 153–171, which recounts the numerous parallels with Greek literature, especially on Socrates' death: "If death is like a departure *(apodēmēsai)* from this place to some other, and if it is true, as some people say, that all the dead are gathered there, what better state can we imagine?" *(apodēmia: Phaedo,* 67B).
27. Mt 16:25; cf. pp. 31–40.
28. Gal 5:13–25.
29. Cf. pp. 35–39.
30. Col 1:22. The expression is found also in Qumran: *1 QSa* 2:5f; *1 QpH* 9:2. It does not have a pejorative meaning (unlike 2:11) and simply designates the physical body of Jesus.
31. 2 Cor 5:21; cf. p. 164.
32. Rom 8:3.
33. Rom 8:5–17.
34. Col 3:5; Paul here has in mind the "members" that have been put into the service of impurity and of the vices by the sinful passions (Rom 6:18f; 7:5).
35. Col 3:15.
36. Rom 14:6; 1 Cor 10:30; 2 Cor 4:15; Eph 5:20; Col 2:7; 1 Thess 5:18.
37. 2 Cor 12:7.
38. 2 Cor 4:11; cf. pp. 252–253.
39. Cf. G. Stählin, "Peripsēma," *TDNT* 6 (1968), 84–93.
40. In Greek, *peripsēma hēmōn genou, ētoi sōteria kai apolytrōsis.*
41. Following the notation of Photius (ninth century), *Quaestio 133 (PG* 101:732–733).
42. *"Lian aggeneis kai achrēstous"* (Aristophanes, *The Frogs* (Harvard: Loeb Classical Library, 1961), verses 730–732: "worthless sons of worthless fathers, pinchbeck townsmen, yellowy scum, whom in the earlier days the city hardly would have stooped to use even for scapegoat victims" *(pharmakoisin).*
43. A means of expiation that corresponds to the *antilytron* and the *antipsychon* (cf. Tb 5:19 [LXX]; 4 *Mc* 6:29; *Ign. Eph.* 1:2; 3:1; Rom 3:2; 4:2).
44. This custom would confirm the hypothesis of R. Girard, *Des choses cachées* (p. 47, n. 129).
45. Origen was not afraid to apply to Christ the name of *peripsēma (Comm. in*

Joh., VI:284, in 1:29 = *PG* 14:296 = *SC 157* [1970] p. 344; XXVIII:161, in 11:50 = *PG* 14:721).

46. Gal 6:17.
47. 2 Cor 4:10, a text quoted and commented on, pp. 252–253.
48. J. Kremer, *Was an den Leiden Christi noch mangelt* (Bonn: Peter Hanstein Verlag, 1956) pp. 154–201.
49. Ex 4:31; Dt 4:29.
50. 1 Cor 7:28.
51. Acts 7:11; Jas 1:27; Rv 2:9.
52. Jn 16:21f.
53. Chrysostom, "Fourth Homily on the Epistle to the Colossians," *PG* 62:326–327; cf. J. Kremer, *Leiden Christi* (above, n. 48), pp. 189–195.
54. Ex 4:15f; Zec 2:12; Mt 10:40f; 25:34–40; Phlm 12.

Conclusion

As the end of this lengthy journey in company with Jesus and Paul, with one and the other having faced death in others and their own individual death, what have we come to? I don't know what you, the reader, are thinking, but I can state that, for my part, a serene joy has come over me, a token of deeper freedom and greater harmony with other people and with the Lord. To my eyes death from this point forward has ceased being a problem, though it still remains a mystery. I cannot yet fully discern this mystery, but even within its darkness it illuminates my life.

Isn't this reason to be astonished? How can it be that the Good News—oriented as it is toward the fullness of life, as well as toward joy in the presence of the Holy Spirit who renews all things—has ended up as it has in recent times? It has been bottled up in tedious catechisms, in a religion more preoccupied with faults than with true freedom, one unable to be easily reconciled with progress and with the flowering of life values. I do, indeed, know the grace of the Vatican II Council, of the efforts made by pastors for liturgy that is alive, of research done by theologians to renew the understanding and language of the gospel in terms of our age's culture, and of the witness of spiritual people who recall the absolute demand of mutual love, the privileged locus of authentic experience of God. Despite all the above, I am aware also of the disaffection of so many of our contemporaries, the *irritations* of psychologists and the *lack of desire* on the part of scientists. On the other hand, I also notice that there is, more than ever before, a thirst for the gospel and a desire to return to its radical demands. Without allowing myself to fall into an easy opposition between faith and religion, I have to acknowledge that a return to the sources brings to the surface the gap that separates the current view of religion from the Good News in its nascent state. Here, then, is the reason why at the very moment when I

am putting the final period to this work, I would like to contrast
what I got from my catechism lessons and what together we have
come to understand better through our encounter with Paul and
Jesus.

THE MEANING OF DEATH

Can we "change death"? Doctors and psychologists are right
to persist in making death more acceptable; for example, by surrounding the dying person with the warmth of human presence.
People no longer want the end to be hidden by camouflage and
rituals that conceal it. People want to rediscover the simplicity of
the past, which is still recent enough since it was characteristic of
the human behavior of those who lived in the nineteenth century
and who were unafraid of familiarity with the deceased. And all
this is to the good. But we can still ask ourselves whether such
a rediscovery is not likely to end paradoxically in a return to con-
ceptualizing death as a "gentle passage" to the Father, while at the
same time we are being robbed by seeing this going to the Father
as nothing other than a gentle passage into nothingness.

This is not the way in which the Christian thinks of "changing
death." Death will be changed if in our eyes it takes on meaning.
Death's meaning has often been presented in a way that today is
often poorly understood. We were taught that since Christ's death
had merited for us reconciliation with God (something that had
been lost following original sin), every Christian death had meaning henceforth because of Christ's. Let us reflect for a moment
on the reasoning process that leads to such a conclusion. Such
reasoning proceeds in the following way. Adam's sin brought
about the death of every person, while Christ's death procured
the salvation of all. In order to claim that sin and salvation are
universal realities, a causal link has to be introduced into the relationship linking one individual with all others. Now, contemporary thought would spontaneously interpret this marvellous fact
as a transferring of responsibility onto the shoulders of an individual—Adam or Christ—which thereby does away with any se-

rious personal involvement. Furthermore, this link between the believer and Christ, even if effected through baptism, still remains an extrinsic one, so that the relationship would have to be expressed with the help of an "imitation" concept. However, we must ask ourselves whether this is an adequate way to take account of the unique solidarity that binds the believer to Christ in definitive fashion?

Jesus did not so present his message. We were able to establish that, in Jesus' eyes, what was meaningful was God alone and God's plan. He grasped his death as situated within the history of Israel. The prophets and Just Ones by means of both their words and their lives had been God's expressions within time. They encountered resistance from other men and women, who condemned them to the death penalty. If God is the one who is to have the last word, why would Jesus be solicitous to specify himself the meaning of his death? Constantly he had recourse to God, the God of the living. Remaining steadfastly faithful to the mission received from God, he could then entrust himself to the faithful God, who would save him from death. Again, in affirming that he enjoyed a unique relationship with the Father and all men and women, Jesus could also declare that everything hinges on the attitude people take toward him and he invited his disciples and those who would believe in his message in the future to make explicit the saving worth of his cross for all humankind.

Jesus called these men and women to "follow" him. He demonstrated that the way to the life that perdures is by way of "self-denial," that very same way he opened up before their very eyes. What he called for was radical engagement on his side and with him personally. That this "following" is no mere "imitation" is what Paul underlined with his choice of prepositions that, in stressing ties to the Risen One, evolved from a being "with" to a being "in" Christ.

If there is one person in whose eyes the reality of death changed it surely was Saul of Tarsus. Jesus, condemned to the cross because of his perfect fidelity, became the source of life for every one. The experience of Paul is that of every believer and that experience

even shares in the very experience of Jesus, though with a difference; Jesus was faced with a death he underwent with complete
trust in God, while Paul came along after Jesus' death, a death he
understood to have been overtaken by the glorious life bestowed
by the Resurrection. In turn, both experiences proclaimed the life-
giving presence of the living God.

To signify that Christ's death had a universal import, the early
community and Paul had at hand for their use the categories of
their religious tradition. Thus they spelled out their convictions
by making use of inherited terminology, either that of Israel's
liberation in the Exodus, or that of the cultic life through which
they celebrated God as their savior. Using categories from their
own era, the first Christians elaborated a certain terminology,
without thereby claiming a definitive status for categories that evidently were adapted to their purposes, but that also equally evidently were contingent by reason of their origin. Moreover, we
have demonstrated the plurality of terminological categories that
were chosen by them to reveal the same mystery.

When the first Christians made use of the concept of causality,
this was only to declare that Jesus' death had been brought about
by our sins; that is, by sinners who could not abide the presence
of the Just One in their midst. Despite this they did not assert
that the death of Jesus was *in itself* the cause of salvation; they
only affirmed a definitive relationship between One and All. Far
from them was any thought of an event that would work magically on all; for this event is only efficacious in those who would
from that moment on live in conformity with their new life. This
is what Paul magisterially depicted by means of his intermeshing
the indicative (You are!) and the imperative (Become!). In no way
is this a case of the "substitution" of the Christ event for my own
life; rather it is an expression of the solidarity made possible with
the coming of the new Adam, a solidarity that demands a whole
new life.

The various sets of symbolic terms employed by Paul help us
to appreciate the significance of God's saving action. Now justified, we have been born into a new life and a new companionship.

Now set free from slavery, we are little by little being transformed into the likeness of our liberator. Now reconciled with God, we are likened unto him who, from now on, enables us to live in communion with him.

Thus, in the believer's eyes, Christ's death possesses full value by virtue of the fact that it has been connected with God's life. It follows that the death of a Christian and, in some definitive way, every human death becomes meaningful to the degree to which it is associated with the death of Christ: death can even become the means to enter the fullness of life. On several occasions we have maintained that suffering and death should be fought against without respite, but we have also maintained that once that certain threshold is reached in one's personal life death is to be welcomed with open hands, just as it was by Jesus. In this way, love gathers our unconquerable weaknesses within its infinite power.

THE TWOFOLD COMPLEXION OF DEATH

Has death in this view lost its terrifying aspect so that it is no longer but a gentle passage to the Father? Have we by faith "tamed" death? Francis of Assisi held dialogues with the one he named "Sister Death" and with the fire with which they treated his diseased eyes: "Be good for me, Brother Fire." This welcome he extended to death and suffering followed closely on the stigmata having been imprinted in his flesh on Mount Alverna, an experience that told of an extraordinary love relationship. For it is only love that tames.

But not all men live like the Poverello. And, just like a wounded lion that never seems to die from its wound but threatens with its growls whoever draws near, so death also remains terrifying. All the data from our readings converge on a central theme: death has a twofold complexion; one cannot eliminate either of its two features.

The Bible had already in the past given death a serene face (going to join one's ancestors) and a hateful visage (premature or violent deaths). In the case of Jesus and Paul, this twofold countenance was constantly discernible in their reactions and statements they articulated in their accounts of death or when they clothed death in mythological guises.

Jesus spoke of death with simplicity, as he would of a normal human condition. Unlike the Old Testament (which for a long time had ignored thought about the resurrection), Jesus drew out of death consequences for the individual: his view of death as a reality that threatens without cease also constituted it as an invitation for conversion while time yet remained, time to look toward the One who is coming. In a sense quite different from the modern view, then, death is in fact the prick caused by desire on our part, an invitation to us to use well the time allotted.

Nonetheless, Jesus was not satisfied merely with welcoming death from God's hand; he struggled against it and suffering. Indeed, not only did he not rebel against it; he showed himself to be death's master. The resuscitations and healings that he worked signified ahead of time that life is stronger than death and that, accordingly, death is not the definitive word about life. Jesus believed in resurrection on the Last Day and he knew that he would soon rise. This twofold complexion appears as well in Jesus' own reactions to death that was either imminent or at hand. Jesus experienced simultaneously in himself both refusal and welcome of the Father's will. In the end, on the cross (according to the theory that we feel to be well grounded) he gave expression to his outlook through a final cry of anguish; by means of this cry he kept covenant fidelity, proclaiming that the Father was his God even in death, even in the loss of the ultimate expression of his being. In saying, "My God, it's you!" Jesus indicated that in dying he did not bring about the death of God.

Paul did not express his own reaction to death when it had drawn quite close to him. Quite simply he himself gave expression to the twofold complexion under which death appeared to him. In doing so he showed that the theory he had developed in the Epistle to the Romans did not lead him to a form of literary "evasion." He did not regard his death either as deliverance from matter, as Socrates had, or in some "pious" way, as do certain Christians who dream of a "gentle passage." Instead, death remained terrible, but faith in God, which had won him over in Jesus Christ, was revealed to be sufficient to hold him amid the darkness. Paul was a true disciple of Jesus Christ.

The real Pauline contribution was of another order—the "theological." Thanks to him we can better grasp that death consists essentially in the "transformation" of our body, which now becomes likened to Christ's glorious body. Death, then, is not essentially the decomposition of the corpse, something to be abhorred, but instead is the entry point to another life, the flowering of life begun here below into a "spiritual" life.

On the other hand, the reality of death possessed another face that was thrust upon Paul in all its brutality. Paul adhered to the Old Testament presentation that saw in Sheol not simply a place where the dead went but a power at work in the world, a power that indeed had seemed to triumph over life. Paul's genius lay in associating this power with sin, which had also been at work. Indeed, it was sin that had unleashed death into the world and this was the reason why, conversely, it was death that symbolized sin. Death, then, is not simply a natural phenomenon, but it also is the symbol of sin at work in the world, wherein we detect its repugnant aspect as that of a violent snatching away.

Paul did not stay put with this view. He actually extended his horizons. He at once took account of both of death's visages when he described creation as groaning in birth pangs. When creation was said to groan, this was not properly speaking on death's account, but rather because creation, which had been made for life, clung to hope: death is a new begetting of the very being of life—a second birth.

THE MYSTERY OF FAITHFULNESS

Death is a mystery. The mystery is that of sin, which it symbolizes. The mystery also of a birth to a full life. Love, which permitted us to tame it, locates us in the presence of a mystery.

When we stand before mystery, it is the same as when we stand before the sun. To look it straight in the face is to be dazzled and even to be blinded; to look at the light it sheds on creation, though, is to be full of admiration and to want to sing.

A shadowy apparition makes me flee; the real thing makes me feel at home. It has been my experience that once it is exorcized, something I had feared no longer frightens me. I come to a freedom that is more radical, more rooted. I am not afraid of death; I am not afraid of my neighbor. On the contrary, I look on death as a friend, even if it entails my one day becoming its victim once it comes and wreaks its violent way. I am not afraid of catastrophes, for their outcome can be situated within a still greater mystery, that of God himself. Not in that of a God who delights in punishing or in chastising but in the God who can help me deepen my being in the purifying fire of suffering, to await in that very secret aspect of my being the One who gives me my very being *and* my becoming.

Well, then, viewed as submerged in the reality of life, what meaning does the familiar presence of death have except the many hints that it gives me of ways to profit from my life time? I can no longer truly reckon death as a marvellous happening that, once it is united to Christ's death, will in an instant be the source of incomparable merit for me. I refuse to isolate death from the life that precedes it and gives it significance. The mystery of death is illumined by the light of the mystery of faithfulness.

In fact, Jesus did not search out death as a means for the salvation of human persons; he accepted death, in sorrow and in submission, as the crowning of his life of faithfulness. Jesus was faithful to the mission received from his Father, that of proclaiming the Good News concerning the God of compassion and concerning love for the brethren. He maintained this stance against enemies who wanted to silence him, by not defending himself with violent means and by entrusting himself without reserve to the God who is faithful.

Did Jesus immediately proclaim the need for the cross in his life, or may we discern a certain progression in his preaching? I must share what, for me, has been a discovery. In my book, *The Resurrection of Jesus and the Message of Easter,* I contrasted the two foundational terms that expressed the mystery of Jesus alive after his death, namely the language of "resurrection" and the language of "exaltation." For I could not, as a result of investigating the nongospel texts of the New Testament, decide which term encompassed the other; it seemed to me that neither one nor the other could claim to be "first." Today, after a more careful study of the gospel data, I think I can state that the language of "exaltation" encompasses the other, the language of "resurrection." Actually, Jesus began by announcing God's Kingdom, by dreaming of its inauguration on earth in continuity with the proclamation of the Kingdom already begun; he did not proclaim from the outset the path of death and persecution. Once a setback came about within his preaching ministry, only then did he reveal that the path to glory would come about by way of death. And, in making use of an allusion to the Son of Man, he held fast to his view of the in-breaking of glory. Glory, exaltation, was always present, encircling with its halo the proclamation of the cross.

Jesus, therefore, did not go looking for death for its own sake, however salutary that might be. And one can only be quite wrong to so interpret the words he spoke concerning his desire to drink the cup of his passion. Jesus simply wanted to be faithful to the end. He understood himself to be within that line of prophets, whose typical experience was one of persecution; for authentic service to God ends up in rousing up men and women's wrath against those who believe the gospel. When the world does not welcome the Word of God, it is because the world is inhabited by an evil power named sin; this is what John expressed so magnificently when he had Jesus declare, "You cannot hear me."

To speak in this way in no way diminishes the salvific worth of Jesus' death; rather it situates his death within a broader context that gives it meaning: the context of Jesus' obedient faithfulness, something Paul and the author of the Epistle to the Hebrews showed so well. Life illuminates death and, in its turn, death crowns life; it is in this relationship that the truth of Jesus' death is to be found.

In attentively considering the interpretations Paul gave to Christ's death, one perceives that the sacrificial and even redemptive understandings of this death hold up only when they are definitively located in relation to Jesus' love and God's love. Put in another way, when the Son surrenders himself and when the Father surrenders his Son, it is in no way *for the sake of* some chastisement nor *for the sake of* some satisfaction; it is *for* his remaining faithful to the mission of love.

So, Paul affirms that the death and the life of Jesus continue to exercise their sway under the form of what he calls the "dying" of Jesus and Jesus' "power of life." This means, then, that at the moment of his Resurrection Jesus' personality burst out in some way into the lives of all those who believe in him. This very presence creates the condition of possibility for the "spiritual" life of the believer. How far removed this view is from certain classical presentations of "mortification." Accordingly, let us explain in what sense, then, death is present in the Christian's life.

Starting from the moment when people isolated Jesus' death from his life of faithfulness, which preceded it, thereby conferring on it some kind of virtue in itself either as an "expiatory" action or as some sort of "ransom," it was only a short step, quickly reached, to deduce from this that Jesus had "desired" such a salvific death and that human suffering was an act meritorious and truly desirable. Projecting these views onto the Christian's daily existence, one was encouraged to consider "mortification" as a desirable path by which one could set about prematurely to kill the flesh, particularly sexuality, and to condemn any kind of joy. Is there any need to stress that such a view came about through contact with a certain ancient philosophy according to which, since the body was the soul's shell, one had to ensure the minimalization of the body's tyrannies? Are psychologists not right in denouncing in such behavior a kind of secret masochism, a concealed need to destroy oneself? Moreover, it is not asceticism, something necessary in every human's life, which characterizes the Christian religion.

In opposition to such an attitude stand what Jesus and Paul teach us. Knowing that Jesus' death was active in his own body, Paul did not ask others to seek this "dying" but rather to let it be actively present in oneself, as a consequence of one's faithfulness to the mission undertaken. The message of the cross has to become incarnate in the messenger who, in turn, becomes crucified. I do not think that one should attribute to Paul a desire to "mortify himself"; his enemies saw well enough to that. But, like a good athlete, he kept his body in a state of watchfulness and availability; what well-bred man would not have done likewise? "Mortification" is something else again; it makes death, Jesus' dying, present in those who are faithful to living and proclaiming the Good News: this is the meaning of the "tribulation" spoken of by Paul. This is a reality, brought about by sin present in the world, which does not support the gospel of God.

One cannot, however, maintain that all suffering is brought about by fidelity to the Good News. First of all, human existence presupposes a law of "natural" growth, a law of pulling away from oneself to be open to another; and this involves real suffering. Also the misfortunes of the world, an inexplicable sickness, all this suffering is brought about by something other than the proclamation of the gospel. According to Paul this "something" is the continuing presence of sin in the world. In fact, the universe exists in a state of servitude, headed for a corruption not of its own making. Just as death symbolizes that sin is at work, one can say that suffering partially symbolizes this same power at work. Just as our death can take on meaning from Christ's death, so also our suffering can find meaning insofar as it is united to Christ's. Beyond suffering and death it is life that mysteriously opens up a path for itself.

The consequences of these reflections are quite important, particularly for the way in which it helps to situate the proclamation of "death-resurrection." A good pedagogy of the faith would not directly highlight the cross and death; to begin with it would be careful to stir up enthusiasm in people with the proclamation of the marvellous Kingdom of God. All too often "resurrection" talk, which presupposes death, has overtaken "exaltation" terminology, which describes the living out of God's plan; too often, also, "mortification" has been presented only as voluntary asceticism, instead of being related in the proclamation of the gospel to unwavering faithfulness.

Finally, the last word belongs to Jesus, who declared, "The one who holds on to life, loses it, the one who is not attached to his existence preserves it for eternal life." That personality, which is Christian (and human) exists in a state of "*ec*stasy," a getting out of oneself without which the individual remains sterilely shriveled up on himself or herself. The one who does not love abides in death.

CHRIST'S DEATH AND THE REVELATION OF GOD

God truly did remain silent. He did not answer Jesus' sorrowful prayer in Gethsemane, nor, when Jesus was face-to-face with his enemies, his last cry shouted aloud on Golgotha. We have not been able to record his voice or to pick up whatever all-powerful intervention could have preserved his Son from death. The historian sees only the pierced side of Jesus.

Should we regret this? Wouldn't it be better for us to admit that we subject God to judgment in categories relating to power and efficiency, as if some ultimate criterion of truth could be found in our specific wisdom and not in the depths of the One whom no one has ever seen?

And what if the silence of God had been more eloquent finally than the speech we would rather have heard? Or the signs, which were meant to reassure us? Would not God then have decided to put a full stop to the direct education of his people?

Trumpets sound, lightnings flash, the earth trembles. But when you entered the womb of the Virgin your step made no noise at all.

(*Palatine Anthology* [5th cent.] I:37)

God does not reveal himself to us more in the thunder of Sinai, nor even in the murmur of Horeb; when he reveals himself, he does so through silence. Once for all he took shape in Jesus, but this shape has disappeared.

It was raised up to the eyes of faith. Henceforth, the Word can come to me through any person in whom the Spirit makes me recognize the very visage of the glorified Christ. The sun that the waters of the sea reflect becomes a myriad of shimmering suns.

Nonetheless, death continues to reap without pity. And God continues to be silent. The shapes of those whom we loved so dearly have disappeared; one day I myself shall disappear from my friends' view. Still, I know the one in whom I have placed my trust. So, it is not with an icy silence that I will respond to God's silence. The Spirit makes me say, "*Abba,* my God, it's you! You who are love, stronger than death."

Appendix:
Beyond Death*

"I believe in the resurrection of the body and in life eternal"—
this is the formula by means of which, like every Christian, I
profess my faith in a life without end after death, in a life that
transfigures earthly life by bringing it to fulfillment without letting anything of what typifies it to be lost.

Now, what is this "body" that the Apostles' Creed mentions?
Is it in fact the body that we see and by means of which we express
ourselves, and does the resurrection consist in our taking up again
the body confined to the earth? Again, just when does this resurrection take place? There is no dearth of theologians who declare
that we will rise at the very moment of our death.[1] If that is so,
why do we still talk about the end of time, which will see the
resurrection of the flesh?

I propose to sketch an outline of this topic by drawing on several conclusions of the exegetical sciences.[2] I would hope as well
to be able to echo the testimony of Christian tradition. These
pages are not simply an articulation of objective data, but are also
a *proclamation* of faith. Even as a historian, I cannot speak authentically of the faith except by giving personal witness and,
thereby, a proclamation.

There are three aspects to this treatment. First of all, I want to
take account of the way in which we think about the resurrection
of the dead according to the pattern of catechisms and of the classical exposition of theology. Then, I will recall the biblical data

---

*These pages were published as "Par-delà la mort . . ." in the journal *Études* (No-
vember 1972), 604–618. They treat a subject that this book has touched on only
briefly, namely the genesis of classical language concerning what takes place
"after" death.

and the terminology by means of which the Semites, who are our forebears in the faith, declared their faith in the resurrection. This will then allow me at a third stage to juxtapose classical terminology with contemporary terminology.

THE ORIGINS OF EVERYDAY TERMS

Classically, people represented the resurrection of the dead as the taking up again of their bodies by the whole of humanity at the end of time. This is the Last Judgment, by means of which the world comes to its consummation—the end of the world. However, let us observe, this view of the final resurrection is not adequate to describe the kinds of destinies awaiting human beings. Account must be taken of the individual's fate; thus classical theology spoke of the particular judgment in which the lot of the soul separated from its body is fixed. From the moment of death the soul is destined either to the beatific vision (and, according to need by way of a sojourn in purgatory), or else to hell; that is, to an existence separated from God. These two affirmations— about the Last Judgment and the particular judgment—raise problems for anyone who tries to see how they can coexist with each other. Sometimes people think they can resolve the dilemma by claiming that, hypothetically, the soul is basically happy even though separated from its body until the end of time. And yet, what would be the extent of a living being's happiness when it is not fully joined in a state of joy with its body?

Underlying this issue is the fact that a representation of "separated souls" has been used officially to specify what happens at death. This took place on the occasion of a theological dispute involving two successive popes toward the end of the Middle Ages. In fact, a Gascon, Pope John XXII, showed himself to be someone quite knowledgeable of the tradition and of certain of the scriptural representations. Accordingly, along with John of Patmos, he assimilated separated souls to the martyrs who waited impatiently beneath the altar until that moment when the number of the witnesses would be complete (Rv 6:9). Also given to taking such descriptions literally were very many of the Fathers who, in order to safeguard the value of matter against the Gnostics, stressed the imperfect nature of the blessedness of the just: Origen, Hilary, the two Cyrils, Chrysostom, Augustine. Even a figure of the eleventh century renowned for his individualistic piety echoed this venerable tradition:

Already numerous among us are those who stand within the courts await-ing the day when their bodies shall be restored to them and the number of their brethren shall be complete. They will not enter without us into that blessed house. I want to stress that the saints will not enter without the ordinary faithful.[3]

St. Bernard was not afraid, then, to assert that the saints wait until the just are all gathered together at the end of time. John XXII drew consequences from these assertions in several quite celebrated sermons, even going so far as to say that, even if it ascended to Heaven at the moment of death, the just soul would not enjoy the beatific vision. Henri de Lubac, in *Catholicism*, a book to which I owe so much, recalls three reasons that guided the Fathers and St. Bernard along this path. First, scripture ties recompense to the general judgment. Secondly, the human person is incomplete in his or her body. Thirdly, belief in milleniarism—that is, in a 1,000-year period that in some way is to prolong this earthly life before the Parousia—encouraged the idea of a period of waiting on the part of men and women until the end of time. The same author has adduced a further motivating factor for such thinking, one that is far more profound than the three preceding ones, for this one stresses the truth rooted in such a representation, namely the Church's faith in salvation's social dimension.

People spontaneously depicted the Church entering Heaven after having won the victory. As long as it was still militant, people thought (more or less confusedly), none of its members could enjoy a full triumph. This, then, was a translation in temporal terms, (and falsely so,) of a very real link in causality.[4]

A false translation—in effect, John XXII went too far in refus-ing the beatific vision to those who were, nevertheless, already the just. He stirred up such a vivid reaction among his contemporaries that, on the eve of his death he retracted his private opinions and professed what his successor would solemnly define. In fact, Benedict XII (from Ariège, in France) published a bull, *Benedictus Deus*, that stated the commonly held faith, one that held that the just at the moment of their death do enter on possession of the beatific vision without having to await the resurrection. This reaction derived from a profound and authentically Christian conviction, namely that the human person could not remain for long in a kind of inertia without enjoying the vision of God. Therefore, it is not enough to project onto Christian destiny the mode by which Jews conceived of the life of the dead prior to the final resurrection, and only then filling it out with some kind of locale; too many New Testament texts affirm that at death we see God. So, St. Paul in his Epistle to the Philippians says, "I desire to die and be with Christ" (Phil 1:21). Moreover, every free creature exists in intrinsic relationship with God the creator. Because of a long and gradual penetration of a certain Neo-platonic type of Hellenism into Christianity, these certainties of faith ended up being expressed in terms of an anthropology that saw in the soul and body not only aspects of being, but substances out of which the human person was composed. As a result, in this view, at death the soul separated from its body to enter eternal happiness or eternal loss.[5] In summary, for Benedict XII and for the catechism that followed, the essential reality was already granted along with the lot of the just soul, which goes to heaven at death. Does it follow from this that the resurrection is an accidental complement to one's essential beatitude? St. Thomas refused to draw such a conclusion: but the nontheologian, little versed in philosophy, could not arrive at a way of reconciling the tension that should have linked the two convictions but that ended up instead by making of the beatific vision and the resurrection two separate realities that were added to or complemented each other. The terms of our problem are no doubt better defined, but the question remains: if everything is given with the beatific vision, what does the resurrection add? Having arrived at such an impasse, ought we not recognize that the problem is poorly stated? Does tension exist between two realities or rather between two complementary representations—two sets of terminology by means of which we struggle to give expression to the totality of the unique mystery of the afterlife?

THE BIBLICAL CONCEPTION IN LIGHT OF SUCH USAGE

Let us recall at the outset that, in spelling out the biblical conception, our aim is not to bring discredit on the terminology that has become familiar to us, but rather to strive to better understand it so as to manifest its true meaning. In effect, the successive sets of language called on by the Church to declare its faith to the men and women of every era must always be related to biblical language. This latter is for this reason privileged even though it depends on Semitic representations that are in no way privileged.

Two basic truths control this biblical conception. The first concerns God. Although we are steeped in a certain naturalistic philosophy, still we believe that we are alive by nature,[6] while as far as the Bible is concerned, only YHWH is the Living One. This living God, who must not be confused with the deities of other religions, is the one who "causes death and brings to life", or, as the canticle of Hannah puts it, "God brings down to Sheol and raises up" (1 Sm 2:6). According to the first theological presupposition, then, *God alone is the living one.* The corollary to this is that a man or a woman is never a living being by nature, but is so only by grace; that is, he or she is in a relationship of dialogue with God. This is the relationship that constitutes the man or woman's very existence. One cannot say "God and I are there," but one must say instead "God is there, and I am also present, thanks to God." I cannot number myself with God, although I exist before God and thanks to God: my life is nothing other than a share in God's life.

The second presupposition belongs to the order of anthropology. Although we readily consider the human person as composed of two substances, a body and a soul (the soul being immortal, the body being matter provisionally put at one's disposal), for the Bible, *the human person is one*; the body is not a part making up a man or a woman; rather, the body is that human person insofar as he or she is exteriorized. In fact, the man or woman reveals himself or herself totally through the soul, the flesh, the spirit, the body. He or she is thought about as an animated body and not as an incarnate soul. The consequence of this truth is that while we too often conceive of death as the separation of soul and body, for the man or a woman of the Bible, when that person dies, he or she goes down in his or her entirety to the subterranean region that is Sheol to carry on there with an existence that is still corporeal, but one that is so diminished that it does not deserve to be called life. When he dies, the human being stops living even though he still exists.

These two presuppositions control biblical notions about the resurrection. The first conclusion, then, is that faith in the resurrection is neither a consequence of nor a complement to belief in the immortality of the soul. While their neighboring peoples, the Greeks or the Egyptians, came very early on to a certain notion of immortality, the Jews did not share this faith before the second century before Jesus Christ. The God of all justice could not leave in Sheol those who had been witnesses to the living God. This is the way Daniel the prophet made his declaration:

And many of those who sleep in the land of the dust of the earth shall awake, some to everlasting life, and some to shame and everlasting contempt.

(Dn 12:2)

Exegetes are agreed in thinking that the determining factor had been the experience of the death of the martyrs during the persecution of Antiochus Epiphanes around 167 B.C. This resurrection terminology, additionally, had been prepared for by a certain number of metaphors or modes of expression that spoke of resurrection not yet as a true resurrection after death but as a kind of rising up out of the jaws of death at the very moment when the sick one was on the verge of losing his life:

> He has stricken, and he will bind us up; after two days he will revive us; on the third day he will raise us up, that we may live before him.
>
> (Hos 6:1–2)

In this text, as in the famous prophecy of Ezekiel 37, which describes the dead standing up and reviving under the breath of God, it is affirmed that God is able to preserve from death: in our time we remain convinced that, despite everything, the life in Sheol after death does not merit being called life. It was in the second century before Christ, then, that the Jews began to believe that God's justice was able to give back life. Resurrection, then, does not consist in the reanimation of the body whether, according to Pythagoreanism, this means giving the being a new body during a transmigration of souls or whether, following a form of Hellenized Christianity, this means one's own body after it had become a corpse. Rather, resurrection means the gift of an entry point to a full life according to a new way of living and expressing oneself. It was in just such a way, thanks to the proper terminology, that Christians were able to describe their experience of Christ as alive, stressing that God raised him from the dead. Already, starting with this first vocabulary, we can measure an enormous gap between it and the Hellenized conception of the immortality of the soul. The resurrection of the flesh meant the resurrection of the entire person; it was not something added on to the immortality of the soul. It *is* the very definition of the final lot of the just.

So much for the fact of the resurrection. Can we be more specific about the nature of this resurrection? The conceptions that the Scriptures or the Jewish texts of the period make available to us are quite a varied lot. They oscillate between depictions of a materialistic kind and depictions that are entirely spiritual. On the one hand, we see, for example, the way in which the *Apocalypse of Baruch*, a Jewish apocalyptic text of the first century A.D. and contemporary with the redaction of the gospels, describes it:

In what way will they come alive, those who will see your Day? What will become of their splendor after these happenings? Will they regain their actual forms?

This question, we observe, is similar to the one Paul has the Corinthians ask, "How are the dead raised? With what kind of body do they come?" (1 Cor 15:35). Here is the reply that the visionary Baruch hears:

The earth will give up her dead . . . as she received them and as I entrust them to her so will she cause them to rise up. For it will be important to reveal to the living that the dead are alive. . . . And when those who today know one another will mutually recognize each other, then the judgment will begin to be carried out. . . . Thus the aspect of those who will have been condemned and the glory of those who will have been justified will be changed. . . . Their splendor will be rendered glorious.

Such a depiction is very close to what the New Testament says. For Paul, equally, the transformation is contradistinguished from the resurrection, at least in regard to the Parousia: "We shall not all sleep but we shall all be changed" (1 Cor 15:51). It was in this way, moreover, that Jesus allowed himself to be recognized by his own. This was the way—somewhat materialistic, even objectivized one might say—in which the Risen One presented himself to his disciples.

According to another tradition, the same visionary Baruch finished off his description of the elect by proclaiming: "They will resemble the angels, they will be comparable to the stars." And, in the same way, to the Sadducees who intended to hold the resurrection and the world to come up to ridicule, Jesus replied in the same terms as the Parables of Enoch (a passage dating from the first century A.D.): "In those days the just will become like the angels of Heaven." We cannot say that materialistic representations won out over "spiritual" conceptions (for spiritual does not mean "noncorporeal"). The interest of this double tendency was to show that human thought strove to depict a state, a condition that in fact is unrepresentable. This is why we assert that this condition has at one and the same time a *material* character, something that means not "spiritual," not "evaporated," not "gnostic" and yet, on the other hand, something that possesses a spiritual character—a conviction that underlines the truth—that in all this we are not concerned simply with an extension of terrestrial life. The Bible, in this way, invites us to remain quite sober in all that pertains to the description of glorious bodies.

Moreover, terminology concerning the resurrection was not the only kind that was used to describe what became of believers after their death. There was extant as well a second vocabulary that tried to state the same thing as the first. This was "exaltation" language.[7] The first set of terms followed a historical type of schema, in which one could speak about what was *before* and what came *after*; in this framework one projected the act of coming into existence along a spatiotemporal line: what came before, and what came after, death. In exaltation terminology, there was a different schema, apocalyptic in origin, that attempted to describe the same reality according to the relationship between what was *below* and what was *above*. A word about the cosmology of the Jews: they conceived of the earth as a *platter* under which there was an underground, the infernal regions (hell), and, above their heads, the dwelling place of God himself. According to a very ancient tradition, one even older than that of resurrection, God is so just that he cannot leave the one who is just to go down into the abyss of death. So it was that the death of the just person was thought of as a removal, an exaltation, an assumption into heaven. Enoch had been transferred (Sir 44:16), Elijah had been carried off into Heaven in a fiery chariot (Sir 48:9). Anterior, then, to the development of faith in the resurrection of the dead, there had come to light a hope of the just one's being taken up into Heaven. Thus did the psalmist pray, "God will ransom my soul from the power of Sheol, for he will receive me" (Ps 49:16) or, in another place, "Thou dost hold my right hand; Thou dost guide me with thy counsel, and afterword thou wilt receive me into glory" (Ps

73:23–24). Always recurring are the verbs "to take" and "to lift up," which express the deep desire never to be separated from God, as one would be when dead or sent down to Sheol. This tradition was developed in the prophecy of the Servant of God who, after having voluntarily undergone suffering, had been glorified and exalted (Is 52:13–53:12). In its turn, the Book of Wisdom echoed this belief (Wis 4–5). It was in line with such a tradition, parallel to a resurrection tradition, that Christians expressed the experience they had shared with Jesus restored to life after his death. It was also in this way, and by means of hymns, for example, that Paul in the second chapter of the Epistle to the Philippians described the fate Jesus underwent after he had freely humbled himself to the point of death, even death on a cross; there Paul did not mention Jesus' resurrection but only his exaltation in Heaven. In so doing—and there are still other texts that preserve in this way echoes of faith in Christ brought to life after death— Christians expressed themselves with the help of terminology that saw this experience in a horizontal way, which highlighted what came *before* and what came *after*. For here there was little interest taken in the end of time, not even an anticipation of the end times in Jesus; no mention was made of ordinary time, which belonged to another, spatial scheme of understanding reality, one that made distinctions between what was *above* and what was *below*. It was from below that the just one had been lifted up to Heaven. To illustrate the enduring merit in such terminology we only have to think of the dogma of the Assumption of the Blessed Virgin Mary, who was "assumed" into Heaven. When this dogma was defined, it was not judged opportune to mention that Mary had died; rather, reference was had then to that datum of the tradition according to which Mary had "fallen asleep." I think that quite profoundly and, no doubt, subconsciously at that time they were adhering to an interpretation of terms that reserved to Jesus Christ alone a resurrection within time. By refraining from asserting that Mary had died, one avoided giving the impression that she had been raised; conversely, they did affirm that she had been exalted *body and soul* in Heaven from the very *end of her life*, even if they did not actually assert from the *moment of her death*. Mary's future state was depicted according to the categories of what was above and what was below, that is to say, according to the second manner of presenting the just person's lot.

In any case, in speaking of resurrection or exaltation, one did affirm that the just person in his or her totality was with God whether one thought then of a resurrection at the end of time or of an exaltation at the moment of death. These two sets of terms are not mutually exclusive; each recalls the other to account for the mystery in all its fullness. Yet, in a certain sense, these are conflicting terms, since one declares continuity into the period after death and the other denies this; one projects the person's fate after death along a temporal continuum, while the other refrains from speaking of time so as to declare at the outset a heavenly glorification.

THE STATEMENTS OF JOHN XXII AND BENEDICT XII

Following this contrast with the biblical data, let us attempt to purify the classical terminology. We will try to do this by specifying the truth sought out by John XXII and Benedict XII.

The intermediate time separating death and resurrection was conceived by John XXII according to the Old Testament's perspective on Sheol. In so doing, he seems to have misunderstood that already in Christ we possess the totality of happiness: the resurrection that will take place for all at the end of time has already been realized in Jesus Christ. But as H. de Lubac has put it so well, John XXII stressed quite rightly an aspect of the truth, the concern to preserve a social dimension in this happiness. In effect, when I state pure and simple that at my death I possess beatitude, I tend thereby to miss a fundamental aspect of Christian revelation, namely that we are all bound to one another and that, by virtue of our temporal conditioning, we cannot think of individual happiness without intrinsically relating it to that of our brothers and sisters. This is, in fact, a matter of semantics; I cannot *declare* happiness without tying it to the presence of all my sisters and brothers. This is the aspect of truth so clearly contained in the notion that people await the resurrection of the dead. Here, then, is the reason why we must say that Christ is at work with us to transform the world. Here, too, is the reason for St. Paul's declaration that Christ himself will come one day to hand over to his Father the world transformed into his Kingdom. It is a mistake to say that Christ is no longer within time and that, according to the saying of John Giono, Christ, all alone in Heaven, enjoys unending happiness. We cannot think or speak of Christ without locating him in time and, consequently, we are quite right to speak of Christ's "hope." Our difficulty is to come to the point of grasping that this is simply a necessity for clarity of thought, one that requires a temporal language to adequately make assertions. Without this kind of projection concerning the end of time, I cannot conceive of the totality of the happiness of men and women. Also, I can and must continue to pray for the dead. This, also, is why I have to continue to throb with hope in my labors for God's Kingdom. This is necessary terminology, then, and it expresses the truth in what John XXII said—a fact that runs the risk of being missed when one dwells on the "essential" beatitude (as it is described) bestowed on the elect at the very moment of death. This also the reason why I cannot agree to assert that we will rise at the moment of our death. In effect, to say that at our death we rise is to miss that part of the truth that is concealed in references to the end of time; to speak of resurrection at the moment of death is to mix unduly two different sets of vocabulary.

Having said this, we now have to search out that aspect of the truth contained in Benedict XII's reaction. No doubt, in this reaction that stresses the reality of this beatific vision at the moment of death, the Pope was adhering to a certain philosophy and a certain belief in the immortality of the spiritual soul, over against the mortality of the material body. But with the help of this less than adequate terminology, he intended to state a fundamental truth. It was that, in effect, the human person is not simply defined by the relationship he possesses with other men and women; he is also, in his very person, in a relationship with God. Immortality is not natural;[8] unlike the view maintained by the Greeks, which saw in the soul an emanation of the deity, immortality is conceived as a gift from God. This means that we are always in relationship with God; immortality consists in the fact that God, from the moment he creates a person, enters into a permanent mode of dialogue with him. This is why at death such a relationship cannot be suppressed. More precisely the just person cannot remain in Sheol; instead his relationship with God becomes more perfect: this is what we refer to as the beatific vision. Consequently, at the base of Benedict XII's reaction may be found an affirmation of the essential worth of the human person. All the while making use of an anthropology that conceives death as a separation of the soul from the body, this view signifies that the man or woman is a subsistent being in relationship with God himself. To speak in this way is to state the equivalent of another terminology, that of the resurrection. Benedict XII found himself dealing with exaltation language to which we had recourse earlier, with the Bible, with our aim of depicting man's lot at the moment of death.

Thus John XXII and Benedict XII represent two tendencies, both of which ought to be respected. In what way? Not in their common anthropology, which adopted the representation of "separated souls," but in their different outlooks toward the kind of "time" that surfaces at the moment of death. With John XXII, I use a language that continues to be temporal, and I locate the afterlife on a continuum of a before and an after. With Benedict XII, I deny this time and substitute for it an affirmation concerning the terrestial-celestial relationship, what is below and what is above.

TOWARD A CONTEMPORARY IDIOM

As a function of the above, let us now try to specify what contemporary terminology about the resurrection would look like. First of all let us recall the following: when one speaks of the resurrection of the flesh, the word *flesh* does not mean the body insofar as it is matter separated from the soul, but rather the human person in his or her mortal condition. Resurrection of the flesh means resurrection of the whole person and this to such an extent that in certain apocryphal writings dating from the period of Wisdom (the first century B.C.), there is even talk of the resurrection of souls,[9] the word *soul* designating not some spiritual essence but the person in relationship with God.

Secondly, the two languages cannot be added on to one another; they must be situated in relationship to one another. The terminology of resurrection does not complete that of the beatific vision, but each is necessary to effect a vision of the mysterious reality that, in itself, escapes our grasp. We do not add up the two languages; rather, we relate them the better to lay hold of the reality.[10]

Thirdly, we ask what will be the function today of our faith in the resurrection of the dead? Here is the importance of grasping well resurrection's double dimension. The resurrection concerns the entire human person: under its vertical aspect, it aims to communicate one's relationship with God, one that could be characterized by the term "the soul"; under its horizontal aspect, it aims to communicate one's relationship with men and women and the universe, one that could be characterized by the term "the body."

Faith in the resurrection of men does not find its true meaning except as rooted in our faith in the resurrection of Jesus through the love of God. Through this faith we are certain that love is stronger than death and that, consequently, *from the moment of death* we are conquerors with Jesus Christ; in Christ Jesus, life has triumphed. The personal relationship that has been inaugurated with God already here below becomes perfect. Dialogue with God is henceforth face to face. Of such a kind is the vertical relationship with God. With regard to the horizontal relationship, it keeps us in what we can call hope. It is the language of hope that can be the most eloquent for us today. Faith, which has allowed me to be joined with God, guarantees the authenticity of my hope; and this hope is not merely individual hope. Having understood that Jesus' resurrection is the affirmation of Christ's lordship in the universe is to state as well, that Christ is *already* the lord of the universe and that Christ is now at work in the universe to establish love over hatred. This conviction of my faith confirms me in my certitude that love is stronger than death, not only for me but also for my brothers and sisters. If I can struggle for the establishment of the reign of love in humanity, this derives from my conviction that I am no longer alone. My solitude is henceforth filled with a presence, the presence of the one who is alive, the presence of a being on whom I depend, a presence through which I enter into deep communion with my brothers. This is the presence of the Resurrected One, which has been granted to me by faith and which therefore does not depend on my humors and my intimate dispositions. This presence always brings me back to Jesus of Nazareth, who lived long ago. This presence opens me up to the future and opens me to a world in which Jesus' unique commandment can finally find its meaning and place: "Love one another." In all truth, because I believe that Jesus of Nazareth came forth alive out of death and remains living beyond death, I am capable of hoping that the world can be transformed. This dynamic creates in me a perfect freedom with regard to all that is passing away since, in principle, I have been set free of the great fear of death. And not set free in words, as if we could abstract from death; but set free in this sense, that, positively speaking, divine life—that is to say, God's love—is already present and active in the midst of all death's ferments, which are at work in me.

If these things are so, a good many questions appear to us not as futile but as secondary. In what does the glorious body consist? Let it be enough to say that after death we will be fully ourselves. How will the identity between who I have been and who I now am be preserved? Theology leaves this issue open. Some have believed that it was necessary to preserve a special relationship with one's very own body, without adverting to the kinds of difficulties aroused by speaking in this way. Others, on the contrary, were brought to the point of thinking that this was simply a question of a relationship to the universe, this universe into

which our body has been restored. In any case, what is certain is
that, above and beyond the apparent discontinuity, a deeper continuity unites the risen one to the man or woman who lived on
earth, a continuity that is not determined by the assumption of
some chemical or organic particle of what had been the body but
rather of two conjoined factors. First and essentially the continuity
is guaranteed by the same God who brought into existence and
who effects the coming back to life: how can God have as the
term of his activity a person other than the one I had been? And
this activity of God's consists in his giving to my "I" the ability
to regain possession of my own identity by means of the body
that I had been. The second factor in this continuity is the fact
that, in the course of my life, love little by little was incarnated
in my very self; my personality was woven out of the love I received and gave. The manner in which I expressed this love
through my body, which was my capacity for being present to
others and to the universe, this very love has shaped my personality forever. Sometimes people raise the problem of relationships
with others; let us be aware that such relationships are not casual,
or additional, but are indeed constitutive of our persons. I was
shaped by the love I received and by the love I gave. And, if it
is true that love alone goes beyond death, we can say that, to the
extent of the openness of my being to the totality of God and
others, I will be forever this person that I have been constituted
throughout the length of my days.

Presented in this way, can our faith in our resurrection still be
called the opium of the people, a consolation of the dispossessed
of the earth? This is a very strange misunderstanding of heaven,
which, far from reassuring me with an illusory security, energizes
my will to action on earth by pressing me to make myself open
to others and to struggle so that love may reign here below. In
this regard, we seem to be very much like the best men and
women who do not share our faith. What differentiates us is the
enthusiastic certainty that causes us to recognize the living Lord
at work here below and the very love of God, that love which,
one day, showed itself stronger than death in raising up Jesus of

Nazareth, the first fruits of our own resurrection. Yes, indeed, within the one body of Christ—without there being any confusion of persons—we will one day be perfectly transparent to God and to others, according to the measure of love we received and gave on earth.

NOTES

1. Cf. *Concilium 60* (New York: Herder and Herder, 1970), with its articles by L. Boros and P. Benoit.
2. And especially the results of our inquiry on *The Resurrection of Jesus and the Message of Easter* (New York: Holt, Rinehart and Winston, 1975). A summary on this topic has been published recently by G. Greshake, *Die Auferstehung der Toten. Ein Beitrag zur gegenwärtigen theologischen Diskussion über die Zukunft der Geschichte* (Essen: Ludgerus Verlag, 1969).
3. Cf. St. Bernard, *In festo omnium sanctorum*, Sermon 3, quoted by H. de Lubac, *Catholicism* (London: Longmans and Green, 1950), 59.
4. Cf. H. de Lubac, *Catholicism*, p. 56.
5. Cf. K. Rahner, *On the Theology of Death* (New York: Herder and Herder, 1961), pp. 21–63.
6. We take here the word *natural* in the meaning it has today, not its traditional meaning (cf. H. de Lubac, *The Mystery of the Supernatural* [New York: Herder and Herder, 1967]; *Athéisme et Sens de l'homme* [Paris: Cerf, 1968], pp. 96–98): what belongs to the very constitution of a human person, apart from God and apart from the supernatural, which is thereby equivalent to something "superadded."
7. On "exaltation" terminology, cf. our work, above, n.2.
8. Cf. the remark made in n. 6 above.
9. Cf. P. Grelot, "L'Eschatologie de la Sagesse et les apocalypses juives," in *De la mort à la vie éternelle* (Paris: Cerf, 1971), p. 198.
10. J. Ratzinger, *Introduction to Christianity* (New York: Herder and Herder, 1970), p. 270: "Originally it was not a question of two complementary ideas (the Greek idea of the immortality of the soul and the biblical message of the resurrection of the dead); on the contrary, we are confronted with two different total views which cannot be simply added together" (modified translation).

Bibliography

The bibliography on this topic is so extensive that I decided not to publish one here. I merely indicate three works that touch partially on the theme treated in this book:

J. Guillet. *The Consciousness of Jesus*, trans. Edmond Bonin. New York and Toronto: Newman Press, 1972.

P. Grelot. *Péché originel et Rédemption à partir de l'épitre aux Romains*. Essai théologique. Paris: Desclée, 1973.

H. Schürmann. *Comment Jésus a-t-il vécu sa mort?* Paris: Cerf, 1977.

Abbreviations of Books of the Bible

Acts	Acts of the Apostles	Gal	Galatians
Am	Amos	Gn	Genesis
Bar	Baruch	Hb	Habakkuk
1 Chr	1 Chronicles	Hg	Haggai
2 Chr	2 Chronicles	Heb	Hebrews
Col	Colossians	Hos	Hosea
1 Cor	1 Corinthians	Is	Isaiah
2 Cor	2 Corinthians	Jas	James
Dn	Daniel	Jer	Jeremiah
Dt	Deuteronomy	Jb	Job
Eccl	Ecclesiastes	Jl	Joel
Eph	Ephesians	Jn	John (Gospel)
Est	Esther	1 Jn	1 John
Ex	Exodus	2 Jn	2 John
Ez	Ezekiel	3 Jn	3 John
Ezr	Ezra	Jon	Jonah

Jos	Joshua		Phlm	Philemon
Jude	Jude		Phil	Philippians
Jgs	Judges		Prv	Proverbs
Jdt	Judith		Ps	Psalms
1 Kgs	1 Kings		Rv	Revelation
2 Kgs	2 Kings		Rom	Romans
Lam	Lamentations		Ru	Ruth
Lv	Leviticus		1 Sm	1 Samuel
Lk	Luke		2 Sm	2 Samuel
1 Mc	1 Maccabees		Sir	Sirach
2 Mc	2 Maccabees		Sg	Song of Songs
Mal	Malachi		1 Thess	1 Thessalonians
Mk	Mark		2 Thess	2 Thessalonians
Mt	Matthew		1 Tim	1 Timothy
Mi	Micah		2 Tim	2 Timothy
Na	Nahum		Ti	Titus
Neh	Nehemiah		Tb	Tobit
Nm	Numbers		Wis	Wisdom
Ob	Obadiah		Zec	Zechariah
1 Pt	1 Peter		Zep	Zephaniah
2 Pt	2 Peter			

Abbreviations of Nonbiblical Writings

Ant.	Jewish Antiquities (Josephus)
Ap. Bar.	Apocalypse of Baruch
Aq.	Aquila's Greek translation of the Bible
Ass. Mos.	Assumption of Moses
Ep.	(Ethiopian) Book of Enoch
4 Ez	Fourth Ezra
LAB	Liber Antiquitatum Biblicarum (Pseudo-Philo)
4 Mc	Fourth Book of Maccabees
Ps. Sol.	Psalms of Solomon
1 QH	Hymns discovered at Qumran
1 QpH	Pesher on Habakkuk, from Qumram

1 QS	(Seder) Community Rule, from Qumran
Sanh.	Sanhedrin Treatise of the Talmud
Sym.	Symmachus's Greek translation of the Bible
War	Jewish War (Josephus)

Standard Abbreviations

cf.	refer to
chap.	chapter
ed.	edition
f, ff	*and the following verse(s),* or year(s)
Fr.	French
Fs.	Festschrift (memorial edition)
Gk.	Greek
LXX	The Septuagint Greek version of the Old Testament
n.	note
No.	number
N.T.	New Testament
O.T.	Old Testament
p	*and (synoptic) parallel(s)*
p., pp.	page, pages
Q	Q-source (German *Quelle*) = the material common to Matthew and Luke
vol., vols.	volume, volumes
v., vv.	verse, verses

Abbreviations of Reference Works, Periodicals, and Collected Essays

Bib.	*Biblica.* Rome: 1920ff.
BZ	*Biblische Zeitschrift.* Paderborn: new series 1957ff.
CBQ	*The Catholic Biblical Quarterly.* Washington, 1939ff.

DBT	X. Léon-Dufour, ed. *Dictionary of Biblical Theology.* 2nd ed. New York: Seabury Press, 1973.
EvT	*Evangelische Theologie.* Munich: 1934ff.
KuD	*Kerygma und Dogma.* Göttingen: 1955ff.
LV	*Lumière et Vie.* St-Alban-Leysse/Lyons: 1950ff.
MD	*La Maison-Dieu.* Paris: Cerf, 1945ff.
MelSR	*Mélanges de Sciences Religieuses.* Lille: 1944ff.
NTS	*New Testament Studies.* Cambridge, England: 1954ff.
PG	J.-P. Migne, ed. *Patrologia Graeca.* Paris: 1857–1866, suppl. 1959ff.
PL	J.-P. Migne, ed. *Patrologia Latina.* Paris: 1844–1864, suppl. 1959ff.
RB	*Revue Biblique.* Gabalda, 1892ff.
RevSR	*Revue des Sciences Religieuses.* Strasbourg: 1921ff.
RSPT	*Revue des Sciences Philosophiques et Théologiques.* Vrin, 1907ff.
RSR	*Recherches de Sciences Religieuse.* Paris: 1910ff.
SC	H. De Lubac, J. Daniélou, L. Mondesert, eds. *Sources Chrétiennes.* Paris: Cerf, 1941ff.
SDB	*Supplément au Dictionnaire de la Bible.* Letouzey et Ané, 1928ff.
TDNT	*Theological Dictionary of the New Testament.* Grand Rapids, Mich.: Eerdmans, 1964–1976.
TOB	*Traduction oecuménique de la Bible. Nouveau Testament.* Cerf/Bergers et Mages, 1972.
ZNW	*Zeitschrift für die neutestamentliche Wissenschaft und die Kunde der älteren Kirche.* Giessen/Berlin: 1900ff.
ZTK	*Zeitschrift für Theologie und Kirche.* Tübingen: 1891ff.

Selected Biblical References

The most significant texts and most important page references are in italics

Genesis
2:7
3:15

Exodus
19:5
24:8

Psalms
16:10
22
22:16
31
31:23
39:13
40:7
49:15–16
63
69:22
73:23–24
88
110

Qoheleth
3:19–21
7:15

Sirach
1:13
11:18–28
38:17,20–21
41:1
41:2–4

Isaiah
11:6,8
25:8
26:19
53
53:10,12

Ezekiel
9:4–6
37

Daniel
12:2

Hosea
6:1–2

Matthew
8:21–22
9:13
9:18
10:28
10:29–31
10:38
10:39
11:23
13:57
15:21
16:24
16:25
16:27
20:28
21:33–44
22:31
22:31–32

23:27
23:29
23:31
23:34–35
23:37–39
25:31–46
26:17–35
26:20–25
26:26–29
26:28
26:36–46
27:45–54
27:47–49

Mark
2:19–20
5:23,35,41
5:38–40
6:4
8:31
8:34
8:35
9:11–13
10:38
10:42–45
12:1–2
14:8
14:22–25
14:32–42
15:33–39
15:34
15:39

Luke
4:24
7:14
9:23
9:24
9:59–60
11:44
11:47
11:47–51
12:4–5

12:6–7
12:37
12:49–50
13:1–5
13:33,34–35
14:27
15:32
16:22
17:25
17:33
22:14–20
22:15–18
22:22
22:25–27
22:40–46
23:28–31,34
23:36,44–47
23:43
23:46
24:7
24:50

John
4:34
4:44
5:24
5:36
11:33–38
12:23–32
12:25
12:27
13:1–20
15:22
15:28
17:4–5
17:19
19:26,27
19:28
19:30

Acts of the Apostles
7:57–60
8:3; 9:1–2

Index

Abandonment by God, 280–81; at
Crucifixion, 126–28; Gethsemane
and, 103–6, 114
Abba (father), 42, 96, 117, 118, 132,
143, 281
Abel, 59, 143
Abraham, 5, 159, 176, 181, 183, 211,
212, 227, 239, 251
Absalom, 41
Acts of the Apostles, 133, 155, 156,
159, 160
Adam, 164–65, 270; Jesus as second,
202–4, 207–14, 220, 255, 272
Afterlife, xxiv, 20, 282–98; biblical
conception of, 286–92; in classical
theology, 283–86; contemporary
idiom of, 294–98; Hellenistic
tradition and, 249; in Jewish
tradition, 25–27, 199; John XXII
and Benedict XII on, 292–94;
present moment and, 25–27. *See
also* Heaven; Hell; Resurrection of
the dead
Agony, 98, 104, 110, 116. *See also*
Crucifixion; Gethsemane; Passion;
Suffering
Andrew, 99
Antiochus Epiphanes, 143, 287
Apocalyptic, the, 27–28; Crucifixion
and, 139; Paul's use of, 218–19. *See
also* End of time
Apostles: the Church's consciousness
and, 246; suffering (humiliation) of,
246, 251–54, 259, 262–64. *See also*
Disciples
Apostles' Creed, 282
Aqiba, Rabbi, 138
Assimilation, 163, 166, 173–78, 192
Assumption of the Blessed Virgin
Mary, 291–92
Atonement, Feast of the Great Pardon
or (Yom Kippur), 186, 189

Augustine, 264, 284

Baal, 116
Babylonian captivity, 169
Banquet, heaven as, 20, 31, 81
Baptism, 89; assimilation of believer
into paschal mystery by, 258;
connection to Christ through, 271;
liberation from sin by, 170; in
Pauline theology, 166–67, 192
Barabbas, 132
Baruch, Apocalypse of, 288–89
Beatific vision, 219, 254, 283–85,
293–95. *See also* Heaven
Benedictus Deus (papal bull), 285
Benedict XII, Pope, 285, 292–94
Benjamin, 159
Bernard of Clairvaux, 284
Bible, the: exegetical versus dogmatic
methods of study of, xxvi–xxvii.
See also Covenant; God's plan;
Jewish tradition (biblical tradition);
Law, the
Blood: of the covenant, 86; in
sacrifice, 66, 186–87, 189
Body: as glorified in heaven, 254–55;
in Hellenistic tradition, 10; in
Jewish tradition, 10, 198, 287; in
Luke, 9–10; in Matthew, 9–10;
resurrection of, 282–92. *See also*
Afterlife; Eternal life; Flesh;
Resurrection of the dead
Boman, Thorlief, 137
Bossuet, 129–30
Bourdalone, 129
Bridegroom, the Messiah as, 53
Bultmann, Rudolf, 49, 92
Burials, 13–14

Calvin, John, 129
Carmignac, J., 100
Celsus, 93

Cemetery, 16, 215, 217
Charity (love): death of Jesus and, 278; judgment and, 23–25; life force of Christ's, 252–53; present experience and, 229; prevenience of God's, 241; reconciliation and, 173–78; shaping the believer, 297; worship through life of, 184
Chrysostom. *See* John Chrysostom
Church, the: apostolic consciousness and, 246; as Body of Christ, 263, 264; God's plan and, 56; interpretation of salvific death of Jesus, 67; in Paul, 175, 263, 264; penitential practices of the early, 53; Resurrection of Jesus as deliverance of, 139–40; social dimension of salvation and, 284; terminology of service in early, 88
Clement of Rome, 246
Clothing, image of new, 255–56
Coherence, criterion of, xxviii, 50, 81
Colossians, Epistle of Paul to the, 174, 259, 263
Communion: Last Supper as, 82–85; in Pauline theology, 177–78
Consolation, tribulations and, 251
Continuity: of life through death, 297; of the material order, 201–2
Corinthians, First Epistle of Paul to the, 86, 160, 171, 175, 177, 179, 188, 198–203, 206, 210, 213, 214, 225–26, 241, 247, 289
Corinthians, Second Epistle of Paul to the, 172, 174, 233, 237, 250–57, 260
Corn gleaned on the Sabbath, story of, 51
Corporate personality, 165, 166; in Pauline theology, 213–14
Corruptible-incorruptible antithesis, 203–5
Corruption, 200, 201, 235–37, 242
Covenant: blood of the, 86; breaking of, 173; disciples as representing the Israel of the new, 84, 116; inequality of partners in Old, 173; Jesus and the new, 79, 84, 140, 148, 228; justification and, 163–64; the Law and sacrifices under the Old, 162; of the living God with Israel, 56; Paul's location of Christ within

Covenant *(continued)*
tradition of, 179–84, 197; in prophetic tradition, 27; radical faithfulness of Jesus to, 148–50, 274; relationship of Christian hope to, 229; Sinai versus Noachic, 234; unbroken by death of Jesus, 138, 140
Creation: community of humankind and, in suffering, 242–43; in Hellenistic tradition, 234; hope and, 235–37, 275; in Jewish tradition, 234–35; as subject to futility, 235
Cross: reconcilation with God through, 258; as the source of salvation, 161, 162; taking up one's, 35–37, 39; universal significance of, 271–72
Crucifixion: end of time and, 139; last words of Jesus, 126–35; quest for meaning of, 135–43; taking up one's cross and, 36
Cup, 100, 115, 277; as God's will, 101–7, 111, 116; hour and, 102–4, 109; trouble and, 103
Cyril of Alexandria, 284
Cyril of Jerusalem, 284

Damascus Road experience, xxxii, 159, 160
Daniel, Book of, 16, 287
Daube, D., 108
David, 41
Death: acceptance of (ecstasy), 40; of believer, 72, 118; continuity of life through, 297; as decay and change, 204; defeat of, in Pauline theology, 213–20; definition of, xxi–xxiii; as dialogue with God, 295; hope in the face of, 215–17; Jesus' views and deeds concerning, xxxi, 3–42, 148–50; Jewish tradition and, 4, 5; judgment and, xxiii–xxiv; meaning of, 270–73; metaphorical uses of the word, xxii–xxiii; mystery of faithfulness and, 275–81; as passage to the Father, 72, 270; as path to glory, 71–72, 151; Paul faces his own, 246–65; in Pauline theology, 198–205; as separation from God, 21, 106, 213; as separation from the

Death *(continued)*
human community, 107; as
separation of the soul from the
body, 294; sin and, 6–9; sleep
distinguished from, 215–17, 249;
struggle (or rebellion) against, 5–6,
242–43; terminology of, xxiii–
xxviii; time intervening between
resurrection of the dead (or
Parousia) and, 247–50, 292–94;
transformation of, in Pauline
synthesis, 151; twofold complexion
of, 72, 273–74; wrenching versus
passage, xxii. *See also* Death of
Jesus; Physical death; Spiritual
death; Violent death
Death of Jesus: believer's death and,
273; early Church's interpretation of
salvific nature of, 67; as expiation,
278; God's love and, 278; God's
plan and, 56–63, 69–72, 179–93;
imminent, 78–118; Israel's history
and, 271, 272; life of faithfulness
and, 276–80; observations by Jesus
on, 63–68, 85–87; Paul's symbolic
terminology for, 155–57, 159–78;
present, 123–43; as sacrifice, xxxii;
threatening, 49–72; universal
significance of, 86, 149–50, 271–72.
See also Crucifixion; Death—Jesus'
views and deeds concerning;
Gethsemane; Last Supper
Dibelius, M., 92
Difference, criterion of, xxviii, 50, 81
Disciples: apostolic work of, 264;
counsels of Jesus to, 84; at
Gethsemane, 99–102, 105–8, 112–
13, 116–17; Jesus' call to, 56; at
Last Supper, 82–85; as Remnant of
Israel, 84, 116; role of, in Mark, 55;
suffering and death of, 262–64;
temptation of, 131–32
Discipleship: general rules of, 113;
persecution and, 34–35, 37;
temptation and, 117
Divine economy, 61, 63, 212. *See
also* God's plan; Law, the
Dogmatician, exegetes' role compared
to, xxvi–xxvii
Duel between God and death, 11–13
Dwelling not made by human hands,
image of, 254–57

Earthly dust-heavenly spirit antithesis,
202–3
Eating, symbolism of, 177–78
Ecclesiastes, Book of, 6, 205
Ecstasy, acceptance of death as, 40
Elijah, 14, 58, 116, 124, 290; Jesus'
invocation of, from the cross, 137
Elisha, 14, 58
End of time, 29–30; Crucifixion and,
139; importance of present moment
for, 25–27; in Jewish tradition, 25–
27; in John, 30; in Matthew, 37;
persecution and, 38–39. *See also*
Apocalyptic, the
Enoch, 199, 289, 290
Epaphroditus, 217
Ephesians, Epistle of Paul to the, 16,
175
Eschatology: the apocalyptic versus,
28; importance of present moment
for, 25–27; in Jewish tradition, 25–
27
Eternal, the, before and after death,
28–29
Eternal life, 31–32, 34, 282–92;
biblical conception of, 286–92; in
classical theology, 283–86;
contemporary idiom of, 294–98;
John XXII and Benedict XII on,
292–94
Eucharist, 64, 66, 83, 89, 177–78; in
Pauline theology, 188, 192–93; as
sacrifice, 85–87
Exaltation, language of, 277, 290–92
Exegesis, xxvi–xxxi; coherence/
difference criteria, xxviii; historical
inquiry distinguished from, xxvii–
xxviii
Exodus, 139, 187, 272
Expiation: death of Jesus as, 278;
definition of, xxv–xxvi; *peripsēma*
and, 261–62; redemption versus, 66;
vicarious, 69. *See also* Sacrifice
Ezekiel, 36, 203, 219, 288

Faith, 30; death of Jesus and, 142–43;
as dialogue with God, 227; in the
face of death, 216–17; historical
inquiry and, 147–48; impotence of
death and, 253; of Jesus at death,
141; judgment and, 22–23;
Resurrection of Jesus and, 295–96;

Faith *(continued)*
righteousness through, 260. *See also* Hope
Faithfulness, mystery of, 275–80
Father, God versus, in Jesus' words, 127. *See also Abba* (father); God; God's plan
Feuillet, André, 254
Final death. *See* Spiritual death
First fruits, 198, 225, 231, 237
Flesh: as heir to sin, 258–59; resurrection of, 288, 294–95. *See also* Body
Food, symbolism of, 177–78
Francis of Assisi, 273
Francis of Paola, 130
Freedom of believer, 248, 257, 269, 296. *See also* Liberation
Free-slave antithesis, 168–72
Future, present versus, 25–27, 29

Galatians, Epistle of Paul to the, 159, 161, 168, 175, 180–83, 211, 258
Galilee, 51–52; Jesus' ministry in, 53–55
Garden of Olives. *See* Gethsemane
Gehenna, 9, 10, 21, 26
Gethsemane, 78, 79, 89–117, 150, 151, 280; Christological and parenetic themes in the tradition, 95–98; as expiation for sins, 114–15; historicity of narrative, 92–95; Jesus-disciple relationship, 116–17; in John, 89–92, 94, 97–107; in Luke, 94, 97, 99, 104, 109–10; in Mark, 94–95, 97–99, 102–4, 108–9; in Matthew, 94, 97–99, 102–3, 108–9; Paul and, 247; synchronic reading of, 98–107. *See also* Cup; Hour
Giono, John, 293
Girard, R., 185
Glory: creation as sharing in promise of, 235–36; death as path to, 71–72, 151; as divine action, 241; of God through Christ, 172; hour as God's plan for, 111; humiliation and, 251–52; Paul's language of the cross and, 162; of spiritual body and heavenly dwelling, 254–57; suffering and hope of, 228–29, 231–33, 238, 242–43; through Resurrection of Jesus, 272

Gnostics (gnostic tradition), 161, 284, 290
God: abandonment by, 103–6, 114, 126–28, 280–81; cup as the will of, 101–7, 111, 116; death as dialogue with, 295; duel between death and, 11–13; faith as dialogue with, 227; Father versus, in Jesus' words, 127; glory of, through Christ, 172; as guarantor of continuity, 201–2; living (in history), 11, 19, 56, 179, 271, 272, 286; prevenience of love of, 241; separation from, 21, 106–7, 213. *See also Abba*; God's plan; YHWH
God's plan, 211–12; Church and, 56; creation in, 235–37; death of Jesus and, 56–63, 69–72, 179–93; for glorification of the Son through the cross, 111; God's law and, 180–84; persecuted Just One and, 271, 272; prayer as providing access to, 240–41, 243; sacrificial expiation and, 184–90; unfolding of history as guided by, 241. *See also* Covenant; Law, the
Goguel, M., 92
Golden calf, the, 173
Golgotha (Calvary), 123, 150, 151, 280
Good Shepherd, 71
Gospels. *See* Synoptic gospels; *and specific gospels*
Grace, 213–14
Grain of wheat, symbol of, 40, 71, 105, 106, 112, 113, 148, 166
Greek tradition. *See* Hellenistic tradition
Gregory the Great, 143
Guilt. *See* Sin

Hannah, 286
Heaven, xxiii–xxiv; as banquet, 20, 31, 81; as being with Christ, 249; body glorified in, 254–55; as dwelling not made by human hands, 254–57; images of, 20; in Jewish tradition, 20; symbolized by earth, 30; viewed as prolongation of life on earth, 256. *See also* Afterlife; Eternal life
Heavenly spirit-earthly dust antithesis, 202–3